Christopher Rowland is Dean Ireland's Professor Emeritus of the Exegesis of Holy Scripture in the University of Oxford. His many books include *Blake and the Bible*, *Revelation: The Apocalypse of Jesus Christ* (with Judith Kovacs), *The Cambridge Companion to Liberation Theology*, *Christian Origins: The Setting and Character of the Most Important Messianic Sect of Judaism*, *Radical Christian Writings: A Reader* (with Andrew Bradstock), and *In a Glass Darkly: The Bible, Reflection and Everyday Life* (with Zoë Bennett).

'This is a rare achievement: a book that sweeps across two thousand years, and combines close scholarly analysis with passionate personal engagement. Christopher Rowland draws us back to the apocalyptic strand in Christianity, marginalised or suppressed down the centuries, with its vision of a heaven on earth rather than in the hereafter. Rowland traces the story from Christ's own time through medieval prophets, German Anabaptists, English Diggers, and William Blake, to the ideals and achievements of liberation theology in Brazil. And like all these radical prophets, Christopher Rowland seeks to inspire as well as inform.'

– Bernard Capp, FBA, Emeritus Professor of History,
University of Warwick

'*Radical Prophet* is a major study of Christian radicalism from the New Testament to Latin American liberation theology. It freshly illuminates the ways such radical writers as Gerrard Winstanley and William Blake, as well as modern thinkers, drew upon and revised messianic and apocalyptic ideas. Christopher Rowland makes a splendid contribution to the intellectual history of Christianity. Historians of ideas, scholars of religion and literary scholars – even general readers – will all appreciate this deeply original and stimulating book.'

– David Loewenstein, Edwin Erle Sparks Professor of English and the Humanities, Pennsylvania State University

'With characteristically incisive scholarship, Christopher Rowland makes a novel cut through the two-thousand-year texture of Christian history to reveal some startling perspectives from the past. Introducing us to disquieting voices from previous ages, he shows how they can feed into a reconstruction of Christian theology for those who cry out for liberation and redress, as so many have done over the Christian centuries. The reader may disagree with Rowland's analyses, but cannot fail to reap rich rewards from the conversation.'

– Diarmaid MacCulloch, FBA, Professor of the History of the Church, University of Oxford

'Identifying the profound, but much neglected, significance of mysticism and of visionary radicalism in the Christian intellectual tradition, *Radical Prophet* gives voice to writers whose hopeful revelations sought material change: not in a future paradise, but on earth right here and now. Rowland brilliantly revises radicalism's association with violence to conceive of it as an apocalyptic, critical and insightful way of experiencing scripture, tradition and the church. From early Christian writings to that of the Digger Gerrard Winstanley, poet William Blake and legal activist William Stringfellow, Rowland focuses on the eschatological as an urgent cry to manifest hope and change. An enthralling and crucial address to both the general and the academic reader, *Radical Prophet* seeks to affirm the politics of liberation theology in a mystical mode by insisting that we must perceive the divine in each other and respond with love to that imperative.'

– Emma Mason, Professor of English and Comparative Literary Studies, University of Warwick

Radical Prophet

The Mystics, Subversives and Visionaries who Strove for Heaven on Earth

CHRISTOPHER ROWLAND

Published in 2017 by
I.B.Tauris & Co. Ltd
London • New York
www.ibtauris.com

ISBN: 978 1 78453 265 9
eISBN: 978 1 78672 238 6
ePDF: 978 1 78673 238 5

A full CIP record for this book is available from the British Library
A full CIP record is available from the Library of Congress
Library of Congress Catalog Card Number: available

Typeset by Free Range Book Design & Production Limited
Printed and bound in Sweden by ScandBook AB

For Catherine,
our children and their partners,
and our grandchildren

Contents

List of Illustrations

Figures

Plate Section

Acknowledgements

As I explain in the Preface, the subject matter of this book has its origin in the various short periods of time I spent in Brazil and the intellectual quest to understand the antecedents in the Christian tradition of what I discovered. The book I wrote 30 years ago marked the first stage of that quest which has gone on ever since. I am grateful for the decade I spent on the Board of Christian Aid and to my many friends in that organisation who helped my learning greatly, particularly Wendy Tyndale, who for many years was head of the Latin American and Caribbean section of Christian Aid's work. Other friends have helped over the years. I have shared common interests with Andrew Bradstock, which led us to put together an anthology of radical Christian writings. Alex Wright played an important part in commissioning that book and it was he who suggested I write the present book. I am grateful to him for his support, guidance and patience; writing this book has taken longer than either of us expected. My work in higher education over the years has enabled me to work with many students whose own commitments, research and writing have helped me to understand various subjects in this book better than I could ever have done on my own. Finally, Catherine has laboured over various drafts and has helped me make this a better book. Her skills as a copy editor are second to none and she has brought some much-needed clarity to my prose. I am profoundly grateful.

As this book neared completion, the news came of the death of Alan Kreider. His friendship and scholarship pervade the whole of this book and were an inspiration to me over many years. His was a radical prophetic voice, which spoke to many of us in these islands, and to others in many other parts of the world, about the neglected richness of the Anabaptist tradition: *erit in pace memoria eius.*

This book is dedicated with love and gratitude to Catherine, our children, their partners, and their children. In particular, I hope that it will enable my grandchildren to understand a little of what so enthused one of their grandparents!

I am grateful to Oxford University Press, Taylor and Francis and to Wipf and Stock for permission to use material in Part 2 (on apocalyptic and radicalism and Thomas Muentzer), Part 3 (on Winstanley's biblical interpretation) and Part 4 (on liberation theology) which was previously published in earlier forms in the following: *The Oxford Handbook of Apocalyptic Literature* edited by John Collins; *Theology and Human Flourishing*, a collection of essays in honour of Tim Gorringe, edited by Mike Higton, Michael Law and myself; *Gerrard Winstanley: Theology, Rhetoric, Politics in Prose Studies* 36; K. Dell and P. Joyce (eds), *Biblical Interpretation and Method: Essays in Honour of John Barton*; and *The Expository Times* which published the article on Thomas Muentzer, *Expository Times* 126 (2015), pp. 417–24.

Also, thanks are due to Harvard Art Museums/Fogg Museum (Sandro Botticelli, *Mystic Crucifixion* – Friends of the Fogg Art Museum Fund, 1924.27, Photo: Imaging Department © President and Fellows of Harvard College); The National Gallery London (Sandro Botticelli, *Mystic Nativity*); and especially The Yale Center for British Art, Paul Mellon Collection, whose Open Access Policy is such a boon for authors, for permission to reproduce images in their collections.

I owe a special debt of gratitude to the team from CEMEP (Centro Missionário de Evangelização e Educação Popular) I met in Valença, Bahia, in September 1990, for permission to use the vivid images they created when my friend, Wendy Tyndale, and I were visiting projects supported by Christian Aid in various parts of Brazil. The images have been much used in my teaching and writing since I first took them, as they so brilliantly encapsulate liberationist approaches to the Bible, better than any words of mine. I am also grateful to Wendy for sharing her reminiscences of that visit with me and for her wisdom and insight about the politics and religion of Latin America.

Preface

Capturing what this book is about in a few words is not easy! It is about radical prophets. Two chapters in the third part of the book specifically explore the ideas of individuals in the modern period who typify the deep-seated radical seam in the Christian intellectual tradition. One of these, William Blake, explicitly stressed the importance of prophecy and is rightly linked with radicalism.[1]

If capturing what a book is about is not easy, choosing a title can be even more problematic. Trying to square the circle of encapsulating what is true to the book, while responding to the legitimate interests of contemporary publishing, that a title is attractive and catches attention, is also never easy. 'Radical Prophet' does manage to hint at the radicalism, and the word 'Prophet' points to protest and an alternative vision. Nevertheless it is important to understand the emphases of the book and the limits of its treatment. It does not pretend to be biographical; it is not a kind of 'lives of the prophets'. Rather, it is an exploration of a crucial, if neglected, part of the intellectual history of Christianity, which should not be relegated to the position of being just a mere curiosity but is central to the Christian tradition, particularly its origins, and in large part explains why Christianity has the history it has.

The study of the 'Radical Prophet: The Mystics, Subversives and Visionaries Who Strove for Heaven on Earth' may suggest the inclusion of other religions in addition to Christianity – one thinks here of the Prophet Muhammad, in many ways the quintessential radical prophet, and Jewish 'messianic mystics' like Abraham Abulafia and Sabbatai Sevi.[2] In a book on the phenomenon of religious radicalism they would have a prime place, but the parameters of this book are much more tightly drawn and reflect the limits of my competence. They focus on particular examples from the history of Christianity. In the Christian tradition, too, there are many others – Leo Tolstoy and Howard Thurman are obvious examples – who might have been included. Such limitations in coverage are a necessary caveat for those who may expect more from the general title of the book than is actually delivered in its pages.

Radicalism involves disjunction and a new start, not just tinkering with things as they are, and that is an important component of this particular perspective on the Christian theological tradition. The word 'radical' in the title is very much part of contemporary discourse, in which 'radical', 'radicalisation' and violence are closely linked. There were those in the history of Christianity for whom participation in the saints' holy war was central to their divine calling, from the Crusades in the Middle Ages via the militant Fifth Monarchists in the seventeenth century (who saw themselves as part of the armies of heaven described in Revelation 19:14), to figures like Camilo Torres who saw his vocation as throwing in his lot with the guerrillas in Colombia. The strand of radicalism which I have considered in this book is on the whole different. Thomas Muentzer and Mary Cary are exceptions. From Jesus to the liberation theologians there can be little doubt of the challenge they posed to the political powers and the elites of the day, but this was not the result of force of arms, and in the case of Winstanley and Blake, such action was explicitly eschewed, as it had indeed been, though more ambiguously, by Jesus. So, radicalism should *not* be identified *tout court* with militant violence, particularly in the context of the Christian tradition. 'Radical' is a word used with approbation and as a tool of criticism and warning, depending on the context. Political parties, for example, particularly those in power, will demonise their enemies as dangerous radicals whose views threaten the fabric of society, while praising their own policies as radically innovative and for the common weal.

It is now 30 years since I first began to write the book *Radical Christianity* (1988), one of the consequences of a life-changing visit to Brazil and Mexico in 1983, which has been determinative for my intellectual life. What that journey opened up for me was a different perspective on the Christian tradition. It led me to historical evidence, some of which I had known little about. The subject matter of this book bears more than a passing resemblance to *Radical Christianity*. Jesus, Joachim of Fiore, Thomas Muentzer, Gerrard Winstanley and liberation theology are all there. That book was an attempt to comprehend what I had seen and heard in Brazil and to relate it to the Christian tradition. One reviewer, not unfairly, considered that the book was a long prolegomenon to liberation theology. It certainly took me into unfamiliar, and revealing, paths which have fructified my life ever since.

The genesis of the present book is different. It has been fortified by further trips to Brazil, to Nicaragua and El Salvador in 1988 and 1990, the fruits of which are discussed in the chapter on liberation theology. My 1990 visit to Brazil enabled me to gain a better grasp of the nature of the popular pedagogy of liberation theology, and I am glad to share that in this book, in all the vivid colour of the newly painted posters which I saw on my visit to a church in Valença one September morning. The research I did with Andrew Bradstock in preparation for the reader *Radical Christian Writings* (2002) helped greatly to broaden my intellectual horizons. But the major difference since 1988 has been my discovery of reception history of the Bible, in particular of the Book of Revelation. My sojourn in Oxford in the 1990s enabled me to meet with the doyenne of scholarship on Joachim and medieval prophecy, Marjorie Reeves. It was a privilege to have Joachim's *figurae* interpreted by her in a series of memorable tutorials. Marjorie also pointed me to writers such as Peter John Olivi. She enabled me to glimpse why Joachim of Fiore deserves to be placed with the 'greats' in the history of Christian theology.

As my historical horizons expanded, I began to engage with the texts and images of William Blake, who only had a brief walk-on part in the 1988 book. Blake's grasp of the reasons why the Christian tradition contains within it the seeds of radicalism and the critique of received wisdom is nowhere better exemplified than in his texts and images. His place in this book has been formative of the thesis of the book as a whole and his words help to set the scene in the opening chapter of Part 1. His challenge to dualism and to views of God which emphasised the transcendent monarch rather than the incarnate Christ and meeting God in others, his prioritisation of 'Inspiration' over 'Memory' and the prophetic protest and hope for a better world all pervade the argument of this book. So, while the shape of the present book is similar to the older book, my immersion in Blake's images and texts has enabled my understanding of the nature of Christian radicalism to come into sharper focus. Elsewhere, the presentation of Christian origins is not too different but is much more focused, with the apocalyptic and the eschatological being placed at the very centre of the presentation of emerging Christian identity, and much more attention is paid to the contextual nature of Paul's theology.

Also, there was my involvement in a research project in Oxford, The Prophecy Project, funded by The Panacea Society (now The Panacea Charitable Trust) based in Bedford, which I jointly directed with Jane Shaw, now Professor of Religious Studies and Dean for Religious Life at Stanford University. The Panacea Society has an archive which had lain in drawers in its houses, charting the character of a remarkable apocalyptic/millenarian movement, which was part of a longer tradition of apocalyptic fulfilment, disappointment and renewed hope. Not only did this introduce me to some of the prophetic byways contemporary with Blake but also it pointed me to an international movement of apocalyptic actualisation whose nature is only now being fully told.[3]

Finally, if the genesis of this book goes back a long way, the actual writing of it coincided with writing another book, in collaboration with my colleague, Zoë Bennett. It covers some of the same ground but does so very differently. For one thing it is a more explicitly, and deliberately, autobiographical, self-reflexive and hermeneutical study, whose contribution owes much to collaborative authorship. But in one respect writing the section on the New Testament helped me get into better focus why I think that Paul is the pioneer contextual theologian. Writing *In A Glass Darkly* (2016) has helped me to see the varying, competing, facets of his prophetic vocation and his role as a community organiser.

More often than not in Christianity, as in other religions, the proponents of difference and change have been prophets, whether or not they have thought of themselves in that way. Some of these men and women were mystics, giving priority to their visions over received wisdom, and finding themselves written off or persecuted as subversives and troublemakers, at odds with convention, appealing to a higher authority, and offering, in place of the *status quo*, a new start and a new perspective on life and society. Mystics and visionaries are closely related. Being a visionary may be understood as one version of what it means to be a mystic. For example, there is a dictionary definition of the mystic as 'one who believes in the possibility of the spiritual apprehension of truths which are inaccessible to the understanding' (*The Oxford English Dictionary*). It may be what Anne Hutchinson described as 'an immediate revelation to my soul' or John of Patmos as 'in heaven an open door', or the Jesus of the Gospel of John as what he had seen and heard with God. All of these examples prioritise 'Inspiration' over 'Memory', to quote William Blake's contrast. As such they may be, though are not always necessarily, subversive of established patterns of thinking and may threaten received wisdom and practice. It is that mix of appeal to the 'apprehension of truths which are inaccessible to the understanding' and appeal to experience and the social and political consequences of that action which is the subject matter of this book. That said, not all mystics looked for the coming of God's Kingdom on earth, just as those with such a hope for the future were not always visionaries.

What is central to the earliest Christian texts is that they bear witness to the beliefs and practices of those whose hopes were not just for some distant future world but also in some sense here and now and in this world. What 'in some sense' means and how it was worked out is the key to understanding the New Testament. There are many texts from ancient Judaism which both predict imminent catastrophe on society and also look for a different kind of world order, a messianic age in which 'righteousness and peace will kiss each other' (Psalm 85:10). What distinguishes the earliest Christian writings from other ancient Jewish texts is that the writers believed that hope for the future could become a present reality in a world order which was at odds with their vision of hope. Those whose lives were shaped by the vision sought ways of allowing that horizon of hope to inform and condition the ways in which they behaved.[4]

There is nothing new in this recognition. In particular it informs the New Testament interpretation of Albert Schweitzer (e.g. his books on Jesus and Paul, 1931), whose own life was captured by the strange eschatological message of Jesus of Nazareth. Unlike some of his contemporaries, he sought to understand it and refused to allow it to be written off as a historical curiosity. Visions and hope for the future and a different perspective on habit and convention pervade this book. Without doing them justice we fail to understand the genesis and nature of one of the major world religions.

The outline of the book

The book is divided into four parts. Three of these are thematic, one of which considers the texts and (in the case of Blake) images of two contrasting examples of radical prophets, Gerrard Winstanley and William Blake.

Part 1, *The Roots of Christian Radicalism*, offers an explanatory introduction and covers the biblical origins, particularly the New Testament. The first chapter ('"Would to God that all the Lords people were Prophets"') offers an introduction to the book and considers the approach taken to radicalism and prophecy, and the important contribution of William Blake to the understanding of Christian radicalism. The second chapter ('Heaven on Earth: The Roots of Christian Radicalism in the New Testament') is an outline of the importance of the apocalyptic elements and the centrality of the horizon of hope for understanding Christian origins.

Part 2, Kairos: *The Unique Moment and Apocalyptic Discernment*, considers a major aspect of radical prophecy, the conviction of individuals who believe themselves to have a vocation to be significant agents in enabling the coming of a new age, the roots of which can be found in the New Testament ('Human Actors in the Divine Drama'). A second chapter ('Subversive Apocalypse') includes the apocalyptic dimension of radicalism, in which appeal to visionary insight or divine impulse relativises the authority of Scripture, tradition and the Church. There is a consideration of the ways in which interpreters of Revelation understood themselves to be placed at a decisive moment in history. Most of these are taken from the ancient and modern periods but the chapter concludes with the writing of one of the most remarkable modern interpreters of Revelation, William Stringfellow.

Part 3, *Contrasting Radical Prophets*, considers the views of Gerrard Winstanley ('Gerrard Winstanley: Responding to an Eschatological Moment in English History') and compares his short-lived writing career, linked especially with the prophetic project in which he and his colleagues dug the common treasury of the land, with that of William Blake ('"From impulse not from rules": William Blake's Apocalyptic Pedagogy'). Blake lived on the fringes of political activity but devoted himself to transforming attitudes and understanding by his images and texts.

Part 4, *Christian Radicalism in Modernity: An Example and a Neglected Perspective*, concentrates on liberation theology ('Liberation Theology: How to Proclaim God in a World that is Inhumane'), one of the most remarkable modern exemplifications of a radical prophecy devoted to pedagogy, political empowerment and the betterment of the situation of poor people in the so-called Third World, but with an influence which has been global in its reach. The focus of this chapter is on Latin American liberation theology, specifically in Brazil, but similar points could have been made via a consideration of both feminist and Black theology. This part of the book concludes with a discussion which is less about radical movements and activists and more about writers on apocalypticism, messianism and radicalism in the Christian tradition, Ernst Bloch, Walter Benjamin and Jacob Taubes ('Apocalypticism and Millenarian Eschatology: Recovering Neglected Strands'). Their differing interpretations of the centrality of messianic and apocalyptic ideas in Jewish and Christian history lend a neglected and much-needed perspective to the potency and vitality of this tradition in Western thought and offer a retrospective consideration of themes surveyed earlier in the book.

Part I

The Roots of Christian Radicalism

Where else does an English writer start an essay on radical prophecy in Christian tradition but with the words of William Blake, which now serve as an unofficial English national anthem, and the biblical texts which inspired those words? Radicalism and prophecy sit uneasily with a culture of stability and conventionality, whether in church or state; but doing justice to the subject of the mystics, subversives and visionaries who strove for heaven on earth can only start with the Bible, so much of which is about prophecy and a radical hope for a different world – and the 'mental fight' involved in bringing this about. The earliest Christian sources suggest that Jesus did not lead an armed revolt; yet, as the image on the cover of this book indicates, his dramatic decision to enter Jerusalem in the way that he did, and especially his reported actions in the Temple, are hardly the stuff of a social dreamer – even if in the end he may have abjured a violent struggle with the principalities and powers. The Gospels, and indeed the New Testament, are about mystics and subversives who in different ways strove for heaven on earth; but more by encouraging a 'mental fight' than by force of arms (though a resort to armed struggle is of course to be found throughout Christian history). Chapter 1 of Part 1 covers the nature of radicalism, and Chapter 2 the way in which the visionaries and mystics helped turn their world upside down. Included, perhaps surprisingly, in this story is Paul: the community organiser. Here was the famous convert helping groups of people who followed an apparently failed messiah (cf. 1 Corinthians 1:20–8) to espouse an ethic of hope for a new age as well as moral change in this one: a message and practice, which – even if that message lost much of its initial eschatological impetus, at least in its original, radical form – slowly permeated the Roman Empire. The centrality of the mystical and the visionary, and the message of hope and its implementation, lie at the heart of the New Testament – which is correspondingly at the centre of the second chapter of this part of the book.

Chapter 1

'Would to God that all the Lords people were Prophets'

Immediately before some of the most famous lines in British poetry, commonly known as 'Jerusalem', which have become England's unofficial national anthem, William Blake writes his manifesto inspired by the prophetic radicalism of the Bible. He makes a deliberate contrast with Classical learning and pleads for a return to the roots, to the Bible. The contrast is based on what he sees as two different epistemologies: one, which resorts to the past, or a too pedantic aping of the past, and the other, which depends on present inspiration. What Blake found in the Bible is the priority of Inspiration over Memory, of the visionary and the imaginative over the traditional and conventional. In these words there is a manifesto for the thesis of this book. They culminate with the stirring stanzas to encourage people to build the New Jerusalem. There is no patient waiting for something to happen, for divine intervention, but the keenly felt need for a struggle to achieve the eschatological goal of building Jerusalem *in this world not some other*:

Preface

> The Stolen and Perverted Writings of Homer & Ovid: of Plato & Cicero. which all Men ought to contemn: are set up by artifice against the Sublime of the Bible. but when the New Age is at leisure to Pronounce; all will be set right: & those Grand Works of the more ancient & consciously & professedly Inspired Men, will hold their proper rank, & the Daughters of Memory shall become the Daughters of Inspiration. Shakespeare & Milton were both curbd by the general malady & infection from the silly Greek & Latin slaves of the Sword.

> Rouze up O Young Men of the New Age! set your foreheads against the ignorant Hirelings! For we have Hirelings in the Camp, the Court, & the University: who would if they could, forever depress Mental & prolong Corporeal War. Painters! on you I call! Sculptors! Architects! Suffer not the fash[i]onable Fools to depress your powers by the prices they pretend to give for contemptible works or the expensive advertizing boasts that they make of such works; believe Christ & his Apostles that there is a Class of Men whose whole delight is in Destroying. We do not want either Greek or Roman Models if we are but just & true to our own Imaginations, those Worlds of Eternity in which we shall live for ever; in Jesus our Lord.
>
> And did those feet in ancient time,
> Walk upon Englands mountains green:
> And was the holy Lamb of God,
> On Englands pleasant pastures seen!
> And did the Countenance Divine,
> Shine forth upon our clouded hills?
> And was Jerusalem builded here,
> Among these dark Satanic Mills?
> Bring me my Bow of burning gold:
> Bring me my Arrows of desire:
> Bring me my spear: O Clouds unfold!
> Bring me my Chariot of fire!
> I will not cease from Mental Fight,
> Nor shall my Sword sleep in my hand:
> Till we have built Jerusalem,
> In Englands green & pleasant Land.
>
> Would to God that all the Lords people were Prophets.
>
> (Numbers xi. 29v)[1]

Blake's rhetorical flourish in his Preface to *Milton a Poem* is the words of one committed to radical prophecy. As the words from Numbers 11:29, 'Would to God that all the Lords people were Prophets', at the end of the closing stanzas, indicate, it is an appeal to all to stir up their prophetic genius, all too easily left dormant or quiescent. The appeal is radical because it means subverting and building a different kind of polity. Striving is key, albeit a 'Mental

Fight' rather than resort to 'Religion hid in War'.[2] Blake was a mystic, a visionary, and in his own way a subversive echoing the vision of heaven on earth bequeathed by John of Patmos. Indeed, he found himself in the profoundly precarious position of being on trial for sedition for what he was alleged to have said to an English soldier when he was living in Sussex.[3] He was not engaged in dissident political activity except by his literary and artistic endeavours. His intellectual struggles have enabled those who have engaged with his texts and images to gain new understanding of themselves and the social reality of which they were a part.

The words derived from Numbers 11:29 do not form part of what most of us know (and sing) as Blake's 'Jerusalem', but they pervade the whole. The first two stanzas set out the problem of the present, not by supposing there was some past golden age (*did* those feet in ancient times?) but by questions which suggest a negative answer paving the way for a response. In the face of present inadequacies there is an invocation to prepare for the struggle to change the *status quo* and build the New Jerusalem in 'England's green and pleasant land'. It is a stirring summons, to oneself and one's peers, to recognise the inadequacies of the present and find the resources not simply to look to the future but to bring a much hoped for different world in some way into the present. 'Building Jerusalem' may not be quite the way in which John the Seer writes in the Book of Revelation, but the notion of building something now which may be tested in the future *is* very much part and parcel of what Paul sees as his task (1 Corinthians 3:13–15). Like Blake, Paul believed that to be a prophet is open to all, and it is a matter of awakening the 'prophetic character'. The programmatic verse in the midst of the speech of Peter on the Day of Pentecost says as much:

> This is that which was spoken by the prophet Joel: It shall be in the last days (saith God) of my spirit I will pour out upon *all flesh*. And your sons, and your daughters shall prophesy, your young men shall see visions. And your old men shall dream dreams. And on my servants, and on my handmaidens I will pour out of my spirit in those days, And they shall prophesy.
>
> (Acts 2:17–18 in William Tyndale's translation)

The priority of prophecy rather than adherence to convention is present also in the writings of others, such as Gerrard Winstanley and Thomas Muentzer. More recently, the emphasis on present experience, 'life', as the priority, rather than the Bible or tradition in liberation theology is in many ways analogous in its appeal to experience. Vision, prophecy, subjectivity, non-conformity, autonomy, and unease with what is received, is key. In Blake's work it is explored with a sophistication and recognition of the strengths and weaknesses of that position. He was impatient with an unthinking subservience to tradition and convention and the 'binding with briars my joys and desires' which resulted.[4] Blake saw in Jesus and the prophets the paradigms of 'the Poetic Genius' and put his finger on what was special for him about Jesus – that he acted 'from impulse not from rules'. This may at first sight seem a strange thing to write when the Gospels are full of Jesus' sense of obligation to the Father (Mark 8:38) or obedience to the divine will (e.g. John 5:30). The crucial thing is that the understanding of the divine will, of what constitutes obedience to the One who sent him, comes through impulse not from rules. It is not appeal to an *external* authority such as Scripture or inherited human wisdom but to the God who speaks 'within' through vision or revelation.

Christian radicalism

'Radical' and 'radicalisation' are words which may obscure as much as they illuminate. They are words which have achieved a certain degree of notoriety in popular discourse of late, linked as they have been with acts of violence in the name of religion. For example, in a document from the UK Government's Department of Education we read the words 'radicalisation refers to the process by which a person comes to support terrorism and forms of extremism leading to terrorism'.[5] Dealing with the negative effects of 'radicalisation' is at the heart of the policy of many governments as they confront Islamic terrorism. Nevertheless, even right-wing governments can boast positively about their 'radical' policies on business and deregulation. Those with the power to control political discourse can use the word however they like, of themselves when it suits and to vilify their opponents at other times. 'Radical' relates to the fundamental nature of something, the root of an issue, and is characterised by departure from tradition, and accepted norms and values, but whether radicalisation *necessarily* leads to 'terrorism' must be questioned. One may forgive some of Jesus' disciples who thought that they might be about to engage in some kind of 'Last Battle' on the night of Jesus' arrest in the Garden of Gethsemane in the light of his entry into Jerusalem and action in the Temple. Jesus' words and deeds could well have sowed the seeds of confusion; more on this anon. There will not be much about violence in this book, though certain topics, such as the militancy of English Civil War rhetoric concerning the war of the saints and Thomas Muentzer's espousal of violence in the pursuit of the exercise of divine righteousness are just two examples among many from the Christian tradition. The temptation is to avoid the words 'radical' and 'radicalisation' altogether, and yet what they signify is not easily captured by other words.

Strange as it may seem, fundamentalism and radicalism are intimately related, with a common strand of nostalgia for an idyllic past. So radicalism is always in a sense reactionary. That should not surprise us given the fact that radicals are people going back to roots, even if their agenda may be change rather than preservation. What distinguishes the kind of move made by those discussed in this book is that it is not about nostalgia for a lost Golden Age, so not the recapitulation of the past. Radicalism is not primarily about faithfulness to the faith once handed down from the fathers so much as a retrieval of a lost way of looking at God and the world. It points to difference, not repetition, therefore, and a longing for a different kind of political arrangement, inclusive, equal and free of status and division. The eschatological dimension, such as we find most clearly enunciated in the New Testament's apocalypse, the Book of Revelation, characterises a deep-seated conviction that there is more to come and, what is more, divinely inspired human agents will have a part in seeing that through to fulfilment. The ultimate revelation is not in the past, but in the future, and the quest for the understanding of that, and what makes it possible, means that the nostalgia of the 'radicals' is inspirational rather than prescriptive.

The widespread conviction in the pages of the New Testament from Matthew to Revelation that a new age had come, that the prophetic promises were in the process of fulfilment and, as a result, different patterns of believing and belonging were appropriate not only required a reassessment of received wisdom but also the articulation of different understandings of what it meant to be part of a new age. This is particularly apparent in Paul's letters, especially 1 Corinthians. But what is central about this text, which in some ways lays the foundations for what was to emerge as Christianity, is the mix of the new and the resort to cultural precedent in the service of community harmony and survival. More often than not, this involved unacknowledged indebtedness to the Jewish Scriptures, in the interests of community formation and maintenance, which sets the pattern of Christian life for two millennia. The mix, therefore, of radical re-think and ready return to 'roots' is typical of emerging Christianity and led to that uneasy compromise between the radical and conservative which pervades the New Testament and becomes more apparent in later Christian literature. It explains the peculiar contours of Christianity. Resort to precedent sits alongside novelty. The resulting, uneasy, balancing act has never been satisfactorily resolved.

The history of Christianity, of the church and its rituals and its support of empire from the time of Constantine onwards, has to be complemented by another, often very different, story, of those who appealed to the messianic 'roots' of Christianity, the disruptive, the non-conformist, the protest against the *status quo*, evidence for which we find in all the canonical gospels. From the prophetic activity of Montanists in the second century, a movement which spread from what is now modern Turkey to North Africa, via monasticism in the early centuries, the radical Franciscans in the Middle Ages, inspired as they were by Joachite eschatology, to the radical Reformation and the millenarian movements of Civil War England, thence to Blake and beyond to contemporary liberation theology, the story of striving to build the New Jerusalem on earth is part of the Christian story that is not often told. This is strange given that the identity of the religion is premised on its convictions about the messiah and the coming of the messianic age; it is after all *Christ* (= Messiah) - ianity!

The apocalyptic, mystical and radical political traditions in Christianity contribute to the non-conformity and challenge to convention, which embrace the Gospels and Blake, and more recently liberation theology. My relationship with a little-known apocalyptic/millenarian group in Bedford, The Panacea Society, which I mentioned in the Preface, and a research project which I co-directed, examining its archive, suggested views which have many affinities with the New Testament. It offered a moment, when something familiar confronts the interpreter, reminding one of a familiar past but seen in a new light.

Appreciation of such apocalyptic relics of the Christian history helps me to understand Christian origins. Blake's summons to build Jerusalem 'in England's green and pleasant land' is one which resonated with an elderly member of the Panacea Society who saw the garden in Bedford as a this-worldly Paradise and Bedford the hub of the New Age.[6] As I got to know more about the antecedents of the group, and in particular the way in which they harked back to the vocation of Joanna Southcott to be mother of the messiah, more and more I had the sense that while I was being confronted by something eccentric, the community and my elderly conversation partner were fired by a seemingly irrational hope for a better world, which so completely shaped their existence. It was a moment of recognition similar to that which is described so movingly in Book 1 of Virgil's *Aeneid*, in which something very familiar is discovered in strange surroundings when Aeneas arrived in Carthage and saw the events, of which he had been a part, evoked in murals in a temple. It touched Aeneas deeply as in this new place the familiar images of his own past impinged on the present, albeit in a very different context. In the case of the Panacea Society archive and its history, I not only discerned the way in which hope has sustained and impelled people, but also saw the familiar story of the New Testament, and writers and adherents struggling to mirror the Kingdom of God on earth. Through them I understood better why Christianity has developed as the kind of religion it is.

The prophetic-messianic tradition

The quest for the 'roots' is evident throughout the New Testament. In its pages non-conformist strands are found alongside those elements supportive of the *status quo*. For example, within the New Testament there is ambivalence towards the Scriptures. It is the mental furniture of the New Testament writers, but the approach to the Bible is what one may appropriately term 'radical', never being content with received wisdom, and allowing the wisdom of experience to determine how one approaches both tradition and sacred Scripture. It is that dynamic which typifies such approaches down the centuries, which make up what one may call the radical strand in the Bible. The New Testament offers a lens through which one can see that the Bible as a whole is pervaded with struggles, between priest and prophet, Temple and prophetic visionaries.

Two words are going to recur in this book: 'radical' and 'experience'. The word 'radical' links with what is 'thoroughgoing', getting back to basics, or ideas and practice which depart from current practices, conditions or institutions. This complements the definition offered by distinguished historian, Gerald Aylmer, in connection with movements at the time of the English Civil War: 'By radical I mean anyone advocating changes in state, church or society which would have gone beyond the official programme of the mainstream puritan-parliamentarians in the Long Parliament and the Westminster Assembly'.[7] The other word is 'experience'. In all my examples, priority is given to experience of one kind or another, whether 'immediate revelation' or 'life', revealed through the vicissitudes of life, or vision or audition, which then become the basis for understanding what has been received as well as life more generally.

Rosemary Radford Ruether rightly stresses the importance of experience as a motor both of contemporary interpretation and also in the tradition which has its roots in experience and is constantly renewed through the test of experience.[8] Like Blake,[9] she stresses the centrality of the experiential in theological reflection in what she terms 'breakthrough experiences' that illuminate the whole of life.[10] There is a 'biblical critical principle', the prophetic-messianic tradition, by which she understands not just a particular body of texts, but

> a critical perspective and process through which the biblical tradition constantly re-evaluates, in new contexts, what is truly the liberating Word of God, over against both the sinful deformations of contemporary society and also the limitations of past biblical traditions, which saw in part and understood in part, and whose partiality may have even become a source of sinful injustice and idolatry.[11]

Religion as sanctification of the existing social order is in contradiction to the prophetic perspective, which stands in judgement upon the injustices of society. She argues that one should not set apart any critical prophetic movement, once and for all established in the past, 'for the prophetic tradition remains true to itself, to its own impulse and spirit, only by engagement in constant restatement in the context of the issues of justice and injustice in its times'.[12] Continuity with the prophetic tradition requires the prophetic critique to involve constant revision in dialogue with contemporary issues and is thus renewed both by the issues of today and by new perceptions of the limits of past traditions, including its own.

The prophetic principle is no guarantee of radicalism. Prophets may just be ideological supporters of the *status quo* as they often are in the Hebrew Bible, or the nostalgic restoration of the institutions of a bygone age like Haggai and Zechariah. Here were prophets like Haggai whose prophetic inspiration endorsed a previous regime based on the Temple. But many prophets claimed their authority to speak on the basis of visions (e.g. Isaiah 6) and did not base what they said on appeal to tradition. But those like Isaiah, Jeremiah, Amos and Hosea, whose words and visions were remembered by ancient Jews as pointing to a society heading for disaster, were at odds with their contemporaries and often paid the price for being so. According to later Jewish tradition, the biblical prophets were co-opted as part of the line of interpreters of the Mosaic law[13] rather than harbingers of a new message which may be at odds with what had been handed down, which subtly subordinates their words and their visions to the criteria of what is set out in Mosaic law. The messianic principle relativises the present and its political arrangements to challenge those arrangements and to insist on something different – and better.

In sum, for this prophetic tradition to remain true to itself, there needs to be constant, *contextually*, driven restatement. That is a contemporary understanding, socially and politically, as well as theologically, aware. Continuity with the prophetic tradition is not simply restatement of past texts but the constant renewal of the meaning of the prophetic critique in the context of engagement with the issues which confront the readers. The heart of Christian radicalism is the conviction that there is community/continuity of experience with the experience of those mentioned in the Scriptures to which those foundational texts bear witness. So, the Scriptures may help frame and assist with comprehending the present experience. I choose my words carefully as it is not a question of validation or authorisation. The political character of radicalism is inherent in the prioritisation of the contemporary experience and the consequent and often inevitable, implicit, challenge to received wisdom and authority.

Christianity is not 'enclosed in a past revelation' for it is 'an eschatological faith'. It lives by the norm of the reign of God in the still unrealised future of creation, not by a fixed, completed past.[14] The emphasis on the yet unrealised future, and the participation in working for this future, are key to the New Testament itself, with roots in the prophetic hope of Judaism. This inspires the critique of the present and a longing, and working for something different. The 'prophetic principle', found, for example, in the prophetic texts and the life and teaching of Jesus, includes a critique of religion which offers an ideological legitimation for the *status quo*, of political, social and economic oppression. There is no suggestion in this model that the Bible as a whole is anything other than a mixed bag of religious, theological, social and political perspectives. Present experience sheds light on those biblical elements allowing them to encourage and to inspire new resistance, faith and hope and the determination not to allow oppression to triumph.

Let me offer two examples of the nature of radicalism anticipating what we find later in the book. The first is the kind of engagement with the Jewish Scriptures that we find in the Book of Revelation. Whatever one's view of the origin of John's apocalypse, its relationship with preceding Scriptures is at most indirect. They function more as an inspiration. The earlier biblical texts are a witness to the experience of earlier prophets which later prophets may share too.

Secondly, consider the extraordinary writing career of Gerrard Winstanley. As with Blake and many others he makes a typical set of moves and choices with regard to the Bible. He writes that he didn't learn what he did in books. Experience of poverty, and the historical circumstances, in which he found himself, pushed him into it, and he had the ability to write and interpret his actions in the way he did. Mark Kishlansky has suggested that Winstanley was 'a small businessman who began his career wholesaling cloth, ended it wholesaling grain, and in between sandwiched a mid-life crisis of epic proportions'.[15] Such a personal crisis befits this unique moment in British history when not only had a king been deposed and executed but also had a commonwealth been set up in place of the monarchy which had typified English polity before 1649 and since Charles II's accession. Winstanley may not have made much of an impact until the twentieth century, but he emerged from the toils of the Civil War to write some of the most remarkable prose of his time, only to lapse back into bourgeois obscurity in comfortable Surrey. Experience, as he put it, 'by Vision, Voice, and Revelation'[16] impelled him to write and interpret in ways which are dynamic and insightful, and his experience shed new light on familiar passages and doctrines. His socio-political context was a factor, of course, alongside his personal circumstances. But in the history of biblical interpretation he was not a 'one-off'. There are many parallels to the way in which he interpreted the Bible and to his choice of passages. While we cannot regard him as being part of a 'tradition' in anything like the orthodox Christian sense, we can discern in his writings something that typifies a pattern which is akin to Radford Ruether's 'prophetic principle'.

There pervades the earliest Christian texts a sense of being uncomfortable in the present age and seeking to live by different values and according to another kind of regime. While New Testament texts were written by those with little or no connection with the ruling elites of antiquity, some, like Luke–Acts, may have been directed to those who came from this background, whether inside or outside, persuading of the 'option' that had to be taken to be part of this movement. Even so, the subject matter made it a challenging read. There can be few more stark reminders of obligations of disciples than the one to be found in Luke 14:26–7. The 'ever the same' which characterised stability and continuity is very clearly interrupted by the Gospel of Jesus Christ. The eschatology of the New Testament, and the ambiguous relationship with the Jewish Scriptures and institutions of Judaism, exhibit a level of non-conformity, which, whatever Christianity became from the fourth century onwards, meant that there remains in the canon of the New Testament a stumbling block to the dominant ideology as rank and status ceased to be of any account (Luke 22:24–7).[17] This was rooted, however, with an eschatological expectation, not of some other heavenly realm but *this* world, in which a great reversal takes place, when the powerful are removed from their thrones, and the lowly lifted up; the radical transformation is nowhere more starkly stated.

Christian radicalism is about rupture, the disruption of conventional wisdom and conduct. It means having the wrong person or thing in the wrong place. For Paul on the Damascus Road the wrong person addressed him from heaven. 'Who are you lord?', asked the hapless, discomfited Saul (Acts 9:5). For Peter at Joppa in his trance he was commanded to sacrifice and eat the wrong creatures that he saw in the sail-like object which descended before him (Acts 10:11–15), and for John on Patmos a slaughtered lamb stood in the midst of the divine throne room – a lamb not a lion turns out to be the messiah (Rev. 5:5–6). But in the case of radicalism this is not only epistemological but also social. The dream or vision prompts action which is counter-cultural and provocative. In the world of flesh and blood it is about taking the divine gospel to the wrong people, about a man who claimed to be the messiah, doing things at times and in places he should not be and consorting with people with whom the respectable and conventionally minded would not expect him to be consorting – with tax collectors, prostitutes and sinners (Matt. 9:10–13; 21:31). Change means *not* repeating 'the same dull round over again'. This is why 'the Poetic or Prophetic Character' is so important.[18]

The theme of this book is about the apocalyptic and the eschatological, visionary insight, and hope for the future and its realisation, especially the present signs of its coming and the centrality of experience. Those features of religion have been a persistent element, for better, in their diachronic sense, or worse, if one thinks that the apocalyptic and the millenarian are in some sense pathological, depending on one's perspective, throughout Christian history. Augustine's brilliant theological treatise, *The City of God*, which succeeded in managing eschatology, has never quite managed to tame its effects, even if the main thrust of Christian theology has largely passed it by. There have been particular moments – in the late Middle Ages, at the Reformation, in the seventeenth century in England, at the time of the French Revolution, and in late twentieth-century Latin America, when those images have been particularly prominent. But there has always been an underworld of this-worldly eschatology fed by apocalyptic conviction. The recurrence of such patterns of religion is because they are licensed by the Scriptures themselves, not least the New Testament. Being a visionary doesn't mean being a social radical, but the figures mentioned in this book, Jesus, Paul and John of Patmos, Gerrard Winstanley and William Blake, are linked with decisive visionary experiences. As Blake puts it in his Preface to *Milton*, it is 'Inspiration' which takes priority over 'Memory'.

The dynamic, which made Christianity such a strange, counter-cultural movement to Jews and pagans alike, has not always been recognised. That Jesus died as a messianic pretender is the one secure fact that we know about him and yet the impact of messianism on the evolution of Christianity has not been fully appreciated by students of early Christianity. While the apologetic concerns of the author of the Acts of the Apostles suggest that the charges of 'turning the world upside down' were inappropriate and even false, any reader of Acts cannot fail to note the disruptive elements in the story, in the later chapters about Paul in particular. For example, the speech of Stephen is hardly an adequate rebuttal of the charge levelled against him that he spoke against 'this holy place and against Moses' (Acts 6:13). The ambiguities which are already present in Nathan's oracle to David in 2 Samuel are made more explicit in Stephen's speech. Though the Greek is not absolutely clear in Acts 7:47, the apparent contrast between David who did not build a temple with Solomon who did carries the implication that this was an act of idolatry: how could God dwell in any edifice made with human hands (Acts 7:49–51)?[19] If Caiaphas was worried that if the hierarchy let Jesus go on as he was, the Romans would destroy their holy place and their nation (John 11:48), how much more was it the case with Stephen, a follower of Jesus who offered a rationale as to why the centre of their life was little better than an act of idolatry, a message which the audience clearly grasped as the subsequent violent treatment meted out to Stephen demonstrates (Acts 7:54–8).

When we look at the Gospels we find a distinctive mix of 'apocalyptic' (see Chapter 4, 'Apocalypse'), in the sense of both the revelatory and also the eschatological. The eschatological dimension, along with the 'unmasking' inherent to apocalypse, is central to the cultivation of criticism which we receive from the Bible. It is a refusal to accept that the *status quo* is the last word, and that the way things are organised in this age does not serve the benefit of humanity, and, indeed, creation as a whole. If 'apocalypse' furnishes the beginnings of a critical language to answer the question 'why?', the language of hope instils that sense of dissatisfaction and complacency, recognising that a cosmos in which creatures are exploited and made subservient to the desires of others does not and cannot constitute the true order of things and that something different is not just to be hoped for but worked for as well. The genius of early Christianity was to add to hope an exploration in the age which was passing away of how the messianic ways inspire transformation and 'show a still more excellent way' (1 Cor. 12:31).

CHAPTER 2

Heaven on Earth

The Roots of Christian Radicalism in the New Testament

Biblical writings give evidence of another perspective on existence and on history through dreams, visions or divinely inspired auditions. That could offer a radically different view of things, of social arrangements, of the nature of obedience to God, and of the relationship between present and future. It is that future perspective, and its impact on the present, which pervades the pages of the New Testament and colours belief and practice. This chapter surveys the evidence which indicates the importance of eschatology in the New Testament writings. This is followed by surveys of the eschatological elements in the Gospels, the Pauline letters, and the Book of Revelation. The chapter would not be complete without a reference to the Book of Revelation. The focus here is the crucial part that it plays in building up a picture of the centrality of eschatology in New Testament writings. We shall return to consider it again in later chapters when we see the ways in which the apocalyptic outlook contributed to the thinking of later generations. The chapter concludes with an assessment of the degree to which the failure of early Christianity's eschatological hopes contributed to a change in the pattern of Christian faith and practice.

Eschatology has been central to most interpretations of the ministry of Jesus as presented in the Gospels of Matthew, Mark and Luke over the last century or so. Eschatology is a word which is not easy to define.[1] Strictly speaking, eschatology has to do with the study of the 'Last Things', those events which will bring history and this world to its close. Yet we have to recognise that we regularly use the word 'eschatology' and the phrase 'the Last Things' in a variety of different senses, some of which extend the meaning to such an extent that the connection with the original, future-orientation to the history of the world, has virtually disappeared. As well as the coming of God's Kingdom on earth we can find eschatology being used to describe the fate of the individual believer's soul after death, the termination of this world-order and a setting up of another, transcendent world, even the critical nature of human decisions. In this book eschatology is a shorthand way of referring to this future hope and its fulfilment *in this world*, which was an important feature of many texts from ancient Judaism and Christianity.[2]

There is little, if anything, in the extant Jewish literature from the period up to the destruction of the Second Temple in 70 CE which resembles the peculiar factors which determined the emergence and growth of Christianity such as we find in the pages of the New Testament. The Christians still looked forward to the coming of the messiah, a belief which they shared with many Jews of their day; but it was more a return. This involved them in dealing with a range of issues which would hardly have affected those Jews who did not share their convictions. For most other Jews, messianic expectation remained largely a matter of theoretical interest only. For the first Christians it had become a matter of decisive importance as a necessary corollary of the coming of the messianic kingdom. For most New Testament writers there is still an unfulfilled element in the process of salvation. Believers may have tasted of the heavenly gift and participated in the Holy Spirit (Heb. 6:4), but the fullness of salvation is still to be experienced by the individual and manifested in the world (Rom. 8:18–25; 1 John 3:2). But the eschatological salvation was not wholly future, for the experience of the Spirit, such a dominant feature of early Christian religion,[3] must be understood as part of the eschatological perspective. In the New Testament the Spirit is frequently linked with prophecy (Acts 2; 2 Cor. 1:22). While there was no unified view of the Spirit's activity in contemporary Judaism, there is evidence to suppose that some Jews thought of the Spirit's activity as part of the past experience of God's people.[4] Thus the inspiration by the Spirit was confined to the era of the prophets in the past and would only be operative again when new prophets arose, in the messianic age. The present age was characterised by the absence of the Spirit, and the future age would be a time when the Spirit, and therefore prophecy, would return. By contrast, importance was given to the present as a time of eschatological fulfilment by the first Christians (e.g. Luke 4:18–21).

Similarly, the resurrection of Jesus was regarded as a sign that the Last Days had started. For Jews and early Christians resurrection was an essential component of the future hope. In the context of Second Temple Judaism, the resurrection of the dead was about the life of the Age to Come (e.g. Dan. 12:1–2). In the New Testament we have hints that a close link exists between resurrection and the eschatological events (e.g., 1 Cor. 15:20; Phil. 3:21). The resurrection of Jesus of Nazareth was the first fruits, an anticipation, in which a key feature of the 'Last Days' (a phrase used in Peter's speech on the day of Pentecost in Acts 2:17) became a reality in the old age. Thus the first Christians were affirming that, for them, the future hope was *already* in the process of fulfilment and was not merely an item of faith still to be realised at some point in the future.

This-worldly eschatology was central to earliest Christianity, and was not confined to the enthusiastic margins of its life, a view of Christianity which has often been challenged.[5] But the evidence suggests that Christianity started out with a messianism very similar to that which is characteristic of Judaism. Eschatological convictions about the inauguration of a new age have as their concomitant a commitment to change which is political, something that we shall explore in this book.

The portrait of Jesus in the New Testament Gospels

According to the Gospel of Mark, Jesus' first words are 'the time is fulfilled; the kingdom of God is at hand; repent and believe in the gospel' (1:15). The phrase, 'the kingdom of God', is a central pillar for our understanding of the message of Jesus. It probably refers to a future age, when the divine will would be revealed in human affairs. The Matthean version of the Lord's Prayer, with its petition that God's Kingdom would come and his will be done on earth as in heaven (Matt. 6:10), is an accurate exposition of the essential features of the Jewish belief concerning the eschatological and this-worldly character of the Kingdom. While Luke 11:20 and 17:21 offer evidence of a present anticipation of the coming eschatological Kingdom, in which the eschatological age was already at work in Jesus' ministry, the dominant perspective is of imminent fulfilment.[6]

Nevertheless, Jesus is presented as the *agent* of the inauguration of the coming divine Kingdom, pre-eminently in the challenge he effected by going up to Jerusalem (Luke 9:51). This differs from texts contemporary with the New Testament, where God's purposes in history were to be worked out and a kingdom of righteousness to be set up without human hand (Dan. 2:34 alluded to in Luke 20:18 cf. Matt. 21:44; 4 Ezra 13:38). Nevertheless, the conviction that the eschatological events had, at least in part, arrived did not necessitate the belief that their complete manifestation in human history would be immediate. Jewish sources suggest that the 'end time events' could be very protracted.[7] The time of Jesus was both the time of inauguration and a period *preceding* the final consummation. Mark 9:1 suggests that there will be a period when his followers would carry on his work. If the words at the Last Supper are any guide, particularly in the version in which we have them in 1 Corinthians 11:23–6, then Jesus interpreted the significance of his death and gave instructions for the repetition of the rite by his followers.[8]

In the gospel tradition we find few descriptions of life in the future Kingdom of God. There is anticipation of participation in the messianic banquet which was to come, when Jesus would again drink of the fruit of the vine from which he had vowed to abstain at the Last Supper (Mark 14:25 and par; Matt. 8:11–12). The messianic banquet was a familiar feature in Jewish views about the future, going back to Isaiah 25:6–8 and reflected in Luke 4:15–24; 13:28–9.[9] Some Jewish-Christians in the later part of the Christian century, like Cerinthus[10] and John of Patmos (Rev. 20), include explicit evocations of a this-worldly Kingdom of God. Indeed, in a saying attributed to Jesus which Irenaeus reports to us from the writings of Papias, we find the belief that the whole of creation would be restored to its pristine condition and would even be in a more glorious situation than it had been at the beginning.[11] Some of these themes echo those to be found in the Beatitudes, where promises are made to the poor, the hungry and the oppressed that their position would be reversed in the future, when the Kingdom of God came (Luke 6:20–3; Matt. 5:3–12).

In the New Testament Gospels Jesus' call to 'follow me' started a process of radicalisation for followers like Peter, whose rather forlorn words suggest the cost of his discipleship (Matt. 19:27–30 cf. Mark 10:28). Jesus' final words to his followers (Matt. 24–5; Mark 13; Luke 21) offer dire warnings of the threat of being led astray, of the need to persevere rather than offering answers to curiosity about the details of the future times and seasons. The words start with the prediction of the end of an era and the destruction of the Temple, for centuries the focal point for Jews. The emphasis is on what is necessary here and now, no better exemplified than by the image of the final assize, with the Son of Man sitting on God's throne separating the sheep from the goats (Matt. 25:31–45). It is those who recognise the heavenly Son of Man in the brethren who are hungry, thirsty, strangers, naked, weak and imprisoned in the present age who will inherit the kingdom prepared by God from the foundation of the world.

In the Gospel of John by contrast with Matthew, Mark and Luke the phrase 'Kingdom of God' almost completely disappears. It is replaced by the phrase 'eternal life' (whose eschatological character is evident from Daniel 12:2). Whatever hope there may be for the future (and there are occasional promises, e.g. 5:25–9), the focus is on the first coming as the critical moment when the eschatological decision is taken (5:24). Throughout the Gospel there are twin emphases on realised eschatology with a lack of concern for the kind of cosmic redemption we find in Revelation. Now, claims to see God are regarded as claims to see Jesus.[12] In John 1:14 we read of the tabernacling of the Divine Word in history, not as an event in the future but in the person of Jesus of Nazareth. The God enthroned in glory (cf. Isaiah 6; Ezekiel 1) is found in Christ who reveals God's glory to humans.[13] In the Gospel of John revelation is located in the person of Jesus, though it does hint that Jesus has a privileged access to information from God, as well as sight of the divine. Jesus proclaims himself as the revelation of the hidden God (14:8; 1:18). The highest wisdom of all, the knowledge of God, comes not through the information disclosed in visions and revelations but through the Word become flesh, Jesus of Nazareth, whose authority relies on the communication he has received from his father. The goal of the apocalyptic seer, the glimpse of God enthroned in glory (1 Enoch 14), is to be found in Jesus (1:18; 6:46; 12:41; 14:9) and, to borrow from the letter to the Colossians, he it is 'in whom are hid all the treasures of wisdom and knowledge' (Col. 2:3).[14]

But there is another aspect of the Gospel of John which should not be missed. It is the presentation of Jesus as a mystic, a prophet, who has access to the divine presence and whose authority depends on what he has seen and heard from God. The Johannine Jesus is willing to flout the law impelled by some higher call. This appeal to a higher authority becomes the criterion for his action, not the Law of Moses. Thus, Jesus claims to offer revelation of God (in his person) and also revelation about God in his words from what he has seen and heard in heaven. Like Isaiah, who *both* saw *and* was sent, two themes which are central to the Gospel of John (Isaiah 6), so Jesus is presented as a visionary prophet who sees God and reports what he has seen and heard, and is sent by the Father. The difference is that Jesus also regards himself as the embodiment of the divine glory.

In a brilliant passage Ernst Käsemann captures the problem posed by the radical prophet as the evidence of the Gospel of John shows. What we find there is a demonstration of the priority given to the immediate divine word and vision over received wisdom. Not only does it encapsulate a feature fundamental to the Gospel of John but captures why it is that Jesus' attitude to authority was deemed to be such a threat to the powers that be (cf. Mark 11:27–33). Like Jeremiah, Jesus found himself on the brink of death for speaking what he believed to be given to him by God, a message which contrasted starkly with what the prophets and priests of his day asserted (Jer. 28 and 29 cf. John 7).

In writing about the Gospel of John, Käsemann draws out something which is characteristic of the radicalism of the New Testament, in which, to quote Blake's contrast, 'Inspiration' has priority over 'Memory':[15]

> In [the Gospel of John] Jesus' opponents characteristically barricade themselves behind the Old Testament tradition to help them cast doubt on and contest the truth of his message [...]. Many generations know of revelation only in preserved form and refuse to accept it in any other. Institutions, confessional movements and entire denominations rancorously strive over religious canned goods. They seriously imagine God would lose his identity if he were not caught and rendered concrete in this way, if he were not committed to inviolable theological formulas and thus become a calculable object in pious interchange. With these efforts grave-watchers of the sacred past calculate who Jesus is and must be, that is, the one who fits the religious concept or traditional program. The Johannine Christ reveals that the guardian of tradition makes himself judge of his Lord and protects himself from a new intervention of God. He no longer need fear any surprises from heaven,

> and on earth he defends the status quo of his convictions thus in effect is totally inaccessible.
>
> The Fourth Gospel unmasks such an understanding of revelation as the caricature of a discipleship to which the Creator summons to service from out of that which was, thus continually to hear the Word as if for the first time and to surrender everything in order to remain with Jesus alone [...]. The sole decisive question is Who is Jesus, and What does he bring us and require of us? Even the Bible is to be measured by this, interpreted on this basis. It is not the letter of the Bible but the One who is proclaimed by it that makes it a divine address to us, the bearer of all promise, the measure of genuine piety. Let rebels and reformers take care lest the explosive power of its summons be smothered by what is merely edifying, lest organizational atrophy and manipulation allow the great theme of Scripture as gospel to be forgotten – that is, the exodus of the once imprisoned into the freedom of the children of God, and the presence of the rule of God over our life and earth.[16]

So who was Jesus of Nazareth, the radical prophet?

Jesus resembled both the holy men who frequented Galilee in the first century CE,[17] and the prophetic figures described by the late first-century Jewish historian, Flavius Josephus.[18] The activity of both Jesus and these prophets prompted large crowds to gather, probably because people saw in their persons and actions new signs of God's liberating activity, echoing past events recorded in Scripture, and the possibility of some improvement in their social and economic situation. Jesus' assertion of the imminence of the Kingdom of God (e.g. Mark 1:15; Luke 11:20) put him in a different position. If we compare him with another Jesus, who was active in Jerusalem in the years before the First Jewish Revolt, about whom we know from Josephus,[19] the other Jesus was a prophet of doom whose incessant proclamation of woe led to his arrest. This appeared to be the sum total of his activity, and he was released by the Romans as a harmless eccentric.

With Jesus of Nazareth it was different. Not only did he have a message of woe (cf. Matthew 23; Luke 11:42–52), but his actions as an exorcist and (from the perspective of the authorities in Jerusalem in particular) a troublemaker, made him a threat to public order.

Jesus picked up on Ezekiel's challenge to 'a rebellious house' (Ezek. 2:7) in his generation, both literally, of what the ruling elite had made of the Temple in Jerusalem (Mark 11:17–18) and figuratively, of those whose hegemony Jesus challenged (Luke 11:45–52). Also like Ezekiel, he saw the heavens opened (Mark 1:10 cf. Ezek. 1:1), which may have been shared with key disciples, Mark 9:2–9. Like the prophets of a previous age he endured persecution and expected to die (Luke 13:33–4 cf. Mark 8:31; Luke 9:44). Like the Son of Man of Daniel 7:13, who was given kingdom, rule and authority, Jesus looked forward to a time when his words and life would be vindicated (Matt. 19:28; Mark 14:62) when he would sit down with his followers and drink wine in the Kingdom of God, so remedying his abstinence at his last meal with them (Mark 14:25).

Whether or not Jesus saw himself as the messiah, the descendant of David, a blend of intense visionary experience and a sense of vocation persuaded him to move from Galilee to Jerusalem, the metropolitan centre of ancient Jewish religion focused on the Temple. A violent incident in the Temple, and a large popular following in the volatile atmosphere of Jerusalem at Passover, were enough to set him at odds with the priests. Jesus died as a subversive at the hands of the Roman colonial power during the prefecture of Pontius Pilate in Judea (26–36 cf. Luke 3:1). In the final days of his life, possibly in the light of the hostility he encountered, he prophesied doom on the Temple and Jerusalem (Mark 13:2; Luke 19:44).

As we shall see in a later chapter, William Blake presents Jesus as a challenger of the *status quo*, particularly the Law of Moses and all that it entails.[20] 'From impulse not from rules' summarises something, which is absolutely essential to the portrait of Jesus in the Gospels. Jesus' authority was not based on wisdom passed down from generation to generation by authoritative teachers, such as we find enunciated in the early collection of rabbinic aphorisms, *Pirke Aboth* (1:1). 'Christ died as an Unbeliever,' wrote Blake.[21] At first sight this might be deemed an example of Blake's bloated rhetoric. A moment's thought will remind us that at the crucial moment in his confrontation with the hierarchy according to Mark 14:62–4 Jesus was accused of blasphemy. What he said had put him beyond the pale of his community – at least according to the judgement of the High Priest and his kangaroo court. He was an outcast, as well as an enthusiast. Blake was right. Central to the story that the early Christians told about Jesus was that he was an outsider and had been consigned thither by the political powerbrokers of his day, abetted by the Roman colonial power.

Jesus gave mixed messages, bringing not peace but a sword (Matt. 10:34), contrasting with love of enemies (Matt. 5:44). The artist Rembrandt's evocation of the event on the cover of the book captures the violence of the disturbance. The vexed, indeed angry, look of aggression on Jesus' face evinces a feature of the Jesus tradition in the New Testament which is not easily dismissed and has to be borne in mind and put alongside the emphasis on the king who comes meek and lowly riding on an ass, as Matthew glosses the account of the entry into Jerusalem (Matt. 21:5). Indeed, it mirrors the aggressive and critical words of Jesus about his opponents which are deeply embedded in the tradition and are found in variant forms in Luke 11 and Matthew 23 but are paralleled elsewhere in the Gospels. The violent look on Jesus' face in Rembrandt's portrayal, as he casts out the traders from the Temple (Matt. 21:12; Mark 11:15–18; Luke 19:45–6; John 2:14–16), is hardly the demeanour of one who loved his enemies. Jesus' actions were sometimes at odds with his words. In the light of this it may be no surprise that when Jesus was arrested some of his followers were armed (Luke 22:35–8; John 18:10), though there may have been other reasons for carrying the potentially lethal weapons which, at least initially, had nothing to do with premeditated plans for an armed struggle. Jesus' followers could have been pardoned for supposing that they were going to be part of some holy war alongside the legions of angels taking on the forces of darkness. The sources indicate a gradually more explicit refusal of violence by Jesus, with the earliest Gospel, Mark, being more ambiguous about what was said at his arrest (Mark 14:43–9). Such mixed messages are comprehensible in the context of the report about the nature of Jesus' activity, which was inspired by his conviction that he was the agent of the new age. We cannot be sure, but it was probably only at the point of his arrest that Jesus finally refused the option of violence, thereby setting an example which has had enormous influence ever since. One can only speculate, but in abjuring violence, there may have been a recognition that the 'anticipation of communism' could not be 'by fantasy' (to borrow the words of Friedrich Engels),[22] and the reality of the constraints of history had to be taken into account – which is exactly what we find in the writings of Paul.

Paul: messianic emissary enabling communities to live in the Last Days

Paul's dramatic vision on the road to Damascus meant that his earlier pattern of beliefs, in which Jesus had been an object of contempt and his followers subject to hostility, had to be completely re-orientated. In the first two chapters of Galatians, Paul sets out the basis of his claim to authority which was based on the conviction of a direct prophetic vocation (Gal. 1:12, 16). Paul's sense of himself is nowhere better communicated than in his account of the dramatic event which turned his world upside down in Galatians 1:11–16 and in which he became a messianic agent. His self-description owes much to earlier emissaries of God, Isaiah of the Exile and Jeremiah and possibly, elsewhere, Ezekiel as well.[23] The words from Jeremiah which are quoted relate to his place in the plan of God and his being marked for this *kairos* moment in the divine economy (Gal. 1:15–16 cf. Jer. 1:5 and Isa. 49:1). Paul rejected the idea that he was merely the intermediary of the Church in Jerusalem and therefore subordinate to their dictates. Like Jesus, his was a response to a divine call and not dependent on human dictates and authority. Paul had transferred from a Jewish group, which still accepted beliefs concerning the future as an article of faith, to a group whose beliefs and practices were based on the Jewish tradition but which claimed that those promises were already a matter of fulfilment and practice. For example, Christians in Corinth were told that passages in the Bible were in reality addressed directly to those fortunate to be alive when the decisive moment in history came about: 'Now these things happened to them as a warning, but they were written down for our instruction, upon whom the end of the ages has come' (1 Cor. 10:11, Revised Standard Version). The dramatic vision and vocation which led to this transference was backed up with a new slant on the meaning of the shared Scriptures (as Gal. 3–4 indicate). This was a key point at which Paul and the bulk of contemporary Judaism parted company: he thought it possible to have an interpretation of Judaism which claimed to remain a part of that tradition without accepting the *literal implementation* of the laws (e.g. circumcision), while retaining items of the Jewish law and its role as a general guide for life (cf. Rom. 15:4).

The fundamental issue for Paul in the Letter to the Galatians is that what is rumoured to be happening is that the community, probably mainly non-Jews, are taking up Jewish practices, presumably on the basis that they have in fact become proselytes. It is that basic fact of which Paul wants to disabuse them. His intention was not to offer them access to his former life in Judaism (Gal. 1:14). Because he was the agent of messiah to the gentiles, it is about access to nothing less than the messianic age (Gal. 1:4). That is a promise to non-Jews as well as Jews and making the nations aware of the promise is fundamental to Paul's understanding of himself. He was not, since the apocalypse of Jesus Christ, which Paul understood as a quasi-prophetic vocation (Gal. 1:15), scouring land and sea making proselytes (cf. Matt. 23:15) but fulfilling the eschatological promises to the nations (Isa. 11:10; 45:22–3; Isa. 60; Zech. 8:20–3; 1 Enoch 90: 30–6). Paul believed that in a vision the heavenly messiah had called him directly to be the emissary to the Gentiles, to summon them to be inheritors of the messianic kingdom, which did not require them to become Jews to be participants.

What Paul was trying to articulate was a new situation, uncharted territory, to which the Jewish traditions had borne witness as a promise, but few, if any, had dared to speak of as a promise fulfilled. The struggle to make sense of the significance of his ancestral traditions required an epistemological shift, matching the shift in the ages which Paul believed he had seen in Christ.[24] Paul had forsaken an interpretation of the Law which was common within *non-eschatological Jewish* groups, for one which is to be understood in the light of the conviction that the age to come is part of the present experience of humanity. The Jewish Scriptures were read in the light of the fact that the age of the Spirit had come. For Paul the present had become a time of messianic fulfilment: 'Behold, now is the acceptable time; behold, now is the day of salvation' (2 Cor. 6:2).[25]

Paul explored a new attitude and a new approach to the moral life, appropriate for the messianic age that had already started, based on the action of the divine Spirit. Romans 8:1–11 and 1 Corinthians 2:10–16 commend a life guided by the eschatological Spirit, which places them above the obligations of the law code. Paul expects that the life of the Spirit will be in continuity with the obedience offered to God, which the Law required (cf. Rom. 8:3). In 1 Corinthians 2:10–16 Paul claims that life in the Spirit enables a person to have the mind of Christ and to understand the things of God. There is now no need for a law code, for the Spirit guides, akin to the law written on the heart prophesied by Jeremiah (31:34) and Ezekiel (36:26–7 cf. 2 Cor. 3:3). Such a Spirit-led life could easily produce the kind of discord found in Corinth, however, manifesting characteristics which Paul regards as antithetical to the life of the Spirit (Gal. 5:16–26).

Throughout the Pauline letters reflection arises from action and engagement, and above all else the constraints of context. It is never abstracted from life. Constrained by the limits of communication that confronted him in his itinerant life-style, the written word became the major means of bringing Paul into the midst of the nascent community. Just as he reminded those to whom he was writing of the way Christ crucified had been publicly portrayed before their very eyes (Gal. 3:1), so now in the reading of his words, though absent in body he was very much present in spirit (cf. 1 Cor. 5:3). His letters, beliefs and practices, which often seem to fit uneasily with each other, *together* help one understand a little of the complex exploratory process involved in the struggle to reconcile, to discern what life 'in the Messiah' might be about.

In sum, Paul was involved in community organisation, enabling what were in effect minority groups to maintain identity and cohesion as they sought to understand what it meant to anticipate life in the Kingdom of God on earth. Paul drew on his own experience, as well as conformity with practices which seemed to have worked in communities, encouraging mutual, and indeed, international, altruism (e.g. Rom. 15:25–9; 2 Cor. 8–9), to build community among those whom he addressed. As 1 Corinthians, epitomised by 1 Corinthians 13, makes clear, Paul above all was keen to ensure that mutual respect was encouraged. 'Judge not that ye be not judged' is Paul's maxim as he seeks to persuade the Roman Christians not to live solely for self. Often as not that meant keeping their heads below the radar (cf. 1 Thess. 4:1–12).

Paul emphasised that final consummation was still to come, and that the present is a time of suffering (Rom. 8:18). The old order is still very much in evidence. So the Pauline corpus in the New Testament can often seem to be socially conservative; see, for example, Paul's statements about 'the powers that be' (Rom. 13:1), and the role of women and marriage (e.g. 1 Cor. 14:34 and 1 Tim. 2). But we may have to understand these *ad hoc* pieces of advice as evidence of Paul's determination to maintain community cohesion at all costs in the difficult situations they were dealing with. In 1 Corinthians, and elsewhere, Paul resorts to the role of a rabbi and offers apostolic counsel to guide his Corinthian readers. This ideology was imposed by apostolic authority on the church in Corinth with little or no explanation.

His language about the believers and the messianic community being temples of the Holy Spirit (1 Cor. 3:16; 6:19) indicate the extent of the inclusion of Jewish culture and custom into the emerging ethos of the nascent communities. In 1 Corinthians 5–6, sexual impurity had to be rooted out of the Corinthian community to ensure that the holy Temple remained undefiled (1 Cor. 3:16; 6:19; 2 Cor. 6:14–7:1). Sins which defile 'the temple of the Holy Spirit' needed to be expunged, lest God's presence depart (cf. Lev. 15:31). Holiness became a central concern (cf. Lev. 10:10; 20:26). Those who practised abominations were to be cut off from the people (Lev. 18:8, 29; Deut. 17:7 cf. 1 Cor. 5:13), though elsewhere (e.g. 1 Cor. 7: 12–16) there is evidence of the emergence of a more inclusive understanding in relation to conduct by a believer with regard to an unbelieving spouse and the offspring of 'mixed' marriages'.[26] But it appears to be the case that, while obedience to the Law of Moses was not necessary for entry into the messianic community, in Paul's case it had an indispensable role for those who wished to *stay* part of that community.[27]

What is striking about Paul's letters is the greater concern for community organisation as compared with what we find in all the Gospels. The gospel tradition says that Jesus may have taught his disciples but the impression we are offered is of a group who may have been committed to him but were puzzled about what was expected of them and indeed what would be Jesus' future. They followed him up to Jerusalem, and according to John 11:16, Thomas says 'Let us die with him'. There is little comprehension of what was going on. That may have been true for many of the recipients of Paul's letters, but it certainly wasn't for want of trying on Paul's part, where there is evidence of a consistent attempt to assist in community formation and how to live as followers of the Messiah in the midst of an age passing away.

The genius of Paul is that he engaged in an exploratory, experimental exercise in organising, advising and admonishing his communities. He wanted them to learn to live together, but also to explore what it might mean to be *messianic*, or as Paul put it, to be 'in Christ'. Paul was the 'organic intellectual' (see below, Chapter 7,

'Experiencing biblical study in the *comunidades eclesiais de base*') of early Christianity who used his intellectual expertise to help map the meaning of messianic practice and communicated it as effectively as he could through letters. According to Acts 17, Paul had a rather dusty response from the Athenians who met on the Areopagus, who according to the author of Acts 'spent their time in nothing except telling or hearing something new' (Acts 17:21). That is not surprising. Paul's intellectual engagement was not just words but was about what it meant to love in deed and truth (cf. 1 John 3:18). Biblical scholarship down the centuries has been too ready to make Paul into an Areopagite, or academician, an embryonic systematic theologian, instead of the pioneer practical theologian his letters suggest he was.

The Apocalypse and the revelation of the future as challenge to the present

The word 'apocalypse' opens the Book of Revelation (1:1), but elsewhere it is 'prophecy' (e.g. 22:10, 18). It continues earlier Jewish prophecy, as evident in the many allusions to these texts, but it also, in key respects, transcends them and even supplants pre-existing prophecy, as John's prophecy is about the definitive moment in history. Also, the earlier prophetic texts offer John the Seer the medium for his visions.

The Apocalypse sets out to reveal, or 'unveil' the true nature of things, whether that be the divine plan for history initiated by the coming of the Messiah or the unjust character of contemporary society and the super-human forces at work in opposition to God's righteousness in the world.[28] The outline of future history and the inevitability of heaven on earth (cf. Rev. 21–2) offer a challenge for a change of heart to engage the whole of life. The Apocalypse advocates prophecy before the world, about the coming reign of God on earth, the millennium (Rev. 20) righteousness of God and the dreadful consequences of ignoring its implementation (e.g. Rev. 10:12). The hope for the reign of God on earth has a distinctive form in Revelation. It is to last a thousand years, hence the description of it as the Millennium (Rev. 20). This belief is also referred to as 'chiliasm', deriving from the Greek word for 'thousand'. What is distinctive about millennial belief is that it is very much 'this-worldly' and so differs from the standard future hope that will be in heaven (after all, according to Revelation 21–2, heaven will be 'on earth' in the new age).

The central theological theme of the Apocalypse is the overcoming of opposition between God and earth, as exemplified by the contrast between the vision of the New Jerusalem in Revelation 21 with the initial vision of the heavenly court in Chapter 4. In Revelation 4 the seer is granted a glimpse into the environs of God. Here God the Creator is acknowledged *in heaven*, and, it is from the God of the universe that the historical process begins which leads to the establishment of a new aeon after the manifestation of divine judgement. In Revelation 4, God is depicted as being in heaven, and it is there that the heavenly host sing God's praise. In contrast, in Revelation 21, God's dwelling is *on earth*; it is no longer in heaven. The contrast between heaven and earth disappears in the new creation. Now the tabernacling of God is with humanity, and they shall be God's people. It is only in the New Age that there will be the conditions for God and humanity to dwell in that harmony, which was impossible while there was rejection of the divine righteousness in human affairs. The 'conquest' of the Lamb (Rev. 5:5–6) is a moment of crisis for the cosmos as a whole. It is the perspective from which all else is viewed – culture, economics, religion, power and status.

After Chapters 4 and 5 we find the picture of a world afflicted but unrepentant (Rev. 9:20). In the unfolding eschatological drama in the main body of the Apocalypse there is involvement of the Seer (Rev. 10). He is instructed to eat the scroll and commanded to prophesy. It is a direct call to participate actively as a prophet, rather than merely be a passive spectator of the terrible eschatological drama that is unfolding, or, even worse, be implicated in an unjust order that is passing away. In Revelation 11 the Church is offered a paradigm of the true prophetic witness. Prophecy is not merely an uttering of oracles but involves the whole of life. Prophets could expect a life of witness, suffering and death, so that whether they live or die would be a repetition of what their Lord suffered (Rev. 11:8). The irony is that in the story of Jesus the holy city is the site of profanity in which the rejection of the prophets is continued (Matt. 23:35–7). The holy city, which according to 11:2 is profaned, is thus the same as Sodom and Gomorrah. It is a telling reminder that there is no unambiguously holy place. That will apply to churches and holy places anywhere. They are all potentially sites of human conflict and the possible profanation of God's way.

Revelation 13, a vision inspired by Daniel 7, offers a terrible vision of the whole world following after in amazement (13:4) and worshipping the dragon. Public opinion goes along with the propaganda of the Beast and its supporters. The pressure is to conform and be marked with the mark of the Beast (13:14). Those who persevere (an important theme of Revelation) are shown that the might of state power is itself extraordinarily fragile, and its affluence, so attractive and alluring, is destined for destruction, destroyed by precisely that power which has maintained it. There are, however, public, social and economic consequences of non-conformity.

In the vision recounted in Revelation 17 John, in the midst of the culture of 'Babylon', a place of exile (Psalm 137 and 1 Peter 5:13), is offered a visionary perspective (17:3 cf. 21:10), which allowed him to see Babylon for what it was and the inevitability of its demise (Rev. 17:2, 4; 18:3). It may seem to the nations of the world that they have achieved great prosperity as a result of Babylon's power (18:3), but in God's estimation things are very different. The political and economic challenge Revelation presents includes the church members. They are not exempt from the judgement meted out on those taken in by the political and economic injustice of the imperial beast and its Babylonian culture. In the letters to the angels of the seven churches (Rev. 2–3), it is the weak and those who are on the point of extinction, like the slaughtered lamb (Rev. 5:6), to whom is held out hope. The faithful are not prosperous churches but prophets and witnesses who find themselves suffering 'outside the gate' (Heb. 13:12), where also their Lord was crucified (Rev. 11:8).

As elsewhere in the New Testament what is crucial in Revelation is bearing witness, following a different vision, not compromising with the beast and Babylon and with those convictions finding ways to endure and so to prophesy. Prophecy turns out to be no easy task, just as it was an agony for the prophet Jeremiah and other prophets (cf. Luke 13:33). Jesus of Nazareth is the faithful prophetic witness, and his followers have to continue that testimony of Jesus (19:10). What dominates is testimony to another way of being in the world and the protest against that which stands against it. What we find in the Book of Revelation is how the petition of the Lord's Prayer is fulfilled, how God's Kingdom comes *on earth*. Revelation is not about 'going to heaven' but 'heaven on earth'. It is a text which encourages a critical distance from contemporary culture both in social relations and the language of its apocalyptic discourse: the powers of the day are viewed as The Beast and the Harlot. John's situation is, as Blake's who was inspired by Revelation, one where 'The Beast and the Harlot rule without controls',[29] but the end of that regime is on the horizon.

The change in eschatological perspective

There is some evidence in the New Testament that there was a problem posed by the delay of the establishment of the messianic kingdom (1 Cor. 15:24–5). In 2 Peter, for example, we have the clearest indication that the community addressed had to wrestle with the issue (2 Peter 3:3–7). Elsewhere in the New Testament, the bulk of the evidence is *much* less explicit. Indeed, one wonders if the problem of the delay of the coming of the messianic kingdom may be more a projection of modern scholarly perplexity about the way the first Christians had coped with disappointment than the textual evidence suggests. This is in large part because of the emergence of an understanding of 'apocalyptic eschatology' in the nineteenth century as being about 'the end of history', which has become so pervasive (see Chapter 4, 'Apocalypse'). A rather different eschatological perspective emerged in the Gospel of John. Here the emphasis is on the new life that can be experienced *now* through belief in Jesus (John 5:24). The emphasis of the Gospel is the relationship which believers can enjoy with Christ and, through him, with God (John 14:23). The promise is not for the Kingdom of God on earth when the disciples will reign with Jesus (Matt. 19:28), but that they will be with Jesus, *in heaven* (John 17:24). It is similar in the letter to the Ephesians (1:23). In Hebrews, too, heaven is the focus of salvation and the orientation of believers. Christ has gone into the heavens, behind the veil, and is there a sure anchor of hope for those who follow him (Heb. 6:19–20). There is a move away from the belief that the goal of the salvation of God is the manifestation of God's righteousness in the world, and more towards an emphasis on the salvation of the individual and his union with the exalted Christ (e.g. John 14:2; 17:24). What emerged was an understanding of Christian discipleship which speaks of an earthly pilgrimage and a heavenly destination (John 17:24 cf. 1 Peter 1:4; 1:9; 1:17). The focus of interest of the believer moves from this present world to the joys of heaven. This world is not to be changed in the present; it is a place of pilgrimage, even, at times, a snare, which might prevent those who seek the heavenly Jerusalem from reaching their true home that is in heaven not a polity to come on earth. Church life, worship and doctrine were the means of keeping the faithful within the scope of the divine saving activity, to ensure that the journey to one's eternal abode was not compromised. It contrasts with Revelation, where the contrast between heaven and earth, the life of the age to come and this age, is only a *temporary phenomenon*. When the Letter to the Ephesians speaks of the Church being 'in the heavenly places in Christ' (Ephes. 1:20; 2:6; 3:10; 6:12),[30] we are seeing the beginning of a gradual switch from an expectation for human history to the experience of that salvation which already exists with God.

Also, the demise of significant actors from the first generation of Christians probably contributed to a sense of bewilderment. Paul's writings reflect the conviction that God had revealed to him the mystery of salvation and his part in it (Gal. 1:12 and 16). The mission to the Gentiles, and probably also the collection for the saints in Jerusalem, were closely linked with an eschatological drama in which Paul saw himself as an agent, an apostle, and so, a crucial actor. Paul thought of himself as an, perhaps *the*, eschatological agent, like the 12, who were told by Jesus that they would sit on 12 thrones judging the 12 tribes of Israel (Matt. 19:28). John 21:23 suggests the shock which a community suffered when the death of one who had contact with Jesus took place. Paul, like the Beloved Disciple, places himself as part of the special group who 'had seen the Lord' (1 Cor. 15:3–9 cf. 9:1). Once that sense of being part of the especially decisive moment in history disappeared, however, the understanding of present activity as an integral part of the eschatological drama and its relationship with the future consummation of the divine purposes gradually disappeared also.

Conclusion

As Friedrich Engels with pardonable exaggeration put it, 'as an authentic picture of almost primitive Christianity, drawn by one of themselves, the book [of Revelation] is worth more than all the rest of the New Testament put together'.[31] The hope of a new age *on earth* was still widely held from the second century onwards, as is evident in the writings of Justin Martyr, Irenaeus, Hippolytus, Tertullian and Lactantius.[32] The expectation was for a time of great prosperity, in which people would enjoy long life, as is evident from the words which the early second-century writer, Papias, attributed to Jesus about a this-worldly hope for the future, in which Jesus said the creation would return to and exceed the perfection of the original creation.[33] This type of belief was the earliest phase of the Christian doctrine of hope in which an earthly Kingdom of God was earnestly expected, echoing the Matthean version of the Lord's Prayer where there is a longing for God's Kingdom to 'come on earth as in heaven'.

Jewish future hopes in the Second Temple period were many and various, though with some common features, but the conviction that eschatology was not just a matter of belief or speculation but a determining principle of life, which might disturb received wisdom and push adherents along uncharted paths of religious and social experiment, is a distinguishing feature of New Testament texts. Whatever may have been the case in the earliest phase of Christianity's existence (and we can only surmise from various hints of enthusiasm we find in passages like Acts, such as the utopian practice in Acts 2:44 and 4:34, and 1 Cor. 12–14), by the time Paul was writing his letters, his eschatological beliefs had been tempered with an expectation that the nascent communities must await a consummation still to come, and meanwhile come to terms with an age that is passing away. The various layers of the theology and ethics of the New Testament are saturated with a perspective, which both recognises the 'penultimate' moment, while at the same time stresses the 'extraordinary' privilege belonging to those who found themselves at that significant moment in history.

So, if there is one secure, and perhaps most important, result of 200 years of historical scholarship on early Christian texts, it is that eschatological ideas are central to the understanding of them. Recent study of the historical Jesus echoes assessments, which go back at least to the work of Johannes Weiss and Albert Schweitzer.[34] Even those who doubt that Jesus was an eschatological prophet recognise that by the time of the canonical gospels Christ was viewed through the lens of eschatology.[35] The development of Christianity was tied up with early Christianity's wrestling with its eschatological inheritance.[36] Eschatological beliefs are the most significant motor of the development of the Christian religion and the formation of the typical contours of Christian theology and ethics in the centuries after the New Testament writings were written. Modern New Testament scholarship, whether historical or theological, offers a series of attempts to comprehend the debt of the New Testament to the eschatological and apocalyptic religion of Second Temple Judaism.

In a typically illuminating essay, W.D. Davies seemed to express relief that Christianity moved away from its apocalyptic and eschatological origins. In comparing the seventeenth-century Jewish messianic movement led by Sabbatai Sevi with the apocalyptic and messianic origins of Christianity he wrote of emerging Christianity being 'spared the more undesirable [apocalyptic] tendencies':[37]

> Early Christianity knew the [...] temptation [of 'apocalyptic' as a pernicious menace], but in its main development, though not all its expressions, it was often spared from the more undesirable tendencies by the constraint of its founding figure. Early Christianity was apocalyptic, but, it was such under the constraint of the *agape* [...] of Christ.[38]

Whatever we think of Davies' appeal to the founder's 'constraint', his view that emerging Christianity moved away from its apocalyptic and eschatological foundations helps us to understand the development of its intellectual tradition and the marginalisation of radical prophecy in the centuries to come.

PART 2

Kairos

The Unique Moment and Apocalyptic Discernment

This section is a consideration of the important way in which key themes in the New Testament were taken up in later Christian thought. We start with the evidence in the New Testament of the importance attached to certain individuals in the events bringing about the coming of the new age; Jesus obviously, but also Paul. It is an issue which was raised at the end of the previous chapter (Chapter 2). The career of the Reformation activist and theologian Thomas Muentzer epitomises this issue of human agency in the Last Things. His self-professed role as 'The New Daniel' is indicative of his sense of prophetic vocation, and his theological justification of the war against the princes is a classic example of the way in which human agents resorted to divine endorsement for violence in their struggle to bring about the Kingdom of God.

In the nineteenth century the acting out of scriptural models is well exemplified by the career of Joanna Southcott, who saw her vocation to act out the prophecy of the Woman Clothed with the Sun of Revelation 12 (an identification made also by others, for example, Ann Lee, 1736–84, founder of the Shakers, Elspeth Buchan in Scotland, 1728–91, and later Mary Ann Girling, 1827–86).[1] Southcott also claimed divine inspiration for an authoritative interpretation of the Bible.

The second chapter on the Book of Revelation has two parts: the awareness on the part of interpreters of being at a particular point in the divine economy on the brink of fulfilment; and the revelatory and eschatological character of apocalypse, which all demonstrate the continuing impact of this important biblical book. By reference to the sequences of sevens they read in the Book of Revelation, Joachim of Fiore and his followers believed themselves to be on the very cusp of a propitious moment, as is also evident in the writings and the art of Savonarola and Botticelli. The chapter ends with a different appropriation of the 'subversive apocalypse' by the twentieth-century writer, William Stringfellow, for the imagery of the Book of Revelation provided a lens through which to focus on what he perceived to be his nation's shortcomings and delusions.

Chapter 3

Human Actors in the Divine Drama

Some of those whose ideas are considered in this book believed that they lived in auspicious times which demanded active response. Such responses are to be found within the New Testament itself, as key figures in the foundational texts of Christianity believed that they had important roles in the divine economy. That is true of Jesus, whose sense of the obligation laid upon him impelled him to go to Jerusalem, and Paul, who saw himself as the one delegated by the heavenly Messiah to be an agent to the gentiles in the Last Days. Such convictions have their echoes throughout history. One example, in a century where the sense of destiny and apocalyptic moment were particularly evident, is the revolutionary prophet who died fighting alongside the peasants in a holy war, Thomas Muentzer. Another example is the remarkable career of Joanna Southcott who in her 64th year believed herself to be called to be the mother of the returning messiah, Shiloh, as the Woman Clothed with the Sun of Revelation 12, and died supposedly giving birth to the messiah in 1814.

Omitted from the discussion at this point is the likelihood that William Blake shared this understanding. As will be pointed out later (Chapter 6, 'Every honest man is a prophet'), in one version of his illuminated books he inserts a date, possibly indicating that he regarded himself the agent of the inauguration of the beginning of the new heaven.

The ultimate 'opportune moment' in the New Testament and the agents who sought to act on it

It is not difficult to find antecedents in ancient Jewish texts to New Testament eschatology, either in the Bible or in texts contemporary with the New Testament (NT), whether like those that are dateable, such as the Dead Sea Scrolls, or those whose transmission may have made them more problematic as evidence (like 4 Ezra or the Similitudes of Enoch, 1 Enoch 37–71). General eschatological parallels to the NT, whether or not they concern the end of the world, or some different future, cataclysmic or otherwise, can be found in plenty. What is not so easy to find are texts contemporary with the NT, which give us the kind of evidence that we have in the New Testament, not just of future hope, but the conviction that the hope is being realised and, what is more, humans have a key role as agents in bringing it about rather than merely heralding it. As already mentioned, there are the so-called 'sign' prophets mentioned by Flavius Josephus[1] (see above, Chapter 2, 'So who was Jesus of Nazareth, the radical prophet?'), whose deeds suggest the kind of actualisation of biblical promises, or, in terms of the crossing of the Jordan, the recapitulation of redemptive events from the past. The problem is that we do not have any records extant which tell us about their views.

It is the feature of inaugurated eschatology in the NT which is so distinctive. The Last Days are here, and that which the prophets foresaw, readers of NT texts are now privileged to see (Luke 10:20; 1 Peter 1:11–12). The sociologist Karl Mannheim wrote of the 'chiliastic mentality'. For him this phrase described the mind-set of those with millennial beliefs, who believed themselves crucial agents in the inauguration of a new age *on earth*. It is with regard to a 'this-worldly' eschatology that sociologists of religion have used the term 'millenarian' for those who have held the belief in a this-worldly hope, thereby reflecting the widespread 'this-worldly' eschatology of the fringe groups in Christian history. People with millennial hopes look forward to an imminent reversal of political arrangements in this age, so that the down-trodden (among whom are the holders of the millenarian beliefs, of course) either become the leaders in the new age or have a share in a quality of life denied to them in the old age.

The sense of importance of the present time, evident in these passages, is captured from time to time in several passages in which NT writers use the word *kairos*. From the pregnant announcement by Jesus at the start of his ministry in the Gospel of Mark (1:15), and the link with his journey to Jerusalem in the Gospel of John (7:6, 8), to the acceptable moment of salvation (2 Cor. 6:2), *kairos* is linked with what Karl Mannheim has termed the 'propitious moment' when that which has been hitherto a dream is translated into reality. Heaven comes on earth in the here and now. Mannheim uses the term 'chiliastic mentality' to describe this break with the past and its culture and values that the dawn of the New Age means.[2]

That propitious moment, in Acts and 2 Corinthians is an eschatological moment, a time of fulfilment (other relevant examples include Luke 19:44; Acts 1:10; 5:6; 8:18; 11:5; Ephes. 1:10; Titus 1:3; Rev. 1:3; 22:10, and possibly Rom. 3:26). The Corinthians were encouraged to believe that they were privileged to be 'the ones on whom the ends of the ages had come' (1 Cor. 10:11; cf. Heb. 1:1–4). The present had become the critical moment, as an eschatological moment had arrived. In the Synoptic Gospels in the NT Jesus of Nazareth proclaims the present moment as decisive in God's purposes with himself as the unique prophetic/messianic agent. But the time of perfection in knowledge, insight and practice is still to come. A distinctive feature of New Testament theology is the 'now' and the 'not yet'. While believers may have tasted of the heavenly gift and the powers of the age to come (Heb. 6:4–5), yet the fullness of salvation is still to be experienced by the individual and manifested in the wider world (Rom. 8:18–25; 1 John 3: 2).

The resurrection of Jesus, especially in Paul's theology, was regarded as another 'propitious moment', in which a feature of the end-time becomes a reality in the old aeon. Thus the first Christians were affirming that for them the future hope was already in the process of fulfilment; it was not merely an item of faith still to be realised at some future point. The experience of the Spirit was also seen as the present expression in the life of the individual and the community of that eschatological reality, which had been manifested in the resurrection of Jesus of Nazareth from the dead. In Acts 2:17 the writer of Acts indicates that the pouring out of the Spirit on the day of Pentecost is a fulfilment of an eschatological promise from the book of Joel (Joel 2:28–9). The age of the divine Spirit, is, in Paul's language, the 'down payment' of the glory which is to come (2 Cor. 1:22; Rom. 8:23). This age was already marked by prophecy and under the guidance of the Spirit (1 Cor. 12–14; 1 Thess. 5:19–20). In the Pauline letters the Spirit is regarded as the motor for moral change and the ethical life. Romans 8:1–11 and 1 Corinthians 2:10–16 commend a life prompted by the indwelling, eschatological Spirit. There is now no need for a law code, for the indwelling Spirit enables obedience to the divine will (Ezekiel 36:26–7; Jer. 31:34 cf. 2 Cor. 3:3; Rom. 8:4–5). Throughout the New Testament there is a strong sense of being on the brink of the fulfilment of anticipated eschatological events that are seen as, at least in part, already taking place.

A central component of the future hope in Second Temple Jewish texts was the belief that, before the age to come finally arrived, there must be a time of great distress on the earth, when the elect may be expected to suffer, succinctly put in Daniel 12:1. It is a theme echoed in the eschatological discourses in the Gospels (Mark 13 and parallels, especially verses 7–13). Paul often writes of tribulations, as, for example, in Romans 2:9, Romans 8:18–23 and 35, and in 1 Thessalonians 3:3 and 7 (cf. Rev. 2:22; 7:14). The travail and persecution endured by believers is viewed by Paul as their undergoing that tribulation which is a necessary prelude to the arrival of the new age. Christians can therefore rejoice in their present sufferings (Rom. 5:3). How long that would last is never specified, and we do well to ponder whether the sense of eschatological imminence in the New Testament is as much about this period as the consummation of all things when heaven comes on earth. On the whole, NT writers do not specify moments when there is a shift in the eschatological events from one stage to another. 2 Thessalonians 2:6–7 and Mark 13:10 are exceptions, though in the former the meaning of 'what is restraining' and 'the restrainer' leaves a reader unclear about what precise moment or personage Paul (if he was in fact the writer of 2 Thessalonians) had in mind.

In the New Testament we find persons and events invested with a decisive role in the fulfilment of the Last Things. An obvious example is the way in which John the Baptist is identified with Elijah who is to come (Matt. 11:14; 17:13 cf. Malachi 4:5), or the Angel who will go before the face of God (Mark 1:2; Exodus 23:20 cf. Malachi 3:1). John's self-testimony, according to the Gospel of John (1:19), rejects identification with Elijah or one of the prophets, though there is identification with the voice crying in the wilderness of Isaiah 40:3 (John 1:23). The Gospel accounts, especially Luke, evince a similar sense of Jesus being a significant actor in the divine economy. References to himself, implicit and explicit, as a prophet (Luke 4:18; 13:33) and perhaps the enigmatic references to what is written with regard to the Son of Man and the necessity of suffering, suggest actualisation of what is written (so Luke 18:31: 'See, we are going up to Jerusalem, and everything that is written about the Son of Man by the prophets will be accomplished'); or the necessity of fulfilling the divine purposes (e.g. Luke 9:22: 'The Son of Man must undergo great suffering'). These passages seem to suggest Jesus being under some kind of compulsion to act in response to a divinely inspired impulse, perhaps even to 'act out' the Scriptures.

As we have seen, Paul believed that he and the communities of believers dotted around the Eastern Mediterranean were themselves living in a critical time of fulfilment of the ancient Scriptures (1 Cor. 10:11). He had the conviction that he had been set apart as the apostle to the Gentiles, commissioned by the messiah to preach the good news to the nations, and acted on that conviction (Gal. 1:16). We cannot be certain about the background for this sense of vocation, in particular whether the participation of non-Jews in the New Age (cf. Zech. 8:20) was a widely held eschatological belief (though it does seem to be implied in Luke 2:29–30). Whoever wrote Ephesians considered that Paul had a special role in the divine economy, enabling Gentiles to know the mystery hidden from all ages (Ephes. 3:1–10). If Ephesians is post-Pauline, we see how a later generation kept alive the soteriological role of apostle and community, and the way he was part of the 'propitious moment'. The New Testament writings communicate to their readers that they are in a time of historical transition in which the coming age of salvation, while imminent, already affects life in the present.

That sense of anticipation qualifies certainty about the present situation, for there is still waiting to be done and patient endurance to be undergone before knowledge and fulfilment finally come. The sense of fulfilment and anticipation brought their own problems. When things go amiss it can be seen as a sign of the work of Antichrist. In 1 John, for example, the presence of dissent and separation marks out the identity of Antichrist as an all-too-human presence in the midst of the community. The application of eschatological imagery to contemporary institutions, persons and events is one of countless examples from the Christian tradition. Antichrist is no remote supernatural figure, but stalks the earth in the opponents of the writer of 1 John (1 John 2:18–20).

Just as the coming of John the Baptist, according to the Jesus tradition, had signalled a shift in the aeons (Luke 16:16), so for Paul, the vision of the resurrected Christ was intimately linked with his own sense of mission within the overall scheme of salvation history. Paul, like the Beloved Disciple, places himself as part of the special group who 'had seen the Lord' (1 Cor. 15:3–7; cf. 9:1), belonging to the circle of privileged eschatological agents (Chapter 2, 'The change in eschatological perspective'). There are hints in the Joachite tradition that certain figures were crucial actors in the divine economy, particularly Francis of Assisi who was identified with the angel of the sixth seal of Revelation 7:2 ('Then I saw another angel ascend from the rising of the sun, with the seal of the living God'), in the period immediately preceding the Sabbath rest for the people of God inaugurated by the Lamb (8:1).[3]

Thomas Muentzer: a New Daniel

The sixteenth century was a time when 'apocalyptic was gospel, good news', an era of expectation that 'the transformation of the word was imminent'.[4] Despite the fact that the Book of Revelation doesn't feature as much as we might expect, the career and writings of Thomas Muentzer (*c.*1489–1525)[5] well exemplify that ethos. He is one of the better-known figures of the so-called 'radical reformation',[6] a gifted preacher and liturgist, even if he is now better known for his later revolutionary activity and the part that he played in the Peasants Revolt of 1525, which led to defeat at Frankenhausen and Muentzer's interrogation, torture and death.

Muentzer was born in Stolberg round about 1489. He seems to have had an academic education. His early career gives no indication of the fiery radicalism to come, though his contact with various nunneries may partly explain the profound influence of the German mystical tradition, particularly the writings of Johannes Tauler. His first contact with Zwickau, the centre of his initial outburst of radical activity, came in 1520 when he was appointed to a supply preachership. Muentzer's anti-clerical sermons contributed to the growing unrest in the city, and he became associated with the revolutionary and radical elements in the city, among whom were the so-called 'Zwickau Prophets', who were preaching that the Last Days were at hand and that a holy war against the godless was due to start.

His relationship with Martin Luther was complex. The two had so much in common, not least their indebtedness to the rich tradition of the late medieval mystical theology of Tauler. Muentzer came to regard Luther as a compromiser, and preacher of a superficial understanding of the life of faith, clinging onto intellectual power rather than allowing for the experiential element of all people to work out what that faith involved. What was crucial for Muentzer, and what links him not only to earlier mystical trends but also to later similar emphases in radical Protestantism, was his emphasis on the movement of the Spirit within the soul, to which a true understanding of Scripture bore witness and which was the basis of the divine life in the believer. This understanding cannot be gained from reading books, but only by experience, and is often to be found in the 'humble folk', and indeed 'outside Christendom'.[7] Muentzer's words anticipate words of William Blake at the end of his poem 'The Divine Image' from *Songs of Innocence and of Experience*: 'And all must love the human form, In heathen, turk or jew. Where Mercy, Love & Pity dwell, There God is dwelling too'. This is, in Muentzer's words, ' the order of God implanted in all creatures', more important than 'mere Scripture'. What is required of preachers is not just the words of the Bible but what they have heard directly from the mouth of God.

After Zwickau, he began an itinerant life, which was to characterise the rest of his life more or less until his death in 1525. He linked up with Lutheran sympathisers in Prague and issued his *Prague Manifesto*, whose basic theme is the need for inner knowledge of God and the close identification of the true believer with God himself, knowledge of which is self-authenticating and does not depend on book faith or intellectual assent to credal statements.

There is an emphasis in his writings on the need for the period of trial which leads to true faith, and a sharp attack on preachers and teachers in the Church for their unwillingness to teach 'the true order of God', which he has set in all his creatures. The problem, in Muentzer's eyes, was the lack of any experience on the part of preachers of the words 'heard from the mouth of God'. God's writing is on the human heart, as he puts it in the Prague Manifesto:

> But St Paul writes to the Corinthians [2 Cor. 3:3] [...] that the hearts of men are the paper or parchment on which God's finger inscribes his unchangeable will and his eternal wisdom but not with ink [cf. Exod. 31:18; Jer. 31:33; Ezek. 36:25–7]; a writing which any

> man can read, providing his mind has been opened to it [...] God has done this for his elect from the very beginning, so that the testimony they are given is not uncertain, but an invincible one from the holy spirit [...][8]

The importance of this immediate apprehension of the divine will is crucial. Muentzer pointed out that if God's word were written only in books, it would be ephemeral rather than eternal. As evidence for this, and for the continuing centrality of prophetic immediacy, Muentzer adduced the prophetic conviction that they were mouthpieces of God, a method of God's communication which is *still* active: 'that is why all the prophets speak in this way – "Thus saith the Lord", they do not say, "Thus said the Lord", as if it were past history; they speak in the present tense'.[9]

After Prague, he was eventually appointed preacher in Allstedt close to the mining areas of Mansfeld. His time in Allstedt was marked by a mixture of radical preaching and liturgical experiments which attracted large numbers of people. Allstedt's relative remoteness from centres of authority meant that local officials preferred to take no action rather than risk an uprising which they did not have the resources to contain. Muentzer's reputation attracted the hostile interest of local dignitaries, the upshot of which was that they resolved to hear him preach in Allstedt. This evoked from Muentzer the famous Sermon before the Princes in July 1524, in which he sought to persuade the princes that they should take up the sword on behalf of the Elect and wipe the godless from the face of the earth.[10]

Whether Muentzer at this point had any realistic conviction that the princes could be won over to his side is not clear. But the tone of some of his letters to the higher authorities indicates that he was prepared to engage in negotiation in order to enable a political environment to be created. But events were to close the door on any accommodation. Muentzer asserted that the authority of the princes over the common people was at an end, and by his unmasking of false belief Muentzer rejected a role for the princes who were merely a prop for the status quo and prevented the common people from perceiving the truth. Muentzer's period in Allstedt came to an end when he escaped on 7 August 1524 and ended up in Muehlhausen, where there was already a political struggle against the establishment.

After further wanderings Muentzer returned to Muehlhausen in March 1525; it was then that the full effects of the Peasants' War began to affect Thuringia. There had for some time been various regional grievances, but underlying it all was a common burden of oppression and discontent in a world of rapid social and ideological change. The peasants ransacked religious houses and terrorised local gentry. There was little concerted action by the landlords. A large contingent of peasants assembled at Frankenhausen. A rainbow appeared in the sky, taken as a divine sign that the God of the New Covenant would give them victory. But it was not to be, and the peasants were routed. Muentzer escaped but was later captured and under torture admitted his aspirations to abolish private property. He was finally beheaded outside Muehlhausen on 27 May having recanted of his theological 'errors'.

It is Muentzer's political radicalism which has marked him down as a forerunner of a particular form of political theology. Very little is known about his hopes for the new age when it came. What predominates is, as Peter Matheson puts it, that 'Muentzer offered one of the most interesting experiments in popular mysticism, in a profound personal piety for every believer'.[11] That can detract from the political, but in effect was the other side of the coin from it – democratic spirituality, translating into the totality of life, social justice as well as the inner life. Also, Muentzer possessed a strong sense of the present as a critical moment demanding action (something not unusual among his contemporaries).

In Muentzer's thought the divine is there to be found in all persons and can be apprehended by those who are sensitive to 'the working of the Divine Order bubbling from his heart'.[12] Muentzer challenged the idea that only those who know the Scriptures intimately and academically could understand the ways of Christ. All nations under heaven, given the right perception of the word within, could find God without the Scriptures. Muentzer considered that *all* the Elect had the Spirit already in their hearts: 'even if a man were born a Turk he might have the beginning of the same faith'.[13] This universalism is a feature of Muentzer's thought. God speaks directly to all; and many from the heathen lands will precede the so-called Christians into the Kingdom. Muentzer did not despise the Scriptures. What he inveighed against was book religion, the submission to the letter of the Bible. That emphasis led him to the contrast between Word and Spirit and to emphasise the latter at the expense of the former.[14]

'A Manifest Exposé of False Faith' relates Muentzer's emphasis on the prophetic and the indwelling Spirit to the Gospel of Luke. It takes issue with an understanding of what the testimony to the spirit of Jesus really means. He alleged that the scholars want to bring it within the walls of the university, thereby reserving for themselves the right to judge on matters of faith. The point is that faith is not easily accessed just by knowing the Bible; it is a struggle as exemplified, in Muentzer's view, by the experience of both Zechariah and Mary in Luke 1–2. Just as with Mary, whose initial response to the angel was to ask how these things could be, that 'faith once first kindled confronts us with things so impossible'. What was required was the stormy movement and heartfelt anxiety. The Bible gives testimony not faith. Indeed, 'if someone had never sight or sound of the Bible at any time in his life he could still hold the one true Christian faith because of the true teaching of the spirit, just like all those who composed the holy Scripture without any books at all'. The problem is that ordinary people have come to imagine that the priests *must* know about faith on account of the books that they have read. Surely, wrote Muentzer, there must be more to relating to God than what we have 'stolen from a book'? Indeed, what is needed is the long discipline of identification with the crucified Christ, the knowledge of God in the Son expounded by the Spirit: 'All we need to do is to be conformed to Christ's life and passion through the overshadowing of the holy spirit [like Mary], so bitterly resisted and so coarsely mocked by this fleshly world'. Thereby is destroyed 'the stolen counterfeit faith', by going through the agony of heart which follows. What one needs to learn is the fear of God from the abyss of the heart, for what prevents the pure fear of God is the human hunger for human favour.

The emphasis on immediate knowledge of God is a key to Muentzer's theology. The goal was to become one of those taught and made godlike *directly*. In this there is no need for academic qualifications to know the true meaning of Scripture; what is needed is experience: 'Even if you had devoured all the books of the Bible, you must still suffer the sharp edge of the ploughshare, for you will never have faith unless God gives it to you, and instructs you in it. If that is to happen, then at first, my dear biblical scholar, the book will be closed to you too'.[15] With such an understanding of God Muentzer was sympathetic towards dreams and visions as an important means of knowing the ways of God. He made a study of those passages in the New Testament which speak of visions being vouchsafed to the first Christians. In several places he compares himself with Daniel (for example, in the Sermon before the Princes), John the Baptist and Elijah.

So, the 'cost of discipleship' was crucial for Muentzer. He opposed the idea that the path of discipleship could be anything other than a stony one and castigated Luther for making faith seem an easy option. The whole process of becoming a disciple involved a period of trial and identification with the sufferings of Christ. It is only through the period of spiritual turmoil that he believed true faith could come. Such inner turmoil of one who faces opposition and uncertainty, however strong the inner conviction may be of the rectitude of his cause, places the experience of Thomas Muentzer alongside better-known saints in Christian history. It is the same kind of inner conflict which led Paul to speak of his close identification between his life as an apostle and the sufferings of Christ.

It is easy to forget that Muentzer's career was not totally characterised by revolutionary activity. His liturgical experiments and the theological directness of his words and hymns promoted community building and the immediacy of the relationship of the believer with Christ. The liturgical experiments in Allstedt show an ability to articulate a pattern of reform which is innovative without being totally iconoclastic. His letters to the leading authorities often reflect a more diplomatic tone, which contrasts markedly with some of his uninhibited invective found elsewhere, which suggests a readiness to explore the possibility of seeking to include the princes in the pursuit of his programme of religious reformation. That said, it is not easy to see that there was any coherent political strategy on Muentzer's part. At crucial moments he was deserted by various groups, and his fiery anti-clericalism jeopardised the possibility of Allstedt becoming an alternative centre of Reformation.

The Sermon before the Princes

A good example of his attempt to persuade the rulers to be part of this reform is his interpretation of magistracy as the execution of justice in conformity with the will of God and the will of the people in his famous 'Sermon to the Princes'. Here we find a rhetorical piece which seeks to urge the rulers to take their responsibility and act as

Muentzer believed Paul wanted in Romans 13 and to act as agents of divine justice. It was Muentzer's opportunity to speak directly to a supporter of Luther and one who had himself come under more radical influences.[16]

Muentzer took as his text for his sermon a passage from Daniel 2,[17] which was the cornerstone of millennial hopes, not least among seventeenth-century writers in England in the Civil War period.[18] In it the Jewish seer both tells and interprets a dream of the Babylonian king Nebuchadnezzar, which the wise men of the court were not able to interpret. The dream is of a statue made of various substances which is hit by a stone made without human hands and shattered, after which the stone becomes a great mountain that filled the whole earth (Dan. 2:35). Christ is the stone made without human hands, insignificant in human eyes and trampled underfoot by humanity. The interpretation offered by Daniel is the destruction of four world empires, which will be replaced by the kingdom of God that will never be destroyed (Dan. 2:44).

Muentzer proceeds to interpret the various parts of the vision of the statue. Christ the Stone which is about to shatter the final empire, a fact which is appreciated better by 'the poor laity and the peasants'. In the face of this destruction, the princes are exhorted to side with Christ the Stone whose empire will replace the kingdoms of the present rulers. What is needed now is for the princes to recognise the incompetence of the clerics, just as Nebuchadnezzar rejected the wise men of his court. Indeed, for his interpretation of the dream, Nebuchadnezzar gave Daniel great power and acknowledged that Daniel's God was 'God of gods and Lord of kings, and a revealer of mysteries' (Dan. 2:47), an indication of the appropriate response of the rulers whom Muentzer is addressing. He indicates to them that 'A new Daniel must arise and interpret for you your vision and he [...] must go in front of the army. He must reconcile the anger of the princes and the enraged people. Christ the Stone is about to shatter the schemes of the Lutheran clergy'.[19] In a daring exegesis of Romans 13 Muentzer pointed out that Paul's reference to rulers not bearing the sword in vain as servants of God to execute wrath on the wrongdoer should be interpreted as an obligation to root out the wicked who are opposed to the ways of the imminent 'Fifth Monarchy' of Christ, to which Muentzer, the 'New Daniel', was pointing. So, Muentzer rejected the argument that judgement must remain in God's hands and reminded them of their obligation to wield the sword as executors of the divine wrath. If the rulers refuse to do so, the sword will be taken away from those who 'confess him all right with words and deny him with the deed'.

This then is the basis for a critique of the Church in forsaking the way of Christ and the apostles in their view that God no longer revealed his divine mysteries by means of word or vision. Muentzer insisted that opponents of visions were in fact opponents of the Holy Spirit, poured out in the Last Days. While he admitted that there had been false prophets and deceivers, Muentzer rebuked the 'learned divines' who reject the contemporary revelation of God and thus attack the Holy Spirit – he had Luther in his sights. The vision comes first and then it is to be tested in the light of Scripture. Knowledge of the Scripture, therefore, is inadequate without the enlightenment that comes from the Spirit. Scripture is a witness to the faith of the writers, and it is the appropriation of that inner illumination that prompted the writing, which is at the heart of true discipleship.

After Muentzer's death a concerted attempt was made to blot out all traces of 'the Satan of Allstedt', as Luther called him. But the sympathy for his convictions is indicated by the fact that shortly before his death, Muentzer had received a letter from one of the 'Swiss Brethren', Conrad Grebel, addressing Muentzer as 'the truthful and proclaimer of the gospel'. Muentzer's reputation as a theologian and liturgical reformer had attracted attention, therefore. The letter indicates the community of interest which existed between Muentzer's ideas and emerging Anabaptism.

Muentzer, in a similar way to other sixteenth-century writers, emphasised the primacy of the experience of Christ. That the Scriptures offered confirmation of this is a pattern of interpretation which has its parallels. One of the most remarkable of Muentzer's contemporaries was Hans Denck who died tragically of plague in 1527. Hans Denck (1500–27) was what would come to be called an Anabaptist, as he had undergone rebaptism as a sign of his own commitment to Christ and his move to a new way of life in which violence was abhorred and attentiveness to the law of God written on the heart became the norm for Christian living. His theological position had much in common with that of Muentzer. For example, in his so-called 'Recantation' (published after his death) he wrote that

> Holy Scripture I hold above all human treasure but not as high as the Word of God that is living, powerful and eternal – unattached and free of all elements of this world; for since it is God himself, it is Spirit and not letter, written without pen or paper so that it can never be eradicated [...] Therefore, salvation is not bound to Scripture however useful and good it might be in furthering it.[20]

This statement puts very succinctly what Denck, paralleling Muentzer, saw as the appropriate place of Scripture. It is a witness, which is important but is not primary, in the life of discipleship. God's presence is in all people, and it is this testimony which takes precedence over the Church or the Scripture, though the latter can bear witness to him. Scripture's authority is dependent upon the confirmation of the experience from within. Nor is Scripture the possession of the experts. The importance of Scripture lay in witnessing to the Word which became flesh, Jesus Christ, who comes again and again, encouraging and challenging. It is the inner experience of God, present in all people, even though they may not recognise it, which is fundamental.

Less than a decade after Muentzer's death, in 1533–5, there emerged in Germany a radical Anabaptist movement characterised by claims to prophetic inspiration and challenges to ecclesial practice and polity, inspired by the apocalyptic ideas of Melchior Hoffmann. Anabaptists initially took control of Münster by conventional means,[21] but the city soon became a magnet for many sympathisers from the region. An eschatological commonwealth was established with an explicit apocalyptic hue. The leaders believed that their authority came by apocalyptic experience. Nowhere is the behaviour better exemplified than in the strange conviction that led one leader, Jan Matthijs, to act on that inner prompting and become like a lamb led to the slaughter as he went out to defeat the surrounding armies, only to be slaughtered before the eyes of his horrified supporters. This is not the mind-set of the military strategist. It manifests faith in the God who had delivered the people in the past and would do so again, the kind of conviction, which, according to Josephus, inspired a prophet in the last hours of the city of Jerusalem in 70 CE.[22]

The eschatological commonwealth in Münster ended in bloody suppression. The Münsterites' hopes for a new age, and the part they might play, impelled them, and political circumstances were such that the kind of action they engaged in could easily have paid off instead of resulting in the catastrophe which ensued for those involved, and the view of Anabaptism as a threat to the bourgeois society of the early modern period. 'Anabaptist' became a term of reproach for subversives and malcontents. After the catastrophe of the siege of Münster in 1534–5 one of the founding fathers of modern Anabaptism, Menno Simons, offered a ministry of consolidation which enabled the refugees of the persecution of the Anabaptists to maintain their identity and their understanding of the radical implications of the Reformation. It has continued in various forms down to the present day, and is very influential in contemporary Christian theology and ethics.[23]

Friedrich Engels also grasped the problematic character of early Christian eschatological thought and practice, and its relationship to later Christian movements is well articulated in his essay about the Peasants' War in Germany.[24] His focus is in large part on the career of Thomas Muentzer but what he wrote about Muentzer applies to many individuals and their ideas discussed in this book, from Jesus onwards. Not only did he encapsulate the problem posed by their thought and experience, and the priority given to inspiration over memory, but also the impact of the horizon of hope:

> [an absolutely propertyless group] questioned the institutions, views and conceptions common to all societies based on class antagonisms. In this respect, the chiliastic dream visions of early Christianity offered a very convenient starting point. On the other hand, this sally beyond both the present and even the future could be nothing but violent and fantastic, and of necessity fell back into the narrow limits set by the contemporary situation. The attack on private property, the demand for common ownership was bound to resolve into a primitive organisation of charity; vague Christian equality could at best resolve into civil 'equality before the law'; elimination of all authorities finally culminates in the establishment of republican governments elected by the people. The anticipation of communism by fantasy became in reality an anticipation of modern bourgeois conditions.[25]

Jacob Taubes could have been writing about Muentzer when he wrote of the revolutionary power of apocalypticism and its explosive mixture of creative and destructive powers, which are not just a speculative matter but also a spur to action.[26] On the fateful day in May 1525 when Muentzer led the peasants in battle outside Frankenhausen it was a sign from heaven which was regarded as a good omen. In the event the peasants were routed, and Muentzer captured, tortured and executed.

Joanna Southcott and her followers and successors

Joanna Southcott was a Devon woman who shot to fame in the first decade of the nineteenth century, in the middle of the Napoleonic wars (she died months before Waterloo), initiating a John the Baptist-like movement summoning people to be sealed in imitation of Revelation 6–7, in preparation for the imminent judgement of God.[27] Her role turned from being herald to initiator of the eschatological age, of which more in a moment. There then emerged a series of prophetic figures and movements. Some, like Richard Brothers, were rival prophetic figures, others, like John Wroe and John 'Zion Ward', and later Mabel Barltrop, believed that they had endorsement to continue Southcott's prophetic ministry. These spanned three continents and persist in different forms until today.[28] At the risk of generalising about what in fact was a diffuse eschatological movement, which Southcott set in train, there is that mix of being part of a propitious moment, when they were either on the very brink of ultimate fulfilment, being key actors in the eschatological drama, or, as in the case of Southcott, both. In the history of Southcottianism, in different ways, key figures saw themselves as fulfilling eschatological roles, either predicted in the Bible or based on biblical passages, much as Christians identified John the Baptist with Elijah, who was to come (especially in Matthew 11:14 and 17:13). Southcott, throughout her prophetic activity, linked herself with Revelation 12 and the Woman Clothed with the Sun, whereas Brothers thought that he was the messianic child born to the woman of Revelation 12 and also the *nasi* (chief prince) of Ezekiel 37, 44 and 45.

It was in the last year of Southcott's life that she sought to actualise her vocation to be the Woman Clothed with the Sun of Revelation 12 and moved into the literal fulfilment, when she believed that she was pregnant with the male child, with whom she identified the enigmatic 'Shiloh' mentioned in Genesis 49:10, and which some marginal comments of the King James Version of the Bible identified with the messiah who was to come.[29] She died supposedly giving birth to her messianic child. Quickly her followers believed that, as the text of Revelation 12:5 says, the messianic child was caught up to heaven. That set in train the series of interpretations of the child's future coming, existing alongside a more suspicious community of faithful Southcottians, who looked back only to Southcott herself and kept their distance from the claimants to visionary endorsement from her, or being the one in whom the divine indwelt eschatologically.

The most dramatic example came with the conviction on the part of the women founders of The Panacea Society in the early twentieth century that Mabel Barltrop (or Octavia as she came to be known) was the incarnation of Shiloh, Southcott's messianic child.[30] Arising from her messianic convictions, from 1919, Octavia believed that she was to take down God's Word *each day* and for the next 15 years, at 5:30 pm she would sit down and write *The Writings of the Holy Ghost*, which were then typed out for her followers to read and discuss each evening. Indeed, that sense of being the last one in a line, doubtless influenced by NT language about a line of prophets, which has come to its end in fulfilment, is particularly strong in the case of Octavia. What is evident in her writings is that the place in which they were living had some special significance (Albany Road in Bedford, the headquarters of The Panacea Society, a garden oasis in suburban Bedford, was the divine Kingdom, the Paradise of God on earth, which they termed the divine domain) and the divine had indwelt their leader with the charisma of prophetic, indeed oracular, wisdom. There was much that concerned present life and much less of utopian speculation about what it might be like in the new age. In this respect it echoes the NT, where the challenges of life in community eclipse a speculative thrust. What mattered was how to conquer and to achieve the life in the New Jerusalem on earth.

So, whether it is Southcott actualising Revelation 12, Brothers as the *nasi* of Ezekiel leading Jews back to Jerusalem, or 'Zion' Ward seeing all the Scriptures fulfilled in himself and his suffering as the travails of redemption which brought light and knowledge for himself as a pioneer and paragon of a new humanity for all people, there is a strong sense of eschatology in the process of being realised. The two-stage character of NT eschatology, with the second stage left unclear, gave the Southcottian prophets interpretative space to think themselves into the divine economy and be messianic agents who would have their part to play in the culmination of the Last Things. Like other millenarian movements they had to deal with the disappointment of their hope, but the sense of the 'now' of salvation remained strong in many parts of the movement.

Chapter 4

Subversive Apocalypse

In the previous chapter we considered individuals who believed themselves called to fulfil biblical hopes and so be actors in the eschatological drama. For example, we noted the way in which the vision of the Woman Clothed with the Sun in Revelation 12 was such a crucial passage for Joanna Southcott's sense of her vocation. In fact, her story straddles both chapters, given her convictions about her eschatological role and the significant place that the Book of Revelation had in it. This chapter looks more specifically at the subversive effects of the apocalyptic spirit, exemplified by Anne Hutchinson's testimony at her trial, and the visionary interpretation of Scripture in the writings of Joachim of Fiore and Joanna Southcott. Deciding when the propitious time had arrived, or was about to arrive, became a central part of the interpretation of the Book of Revelation pioneered by Joachim of Fiore, as he and his successors determined at what point they were situated as the scroll of history unfolded. That sense of being in such a moment has a unique artistic exemplification in Botticelli's 'Mystic Nativity', written as it was in the wake of the prophecy of Savonarola in Florence and his execution. The chapter concludes with a consideration of one of the most remarkable modern interpreters of Revelation, William Stringfellow, whose political critique drew heavily on the imagery of Revelation.

Apocalypse

'Apocalyptic' lies deep within the biblical tradition, and indeed the culture whence the Bible emerged. There, dreams and visions and auditions were recognised as constituting that liminal time when the boundaries between the human and the divine were blurred and an epistemological experience was possible, which was less common in the normal circumstances of human life. It was God's way of communicating, as Numbers 12:6–8 puts it:

> 'When there are prophets among you, I the LORD make myself known to them in visions; I speak to them in dreams. Not so with my servant Moses; he is entrusted with all my house. With him I speak face to face, clearly, not in riddles; and he beholds the form of the LORD.'

The term 'apocalypticism' comes from the Greek term *apokalypsis*, meaning 'revelation', 'unveiling' or 'disclosure'. In modern scholarship, it is used to designate a pattern of religion found in different forms in a variety of religious traditions.[1] It is frequently employed to describe a belief system in early Judaism that claimed to derive from dreams, visions or otherworldly journeys, modes of revelation that convey mysteries of the heavenly world and/or insight into the course and climax of history. Within Christianity and Judaism, apocalypticism has played a significant part in both mainstream and fringe religion. It is rooted in the prophetic and wisdom books of the Hebrew Bible and, according to some scholars, is also indebted to the blending of religious ideas that became prominent in the early Hellenistic period, probably influenced by Platonic dualism, and the contrast between seen and unseen, earth and heaven.[2]

What distinguishes apocalypticism as a religious outlook is its peculiar hermeneutical and epistemological basis. Theological understanding does not come by the exercise of established methods of reading and interpretation in which analysis and the application of established hermeneutical techniques are rigorously applied. Revelation is not dependent on an interpretation of tradition which excludes the imaginative and the unexpected. The closest analogy is the dream, which the dreamer does not create, even if the components of the dream may themselves be contingent upon past experience, whether religious or otherwise.[3] The mode of reception may be passive as in a dream. But it could involve preparation on the part of the recipient conducive to the reception of a dream or vision (such as fasting), but then the moments of revelatory insight come to the would-be visionary (cf. Dan. 10:1–3; 4 Ezra 6:35; 9:26).[4] What characterises it is that 'good' interpretation does not exclude the imaginative connections which might be made in the visualisation which imaginative engagement may encourage. Scripture might be a launching pad for what comes to the reader of sacred texts. For the visionary, there is the sense of something being 'given', of 'standing outside' themselves (so in ecstasy, cf. Acts 10:10) or being 'snatched away' (cf. 2 Cor. 12:2–4).

There are two major approaches to the understanding of apocalypticism in modern discussion. One concentrates on the *contents* of early Jewish texts and attempts to construct some kind of synthesis of religious ideas. It more or less continues the kind of synthesis typical of what became known as *Apokalyptik*; it understands apocalypticism as basically an eschatological belief system characterised by dualism and expectation of a new and better world breaking in and from beyond into this world and swamping it with its glory. 'Apocalyptic eschatology' and the radical disjunction between this world and the world to come emerged as a central feature of the understanding of New Testament eschatology in the nineteenth century and has exercised a pervasive influence on scholarship ever since.[5] The other approach starts from consideration of the *form* of revelation described in the relevant texts, whether the disclosure comes through vision, audition or dream.[6] It is understandable why it is that 'apocalyptic' is used as a generic term, because of the character of the *contents* of the Book of Revelation. But that must be complemented by an understanding of apocalyptic which attends to the revelatory form of apocalyptic literature and any visionary experience to which it bears witness. Subsequent study has confirmed that the neat distinction between prophetic and apocalyptic eschatology needs to be questioned.

Although the book of Revelation is the only apocalypse in the New Testament, many other New Testament documents are pervaded with language that may be termed apocalyptic. The Jesus of the Synoptic Gospels may have allowed a sense of his own divine vocation to take him to Jerusalem. It was *necessary* for the Son of Man to suffer (Mark 8:31; 9:31; 10:33). The Johannine Jesus claims not to have spoken on his own authority, for 'the Father who sent me has himself given me a commandment about what to say and what to speak. And I know that his commandment is eternal life. What I speak, therefore, I speak just as the father has told me' (John 12:49–50). Apocalyptic radicalism is typified by the conviction of an impetus for appropriate behaviour or insight into human affairs, even when, as in the Gospel of John, it runs counter to received wisdom.

Visionary material is central to the representation of Christian origins in these texts, whether it be Paul's own testimony to his apostleship in Galatians 1:12 and 16, or the Acts of the Apostles, where the role of the visionary is stressed in the unfolding of the divine economy in this highly selective account of Christian history. Indeed, as we have seen, for Paul, the apocalypse of Jesus Christ was the basis for his understanding of the fulfilment of the divine purposes and his role within it.

But it is the last book of the Christian New Testament which has been the inspiration for later Christian radicalism. Its mix of visionary experience and political protest is unique in its intensity and directness in the New Testament. John's ecstatic experience takes him into the divine court to see what the biblical prophets, Ezekiel and Isaiah, had seen and the mystery of the future of the universe in a slaughtered Lamb. The visions which follow culminate in a vision of heaven on earth in the New Jerusalem, as the political and economic powers of the day are unmasked and their end predicted. This is seen in the visions of the beasts from the sea and the land, and Babylon seated on the seven-headed beast in Revelation 13 and 17 respectively. In both of the last-mentioned visions, images from Daniel in particular are taken up and become part of a devastating political critique of the manifestation of imperial power and oppression of the Roman Empire in the days of John the Seer. We shall see later how these images were used in a different era and situation, but with the same political force. It is prophecy in the style of a biblical prophet, with the same denunciatory power. Unsurprisingly, its effects pervaded Western culture and its political protests. The prophecy of Revelation was not the last word, however. Why indeed should prophetic inspiration and divine revelation stop? So, for example, not only did the second-century Montanists look to Revelation 21 for their idea of an earthly kingdom,[7] but they also claimed additional revelation from the Spirit-Paraclete. Such claims parallel similar claims to revelation in the Gnostics texts, which have been found in the Nag Hammadi Library. These only increased suspicion of apocalyptic claims and texts among the merging orthodox circles.

With regard to radicalism, S.T. Coleridge put his finger on an issue which is crucial to religion and is endemic to the Bible: that sense of communion with the divine, a form of knowledge, for which previous experience can only partially prepare one, and whose impact may mean bypassing the exercise of normal patterns of rationality. As Coleridge himself recognised in his expression of suspicion, it could 'be a menace to society'.[8] In his attempt to distinguish between the 'fanatical' and the 'safe' forms of mysticism, he thereby points to a crucial feature of the radicalism of the prophetic and the messianic. Anyone may be called to be a prophet, as Amos pointed out to his critics. Indeed, he was no member of a prophetic guild (Amos 7:14), but God had spoken; what else could a responsive person do but prophesy (Amos 3:8)? Such convictions are deep-seated in the various texts that the earliest Christians preserved about themselves, and have achieved an authoritative status in the developing religion, notwithstanding the reserve often expressed about the prophetic in those same texts. Coleridge's ambivalence about prophetic claims pervades the Bible (Deut. 13; 1 John 4:1). Paul in 1 Corinthians urges the recognition of the prophetic, but comes up with all kinds of tests and controls, not least some kind of oversight by himself as a paradigm and mediator between groups of what counts as authentic behaviour (cf. 1 Cor. 14:34). But there could be no denying that the very genesis of Christianity concerned one in whom spirits were at work, though the brokers of power decided that they were of Beelzebub (Mark 3:22). Indeed, in the Johannine version of the Jesus story, Jesus appealed to what he had seen and heard from God over against the appeal of his opponents, to received wisdom going back to Moses (John 9:28–9). What was true of Jesus was also true of Paul, by his own testimony and that of others. The prophetic, the apocalyptic and the mystical are essential ingredients of Christianity and have deep roots in its foundation texts.

Anne Hutchinson's testimony: the primacy of apocalypse in the seventeenth century

There is a dramatic moment in the trial of Anne Hutchinson (1591–1643) in New England in 1637 when she explains to her interrogator the priority she gives to 'speaking what in my conscience I know to be truth':

> *Mr. Nowell.* How do you know that that was the spirit?
>
> *Mrs. H.* How did Abraham know that it was God that bid him offer his son, being a breach of the sixth commandment?

> *Dep. Gov.* By an immediate voice.
> *Mrs. H.* So to me by an immediate revelation.
> *Dep. Gov.* How! an immediate revelation.
> *Mrs. H.* By the voice of his own spirit to my soul.

Here she appeals to Genesis 22 and the priority of 'an immediate voice', which was the basis for Abraham sacrificing Isaac. The example of Abraham offered a precedent for appealing to 'an immediate revelation, [...] the voice of [God's] own spirit to my soul', which settled a matter as far as she was concerned. In the opinion of those judging her, this clear enunciation of her convictions, at the climax of what had hitherto been a very measured response, was the basis for her condemnation. So, John Winthrop in his summing up thanked divine providence for making Hutchinson 'lay open her self and the ground of all these disturbances to be by revelation'.[9]

There was a crucial turning point in Anne Hutchinson's trial, when she intervened and was allowed to do so by the governor of Massachusetts. The original charge levelled against Anne Hutchinson was as a woman promoting the 'covenant by grace', preaching of John Cotton and John Wheelwright, the latter of whom was related to Hutchinson by marriage and was also banished for his views. As suggested, Hutchinson's reported admission at her trial put the matter on another level of theological significance, however closely related it might have been. It was not just about a 'covenant of grace' as compared to a 'covenant of works', but the relative weight given to 'immediate revelation' as compared with Scripture *of any kind*. To use Blake's terminology, it had become about the priority given to 'Inspiration' over 'Memory'.[10]

The decisive moment came when she, seemingly spontaneously, shared with the court her fondness for what governor Winthrop, writing to friends in England, termed 'bottomlesse, revelations, as came without any word [of Scripture] or without the sense of the word'.[11] What is more, though she justified such revelations, she used the word 'immediate' of them, which suggested the subordination of the words of Scripture to revelation and conjured up what her opponents considered antinomian, Familist, and smacked of all the worst excesses of Anabaptism. According to Winthrop, Hutchinson became the cause of the colony's troubles and her supporters became, at worst, followers of this dangerous ringleader. Though Hutchinson's testimony is laced with scriptural support, the basic conviction is there, that it is immediate revelation which not only inspires her use of the Bible but also the typological identification with biblical figures.[12]

The 1630s Antinomian Controversy in New England is the tip of the iceberg of a network of beliefs, which reverberated around Old England in the following decades, and in which the primary place was given to the apocalyptic, viewed in its epistemological, rather than eschatological, sense. For example, the importance of 'immediate revelations' is confirmed and justified by Anne Hutchinson's English contemporary Gerrard Winstanley, who wrote 'if you say that visions and revelations are ceased [...] then you erre mightily'.[13] He himself repeatedly set great store by his trance experience, with the command to dig the common land, and wrote of the fundamental importance of 'Vision, Voice, and Revelation' as the basis for the action of the Diggers.[14]

These two examples encapsulate a radicalism which is less about 'back to roots' and more like William Blake's view of Jesus, as one who 'acted from impulse not from rules'.[15] It refers to a broader conviction, which may rightly be termed 'apocalyptic', in which there is 'immediate revelation' of the divine, which comes through a medium other than study of sacred texts, nor does it resort to that which has been handed down.

Apocalypse, disclosure, by the promptings of the Spirit, visions and auditions are evident throughout the New Testament texts. Luke's report of Jesus seeing 'Satan fall like lightning from heaven' (Luke 10:18) suggests a visionary illumination of all that was being experienced in the struggle with the evil powers, in the actions of both himself and the disciples. In the Acts of the Apostles, visions provide the dynamic for the spread of the Gospel. Paul's experience on the Damascus road, repeated in three versions in Acts, emphasises the providential nature of this event in the divine economy. Likewise Peter's vision of the descending sail and instruction to sacrifice and eat animals prepares him for his journey to Cornelius, explanation of which is required by the elders in Jerusalem in Acts 11. In his Letter to the Galatians, Paul emphasises the importance of apocalyptic elements as the basis of his practice (Gal. 1:12 and 1:16; cf. Acts 22:17). In the revelation of the divine mystery, Paul regarded himself and his companions as stewards, with the privilege of administering the divine secrets (1 Cor. 4:1).

Visionary insight into the meaning of the Scriptures

In this age, one can only see in a glass darkly (1 Cor. 13:12).[16] Scripture, rightly interpreted, provides a resource for the discernment of the character of life at the end of the ages (1 Cor. 10:11; Rom. 15:4). For some, its meaning may remain opaque. There is a veil that prevents understanding (2 Cor. 3:14–18). With the benefit of the divine Spirit, however, the reader can pierce the letter to see what the Spirit might be saying through the words (2 Cor. 3:6).

With the possible exception of 2 Corinthians 3:14–16, and possibly 1 Corinthians 2:10–16, there is nothing quite like this inspired understanding of Scripture in the New Testament (NT). Of course, in almost every book in the NT there is evidence of an attempt to relate the events, in which the writer believed he was involved, to the Jewish Scriptures, but *how* that understanding came about is not always clear. Paul writes of having recourse to mysteries which solve doctrinal problems about the economy of salvation, the eschatological position of Israel (Rom. 11:25) and the nature of the resurrection of the body (1 Cor. 15:51), but we do not find the reference to the kind of inspired exegesis which is presupposed in the Habakkuk Commentary (from the Dead Sea Scrolls) and in the examples considered from Joachim of Fiore and Joanna Southcott. Not even Revelation, dependent as it is on prophetic passages and much else in Scripture for its imagery, is the same. The claims to visionary experience, for example, in Galatians 1, or even Revelation 1, are much more akin to the accounts we have in some parts of the Southcottian movement, where a commissioning vision validates the position of the recipient of the vision and is the basis of authority.

It is the unveiling, the transformation of opacity into clarity that Joachim of Fiore (1135–1202) describes in a decisive apocalyptic moment. The origin of Joachim of Fiore's understanding of the meaning of the Book of Revelation occurs in a visionary or even mystical experience, akin to the later visionaries, when he, like John on the Lord's Day, understands the meaning of the text, as mystical insight comes to him after a long period of struggling to make sense of the text:

> Having gone through the preceding verses of the Apocalypse to this place (Rev 1:10: 'I was in the Spirit on the Lord's day') I experienced such great difficulty and mental constraint beyond the ordinary that it

> was like feeling the stone that closed the tomb opposed to me [...] After a year, the Feast of Easter came round. Awakened from sleep about midnight, something happened to me as I was meditating on this book, something for which, relying on the gift of God, I am made more bold to write [...] Since some of the mysteries were already understood, but the greater mysteries were yet hidden, there was a kind of struggle going on in my mind [...] Then on the above-mentioned night, something like this happened. About the middle of the night's silence, as I think, the hour when it is thought that our lion of the tribe of Judah rose from the dead (Rev. 5:5–6), as I was meditating, suddenly something of the fullness of this book and of the entire agreement of the Old and New Testaments was perceived by a clarity of understanding in my mind's eye. The revelation was made when I was not even mindful of the chapter mentioned above.[17]

By means of this insight Joachim describes how he found in the Apocalypse the key to the inner meaning of Scripture and the whole history of salvation. In his meditation upon the Apocalypse, the spiritual insight that informed the prophets of old was again at work; as Joachim explained to the Cistercian abbot, Adam of Perseigne, 'God who once gave the spirit of prophecy to the prophets has given me the spirit of understanding to grasp with great clarity in his Spirit all the mysteries of sacred Scripture'.[18]

Like Joachim of Fiore before her,[19] and indeed the Teacher of Righteousness mentioned in the Dead Sea Scrolls, to whom 'God made known all the mysteries of the words of His servants the prophets',[20] Joanna Southcott distinguished between Scripture and her own inspired interpretative role.[21] While she affirmed that all truth was contained in Scripture, she believed all had not been made clear until the right time. That time had come with her, and 'the words closed up and sealed till the time of the end' (Dan. 12:9) were now made clear. She believed that Christ came as the Paraclete in her, whereby God used prophets to clarify what is in Scripture. A decisive experience for Southcott took place in 1794 as she was reflecting on Revelation 21. Like John on the Lord's day, Southcott identified with John being 'in the Spirit', and, later, as she put it, 'earnest in prayer', she was told, that like John, she saw the New Jerusalem descending and was visited by the Spirit. In *The True Explanation of the Bible* (1803–4), Southcott collected interpretations of biblical passages in which her meditations on issues thrown up by her reading were followed by the Spirit's endorsement and comprehensive interpretation of the meaning and relevance of the passage. Southcott regarded the Bible as a book that could not be understood by either learned or unlearned. The seals could only be broken and the meaning revealed by the Woman, written about in Revelation 12, Joanna Southcott.

It is likely that the reason for the particular interpretative approach favoured by Southcott (and indeed her contemporary Richard Brothers) guaranteed the supreme authority of Scripture and revelatory insight concerning its elucidation.[22]

Plotting a position in the climax of history: Joachim, Savonarola and Botticelli

Joachim of Fiore (c.1135–1202)

The later Middle Ages saw the emergence of another influential reading, by reformer Joachim of Fiore. Joachim saw the Apocalypse as a key to both the entire Scripture and the whole of history.[23] He broke decisively from the Augustinian tradition. The classic text of Christian orthodoxy, Augustine's *City of God*, subtly transformed the central contrast of the Book of Revelation, between the earthly and heavenly into the fundamental dialectic of the Christian life, but in the process millennial elements of the present constitution of the Church are reinterpreted, reducing their potency.[24] But Joachim opened up possibilities for readers of the Apocalypse to discern their place in God's saving purposes, as set out in Scripture, and made human history the arena of the fulfilment of eschatological events. His influence was to be pervasive.[25]

Joachim incorporates Revelation's patterns of sevens into an overarching Trinitarian view of history: the age (*status*) of the old covenant belongs to the Father, the age of the Son began with the New Testament and continues through Joachim's day, and the coming age is of the Holy Spirit, to be characterised by an outburst of spiritual activity in the form of monastic renewal, a time that was imminent. The enlightened reading of the Apocalypse offers the key to the reading of the Bible as a whole and to the interpretation of history.

Joachim's historicising pattern of interpretation of the Book of Revelation is exemplified by his diagrammatic interpretation of the Revelation's visions, for example, the Red Dragon of Revelation 12:3. The dragon's seven heads are identified as persecutors of the Church. Between the long necks of the dragon's heads appear captions detailing the seven persecutions of the Church, Herod, Nero, Constantius, Muhammad, Mesemoth, Saladin. With him the Sixth Persecution began, and with Gog is the final Antichrist.[26]

Saladin, the contemporary tyrant (*c*.1138–93), is represented as a larger head and is singled out by the crown above his head confirming the fact that he is the regnant opponent. The seventh, even larger head represents the last and greatest Antichrist still to come. The sixth and seventh heads are joined at the neck, explained in one of the accompanying notes as an intensification of the Church's tribulation in the sixth age when there is a double persecution: there must be seven persecutions but the 'silence in heaven for half an hour' (Rev. 8:1), when the seventh seal is opened, signifies the Sabbath of history. The space between the menacing seventh head and the curled tail labelled Gog expresses Joachim's belief that victory over the Antichrist will be followed by the Sabbath age of history, the third *status* of illumination and liberty, which will last until the appearance of Gog heralds the end of the world. After this millennial period of peace, Satan will be released (Rev. 20:7); the flick of the dragon's tail will mark the prelude to the Last Judgement.

In another of Joachim's *figurae* we find an example of the way in which the eschatological future of Revelation 21–2 is construed. In it we have a monastic-inspired 'heaven on earth' evident in the New Jerusalem.[27] It is a plan for the new society of the third age.[28] At its centre there is the foursquare pattern of John's city (21:16), with four quarters for the monastic residents of the celestial city. At the foot of the diagram, admittedly outside the wall of the city, are the clergy who serve the secular community and below them are the married with their sons and daughters, sharing a life in common.

This *figura*, and its commentary, with its inclusion of practical details of food and clothing and religious practices, as well as its spatial measurements, is very much 'this-worldly' and evokes the kind of ideal society outlined, for example in the Temple Scroll (11QTemp) from the Dead Sea Scrolls. In Joachim's New Jerusalem people live in their own homes, but according to a lay religious rule, fasting, working with their hands, giving to the poor and obeying their spiritual mentors. In its recognition of the importance of the laity, this vision was prophetic of future developments when, in the age of the friars, there were many lay fraternities of various kinds (e.g. Beguins and Beghards). This picture of a future society might be called utopian were it not that Joachim believed that such a state of bliss on earth was a clear future reality.

Joachim's interpretation initiated an extraordinary outburst of self-aware eschatological enthusiasm in the centuries after his death, in which various persons and events became the signs of hope. Peter John Olivi's name is not so well known, but he ranks with the giants of medieval theology.[29] He is more familiar for being an eschatological enthusiast whose influence on late medieval popular religion was immense. Yet despite being an enthusiast, Peter Garnsey has written of him: 'there is a lot to be said for the commentator, who, while committed to a particular viewpoint, presents his case by means of an intelligent, elaborate and wide-ranging argument, along the way acknowledging, even seeking out, alternative interpretations and showing a readiness to make concessions'.[30] What is striking about Olivi's theology is the mix of philosophical interest and apocalyptic interpretation very much in the Joachite tradition, but, as his major modern interpreter, David Burr, has pointed out,[31] while he considered that he and his contemporaries were part of an eschatologically significant generation, he seems to have believed that many hundreds of years might have to elapse before the eschatological hope could be realised. A sense of eschatological urgency and of being part of the propitious moment could go hand-in-hand with a refusal to expect the imminent climax of all things. In Joachim's, and a century or so later, Peter John Olivi's interpretations of the Apocalypse,[32] the sixth and seventh ages assume great importance as a time of anticipation and struggle, and it is at that moment they seem to locate themselves, a period of conflict with the forces of Antichrist, and an outburst of activity in the form of spiritual renewal. The sense of anticipation prompted various patterns of moral renewal. Here, eschatological reading of Scripture was not only about learned prognostications but, instead, intimately linked with the renewal of the Church as the witness to the coming Kingdom. Olivi was one of the most daring of the commentators in the Joachite tradition. His writings were investigated and condemned by the papacy in 1326, in part because of its enormous popularity, particularly among Beguins and radical Franciscans who sought to keep Francis' rule of poverty literally.[33] Immersed as he was in the conflict over poverty, which dominated the early history of the Franciscan order, Olivi saw the forces of evil concentrated in a worldly Church, a present, or at least imminent, reality, which he identified with the whore of Babylon (Rev. 17). Such views contributed to the intense social upheavals of the later Middle Ages, which were fired in part by apocalyptic revivals[34] and persisted well into the early modern period.[35]

Joachim's readiness to link his situation with a particular point in the unfolding apocalyptic drama outlined in the Book of Revelation gave him, and those who followed his teaching, a sense of destiny, of being at a propitious moment in the divine economy. It spawned intense debates in the Franciscan order and an emerging criticism of the Church and the implicit identification of it as Babylon. This was to loom large in protestant polemics down the centuries. It made Joachite eschatology, with its emphasis on history as the arena of God's saving purposes, politically far from conformist and a significant departure from Augustinian-dominated interpretation.

These medieval apocalyptists in the Joachite tradition echoed something of central importance about the eschatology of the New Testament. Joachim's eschatological reading of the Apocalypse picks up elements at the heart of NT theology. His strong sense of his time was of great significance in human history, and in particular the emphasis on being at a stage of salvation history, 'when (to use Paul's words) salvation is nearer to us now than when we first believed' (Rom. 13:10), is typical of many NT writers' sense of their place in the divine purposes. In the Book of Revelation the present moment is of great tribulation, which must precede the messianic age, during which period the prophets prophesy and many must wash their robes and make them white in the blood of the Lamb (Rev. 7:14). In the space between the sixth and seventh trumpet blasts John is called to prophesy (Rev. 10). In Rev. 11:14–15, 'The second woe has passed (cf. 9:12); behold, the third woe is soon to come'. With the seventh angelic trumpet blast, a decisive moment in the apocalyptic drama arrives as messianic salvation is proclaimed: 'there were loud voices in heaven, saying, The kingdom of the world has become the kingdom of our Lord and of his Christ, and he shall reign for ever and ever'. Also, Joachim's Trinitarian view of history led him to a view of the activity of the Spirit, which, in its emphasis on the present, innovatory role of the divine Spirit and the changes which it opened up, captures that eschatological character which is at the heart of many New Testament texts.

Savonarola and Botticelli: depicting the Kairos

Girolamo Savonarola (1452–98) was a Dominican preacher whose fiery message demanding reform and a 'bonfire of the vanities' electrified Florence.[36] His opposition to Rome, his predictions and his influence led eventually to his trial and execution in 1498. Like Joachim he was an interpreter of the Bible, an activity which is apparent in his preaching, but his preaching was based on a visionary experience, expounded in his *Compendium of Revelations*. Like Joachim he used the sequence of sevens from the Book of Revelation and located himself at the end of the fourth age immediately preceding the fifth age and the coming of Antichrist. He gave Florence a special role in the divine economy. A penitent population of Florence took the place of Joachim's *viri spirituales* as the pioneers of the new age to come.[37] Savonarola was in many respects a typical radical prophet. His fiery preaching of repentance was very much in the spirit of the biblical prophets with the aim of averting the divine wrath from Florence. He heralded in an apocalyptic century. Reading the signs of the times Savonarola used the opportunity to call for political and individual reformation of Florence and its people. But in the following pages it is less the career of this prophet and more his effects, in the form of his likely influence on the artist Alessandro Botticelli in two remarkable paintings, that will occupy our attention (see Plates 1 and 2).

Despite its damaged state, what is evident in Botticelli's *Mystic Crucifixion* from the Fogg Art Museum, Harvard University (see Plate 1) is the stark contrast between light and darkness, at the centre of which is the crucified Jesus. In portraying the death of Jesus as a defining moment of apocalyptic significance, Botticelli picks up on themes in the Synoptic Gospels, in Matthew, where the resurrection from the dead is linked with the moment of the death of Jesus along with events like the darkening of the sky (Matt. 27:45, 52–4), and in Luke which has Jesus' death being marked by an eclipse of the sun (Luke 23:44). Indeed, in the presentation of the crucifixion in the Synoptic Gospels there appears to be a fulfilment of Jesus' predictions of darkness and cosmic disturbance (Matt. 24:29) taking place at the moment of Jesus' death and noted similarities with the Book of Revelation (Rev. 6:12; 8:12; 9:3).

The crucified Jesus, dead, hanging on the cross, divides the picture. On the right are dark clouds. There appear to be angels holding white shields with red crosses as they fight seven brown devils armed with burning faggots and torches. The shields of the angels bear the symbol of the people of Florence. On the left is brightness, with Florence shining in the background, easily recognisable from the cathedral and the Campanile.[38] At the foot of the cross is a woman with flowing ginger hair clinging to the cross. This is widely interpreted as Mary Magdalene, who was one of the women who witnessed Jesus' death (Matt. 27:56, 61) and who, it is suggested, is thought to symbolise a penitent Florence. The apocalyptic and eschatological significance is heightened by the appearance in the left-hand corner of the picture of what seems to be an enthroned God with a book open before him, presumably the book of judgement (Rev. 20:11–15, or Dan. 7:9–10). The Final Assize takes place at the cross as the clouds move away and Florence is bathed in glory. Suffering and tribulation are the context for the renewal of a penitent Florence.

The presence of Mary Magdalene, the forgiven sinner of tradition, at the foot of the cross, on Florence's side of the picture, denotes the act of penitence and, perhaps also, intercession, which must precede the eschatological renewal.

In 1500, itself a significant year, Sandro Botticelli painted *The Mystic Nativity,* which hangs in the National Gallery, London (see Plate 2) and which is an allegorical reading of the Nativity. A closer look at the picture will reveal a caption in Greek capitals which explicitly links the picture with Revelation 11–12, and also with the political upheavals in Italy and also Florence, which came about as the result of the apocalyptic preaching of Savonarola, as this translation of the Greek inscription in 'The Mystic Nativity' shows:

> I, Alexandros, was painting this picture at the end of the year 1500 in the [troubles] of Italy in the half time after the time according to the chapter of St. John in the second woe of the Apocalypse in the loosing of the devil for three and a half years. Then he will be chained, and we shall see him [trodden down], as in this picture. (Translation by the author)[39]

The time in which Botticelli found himself, 1,500 years after the birth of Christ, was one which, he believed, stood on the brink of the new age. Botticelli writes of the troubles in Italy. The inscription implies that within a period perhaps of two years a reign of peace was to occur. In the inscription he links the ascent of the beast from the bottomless pit in Revelation 11:7 with the loosing of the devil after the millennium (20:3, 7). Botticelli writes of the second woe of 11:14, after which, in Revelation 11, the loud voices in heaven proclaim that the kingdom of the world has become the kingdom of the Lord and of the messiah. Here Botticelli reads Revelation 11–12 as a prophecy of the eschatological realities of his day, in which the period of Antichrist prefigures the return of the messiah and the overcoming of the powers of darkness. It is the coming of this kingdom, which is signified in the vision of the woman in Revelation 12 who gives birth to the messiah. The bruising of the serpent's head of Genesis 3:15 may be depicted in the form of the little devils which crawl away into their holes, reflecting Revelation 6:15–16. The picture relates Christ's first coming with his imminent, eschatological, coming. We the viewers are led up the path to the central scene of the picture framed by the dawn sky. The embrace of angels and humans sees Florentines rejoicing with the heavenly world at the millennial glory which is to be revealed. Past and present are brought together as Florence becomes the epicentre of the apocalyptic deliverance, which is about to come upon the world.

Like Milton after him, Botticelli interprets the first coming of Christ as itself an eschatological event, in which the powers of darkness are overcome and a new age begins.[40]

William Stringfellow (1928–85)

William Stringfellow was one of the most remarkable modern apocalyptic interpreters. His life echoes his theology. He did theology, as one book has put it, 'underground',[41] in the shadows, among the marginalised, among the disaffected, outside the mainstream of biblical scholarship, testifying to the radical political importance of the apocalyptic and eschatological, and was a pioneer of the tradition typified by liberation theology. Stringfellow was a lawyer in Harlem and worked with the disowned and dispossessed, in a predominantly African-American and Hispanic subculture, marked by poverty and lack of access to basic services. He was a civil rights activist and protester against the war in Vietnam and champion of the struggle of African-Americans against white supremacy. William Stringfellow tried to do that by interpreting the 'powers and principalities' mentioned in Ephesians 6:12

(thereby anticipating much recent discussion along similar lines) and elsewhere in the NT as the kinds of superhuman forces of death at work within his own time and place, the USA. In *An Ethic for Christians and Other Aliens in a Strange Land,* Stringfellow sought 'to treat the nation within the tradition of biblical politics – to understand America biblically – not the other way round'.[42]

What was crucial for Stringfellow was that the Apocalypse does not offer a timetable for the end of the world but a template by which one can assess the theological character of the world in which one lives. The Apocalypse's stark contrasts offer an interpretative key with which to understand the cosmos under God and the situation of his nation in the 1970s and 1980s. In this respect, Stringfellow follows in a long tradition going back at least to the ancient Christian writer, Tyconius (fl. 370–90), who was such an important influence on Augustine's biblical interpretation.

Babylon and Jerusalem become types of two different patterns of life and assist readers with their understanding of reality here and now. Babylon and Jerusalem are figures but represent the inadequate reality and the potentiality of every society to be something better, 'a community of reconciliation, sanity, freedom, peace'.[43] The problem with 'Babylon' is that of most societies, that is, their complacency, that they believe that 'Jerusalem' already exists in their midst when it does not. The 'marks of Jerusalem' may appear anywhere, however momentarily, and are not tied to the churches. Living in Babylon requires the cultivation of a counter-culture. *An Ethic for Christians and Other Aliens in a Strange Land* offers a vision of what it means to be an alien in a strange land, like the Jewish exiles in Babylon, and to learn how to go on singing the Lord's song in a strange land (Psalm 137:4 cf. Dan. 1:8–21). It offers a vision of a prophetic church, an anticipation of the end of time.[44]

Stringfellow emphasised the particularities of every situation and did not expect to go to the Scriptures as if to a self-help manual which would offer off-the-shelf solutions. Nor was he interested in abstract principles or grand theories to apply to human situations. For him, the ethics of biblical people concern events not moral propositions: precedent and parable, not proposition or principle.[45] There is no norm, no ideal, no grandiose principle from which hypothetical, preconceived or carefully worked out answers can be derived because all issues are incarnate in the phenomena, events, people and institutions of this world at a particular time and place. Time and history must be respected as the context of decision-making.[46] The biblical text becomes a catalyst for interpretation and a gateway to new understanding. What is demanded of the reader is imaginative participation in order to explore the ambiguities, tensions and problems that the text offers. So, Stringfellow, like his ancient predecessor, Tyconius, allowed the imagery of the Apocalypse to be juxtaposed with the interpreter's own circumstances, whether personal or social, so as to allow the images to inform understanding of contemporary persons and events and to serve as a guide for action. Like the parables of Jesus, which only with difficulty can be tied down to one particular meaning, this method offers a mode of moral reasoning which prompts and tantalises in ways which are unpredictable in their effects and may offer those who persevere a means of understanding reality and thereby illuminating the action and commitment on which they are already embarked. Stringfellow's biblical interpretation anticipates much of what we shall consider in the chapter on liberation theology but in his interpretation of the Book of Revelation he manifests, in his time and place, the power of the subversive Apocalypse to continue to be a lens on contemporary values and political priorities.

Conclusion

Apocalyptic symbol, visionary experience, and social and political movements together may make a potent mix, prompting and inspiring social revolt. Hopes for the future are seen to be realised in the present. Acting on such beliefs disrupts patterns of behaving and relating. The present moment was in the biblical accounts in some sense the climax of history, when the major actors were expected to 'sit on thrones judging the twelve tribes of Israel' (Matt. 19:28), and indeed might well have acted out such promises. In the lives of the later millenarians we find repetition of the kind of paradigm that we have in the New Testament. What is more, they are not just interpreters of sacred texts or prognosticators of the fulfilment of its promises, though the Scriptures may be the motor of their visions and their hope. They themselves live out the promises, and they believe themselves to be dwelling in the midst of their fulfilment and so act accordingly. It is the present 'apocalyptic moment' in which the impulse of the vision, dream, audition or intuition leads to the disturbance of the *status quo*, and received wisdom is subordinated to apocalyptic insight. This comes not by resort to the memory of the past, hierarchy or appeal to sacred Scripture. Such a pattern is endemic to all the Abrahamic religions. After all, their founding narratives are about revelations of the divine, in words delivered by human agents. The Jewish 'messianic mystics', particularly Sabbatai Sevi, all manifest similar characteristics, with the inspiration of mystical visions becoming the basis for social action.[47] Radicalism involves the invocation of such revelatory moments, with the possibility of additional revelations to supplement and perhaps even qualify what has already been seen. This after all is the heart of what Christianity and Islam, even Judaism, in their different ways say. It is the acceptance of the central status of the apocalyptic moment, and the subordination of all else to it, that makes apocalypticism such an important motor of radicalism in the history of religion.

Part 3

Contrasting Radical Prophets

Gerrard Winstanley and William Blake

In this part, we consider two English prophets. One of them, William Blake (1757–1827), explicitly set out to write prophecies and saw himself as standing in a long prophetic tradition, inspired by the Bible and in the light of his own visionary experience. The other, Gerrard Winstanley (1609–76), made less explicit claim to being a prophet, though he used prophetic biblical language to explain his vocation and his actions. The political character of Winstanley's and his fellow Diggers' actions from 1649 to 1651 is not in doubt, attracting opprobrium from local landowners and the suspicious interest of the Council of State set up after the end of the British monarchy on the execution of Charles I. The end of the Digger experiment did not come about, as has been suggested, because of the collapse of a social experiment, and the emergence of unequal power relations such as were outlined by George Orwell in *Animal Farm*, but because of the 'what we have we hold' ideology and the opposition of local landowners, thereby aborting an embryonic commonwealth in England which seemed to the elite to be a threat to their power and wealth.[1]

The editors of the first complete edition of Winstanley's works wrote of Winstanley as 'among the most original and boldest interpreters of the Bible in seventeenth century England' and that he 'compares with the finest writers of that glorious age of English non-fictional prose that extended from [...] John Donne and Francis Bacon, through [...] John Milton, to [...] Andrew Marvell and [...] John Bunyan'.[2]

Quite an endorsement from scholars who know the whole gamut of seventeenth-century English literature so well! The reference to his 'original biblical mythmaking' makes a comparison with Blake entirely appropriate, given the latter's original and peculiar biblical mythmaking. If Winstanley's radicalism was honed for a short period in the fires of political activism, Blake, as a visionary, printer, artist and engraver, who found a way of exploring his rich imaginative world through the juxtaposition of texts and images, left us a prophetic legacy which is unique in the history not only of radicalism but also Christian theology.

Chapter 5

Gerrard Winstanley

Responding to a *Kairos* Moment in English History

> [...] our actions and conversation is the very life of the Scripture, and holds forth the true power of God and Christ. For is not the end of all preaching praying, and profession wrapped up in this action, (namely, *Love your enemies, and doe to all men, as yòu would they should do to you, for this is the very Law and the Prophets*). This is the New Commandment that Christ left behind him. Now if any seem to say this, and does not do this, but acts contrary, for my art I owne not their ways, they are members that uphold the curse.[1]

Each May an unusual event takes place in Burford to commemorate the Levellers, shot outside Burford Church in May 1649. There is a plaque on the church wall commemorating Cornet Thompson, Corporal Perkins and Private Church and the metal cover of the font still bears the scratched names of those Levellers who were imprisoned in the church. Taking part in that event, when I was, on several occasions, privileged to read the commemorative narrative, and participate in the procession of modern 'Leveller' sympathisers through the streets of Burford, was always inspiring, as were the speeches by the likes of the late Tony Benn. In my commemoration of the executed Levellers, I always used some words of Gerrard Winstanley (1609–76), who described himself as a 'True Leveller'.

Winstanley's extant writings end over 20 years before his death. We know so little about his early life, and little about what became of him after he shot to fame in the immediate aftermath of the execution of Charles I in 1649. In the midst of what Mark Kishlansky described as a 'mid-life crisis of epic proportions'[2] there was produced some of the most brilliant political theology ever written.

The writings of Gerrard Winstanley have a central position in any study of Christian radicalism, not least with regard to his interpretation of the Bible. Most of what we know of his writing career occupied a few years of his life, and many of his extant writings are linked with his active involvement in digging the common land. Whilst his views were crystallising before this experiment began, in the wake of the execution of Charles Stuart in January 1649, the subject matter of his writing was given a particular rationale by his involvement with the Diggers.

Central to Winstanley's theology is his interpretation of the story in Genesis 2–3, the story of 'The Fall'. It is an exposition of the way in which individual desire gets institutionalised socially and politically by those who seek ways of keeping for themselves that which they covet and find a variety of ways, social, ideological and legal to hang on to what they have gained. In contrast to this 'dis-ease', Winstanley regarded the present moment in which he lived as an opportunity to enable a revolution in the way society was organised. The Second Coming of Christ would be the perfect society when 'the rising up of Christ in sons and daughters, which is his second coming' takes place. Winstanley's hermeneutics encapsulate features that are analogous to modern political movements like liberation theology. What Winstanley wrote emerged out of suffering and professional disappointment, a sense of vocation and a commitment to action, all of which led to the awareness of the indwelling Christ prompting a string of writings inspired by the Bible. The mix of claim to inspiration, rather than appealing to precedent, and the strong conviction that a new world was already on its way and was liveable now, are at the heart of the New Testament.

In his tract *The New Law of Righteousnes* Winstanley wrote of the present as a moment when the reordering of society in line with God's purpose is now imminent.[3] As we shall see, he was prompted by a revelation that he and his companions should dig the common land, thus claiming what they regarded as their rightful inheritance.[4] The action of the Diggers provoked hostility from local landowners and complaints to the Council of State. They were finally driven off the land in the spring of 1650.

'Thy sons and thy daughters shall prophesy': setting the scene

Winstanley's outburst of radical writing is the lightning flash across the theological sky of the 1640s and early 1650s. Few could emulate the power of his words, but many of his ideas were shared by others. It is important to note that prophetic context, as Christopher Hill reminded us nearly 50 years ago in a wonderful book which has been an inspiration to many of us.[5] For example, one of the most colourful figures of the English revolution is Abiezer Coppe (1619–72).[6] Coppe's *The Fiery Flying Roll* mixes personal experience and fiery rhetoric to produce one of the most remarkable texts of any in this period. Coppe came to identify God with himself in what comes across as an extraordinary emotional upheaval, every bit as life-changing as Saul's vision on the Damascus road. It needs to be put thus, to take account of the 'rhetoric of enthusiasm'.[7] Abiezer Coppe, like other contemporaries, sees the upheaval of his day as heralding a time when 'all Forms, appearances, Types, Signes, Shadows, Flesh, [...] shall melt away (with fervent heate) into power, reality, Truth, the thing signified, Substance, Spirit'.[8] Like his contemporary, Gerrard Winstanley, Coppe challenged the hegemony of learning from books: 'better scholars they, that have their lessons without book, and can read God (not by rote) but plainly and perfectly'.[9] From the perspective of this experience, he learned affinity with people on the margins of civilised society and the iniquity of social distinctions, for the eyes of the divine view all flesh equally. Coppe regarded Ezekiel as a kindred spirit, 'his Brother'. He noted that Ezekiel was 'son of Buzi', which Coppe interpreted as 'son of contempt' (בוז means 'contempt' in Hebrew). Contempt seems to have been the way in which the 'Sects of Professours' viewed Coppe's 'strange Postures'.[10] Coppe, like Ezekiel, believed he performed outlandish 'pranks' and was a sign to his generation, just as both Ezekiel and Jesus said they were (Ezek. 24:24, 27; Luke 11:30).

1. It is written in your Bibles, Behold I and the children whom the Lord hath given me, are for signs and for wonders in Israel, from the Lord of Hoasts, which dwelleth in Mount Sion, Isa 8.18.

   And amongst those who were set thus, *Ezekiel*, seems to be higher then the rest by the shoulders upwards, and was more seraphicall then his Predecessors, yet he was son of *Buzi* (Ezek. 1.) which being interpreted is the son of contempt; it pleases me [right well] that I am his brother, a sonne of *Buzi*.

2. He saw [and I in him see] various strange visions; and he was, and I am set in several strange postures.

   Amongst many of his pranks – this was one, he shaves all the hair off his head: and off his beard, then weighs them in a pair of scales; burns one part of them in the fire, another part hee smites about with a knife; another part thereof he scatters in the wind, and a few he binds up in his skirts, &c. and this is not in a corner, or in a chamber, but in the midst of the street of the great City Hierusalem, and the man all this while neither mad nor drunke, &c. Ezek. 5.1.2.3, 4. &c. as also in severall other Chapt. amongst the rest, Chap. 12.3. &c. Chap. 4.3. Chap. 24.3. to the end. This *Ezekiel* [to whose spirit I am come, and to an innumerable company of Angels, and to God the Judge of all].

3. [I say] this great Courtier, in the high Court of the highest heavens, is the son of *Buzi*, a child of contempt on earth, and set a sign and wonder (as was *Hosea*, who went in to a whore, &c.) *Hos*. 2. when he (I say) was playing some of his pranks, the people said to him, wilt thou not tell us what these things are to us, that dost so, *Ezek*. 24.19, with the 3. verse and so forwards, when he was strangely acted by that omnipotency dwelling in him; and by that eternall, immortall, INVISIBLE, (indeed) Majesty, the onely wise God, who dwells in this visible forme, the writer of this Roule, [who to his joy] is numbered amongst transgressors.

4. The same most excellent Majesty (in this forme) hath set the Forme in many strange Postures lately, to the joy and refreshment of some, both acquaintances and strangers, to the wonderment and amazement of others, to the terrour and affrightment of others; and to the great torment of the chiefest of the Sects of Professours; who have gone about to shake off their plagues if they could, some by crying out he's mad, he's drunk, he's faln from grace; and some by scandalising, &c. and onely one, whom I was told of, by threats of caneing or cudgelling, who meeting me full with face, was ashamed, and afraid to look on me, &c.[11]

This treatise is not just about Coppe being indwelt by the divine, but also his identification with the poor.[12]

Coppe and Winstanley were in their different ways prophetic signs for their generation. Their deeds mattered, perhaps as much as, if not more than, their words. Winstanley had his visions and trance-like experiences – indeed, they were crucial to his call to dig the common land – nevertheless what comes across in Winstanley's writing, for all the similarities with Coppe, is psychologically and temperamentally poles apart in the form and content.

'Visionary women' in the aftermath of the abolition of the monarchy continued to face deep-seated cultural prejudices, notwithstanding the breakdown of barriers during the Interregnum.[13] Anna Trapnel was no exception. She went into a visionary trance in 1654 in the centre of London. Visionary mysticism and prophetic political critique coincide, though 'her public voice [...] was just as much the fruit of her own intelligence and political activism as it was the product of a disembodied trance state'.[14] Trapnel started as a supporter of Cromwell, regarding him as Gideon (Judges 6–8), but, echoing biblical prophecy, began to condemn the failures of Cromwell's regime in the light of her Fifth Monarchist convictions about the rule of the saints (cf. Matt. 19:28).[15] Anna Trapnel regarded Cromwell's rule more as the last empire of Daniel's prophecy (Dan. 2 and 7) than as the dawn of the reign of King Jesus. Much as the followers of Joachim of Fiore did, Trapnel positioned herself still living in the time of the rule of Babylon. It was the time when the task of the true saints was primarily to bear prophetic witness. Details of her prophecy were written down at the time in *The Cry of a Stone*.[16] She pleaded with Cromwell to recognise the dominion of Christ and to establish a polity which allowed the common people to have their proper stake in the divine commonwealth. But, as with Winstanley, there was a clear sense that an opportunity, a *kairos*, was in danger of being missed. Her words of condemnation of Cromwell are in the spirit of Amos or Elijah. Cromwell was 'backslidden', because of 'his great pomp, and revenue, while the poor are ready to starve, as he was 'providing great palaces' for himself. 'Oh this was not Gideon of old,' she said. She pleaded with God, 'Tell him, Lord, thou art come down to have a controversy with him'.[17] The name Gideon had been given to Cromwell, but that name had now been taken from him since he had taken to himself many of the trappings of his royal predecessor and shut out King Jesus.[18]

The proper recognition of the voice and status of the women prophets is clearly stated in words which link Trapnel's visions with those of John of Patmos, as she presumed to 'meddle to declare the matters of the King', and also we read of the claims to status close to the throne of God for her and her other handmaids. They become 'the elders' around the throne of God (Rev. 4:4). Not only John of Patmos, who shared the prejudice of his own day in his suspicion of the woman prophet 'Jezebel' (2:20) but also Anna Trapnel's male contemporaries, possibly including Winstanley, were not so unequivocally supportive of women's participation in anything like the way in which they were committed to equality in other areas of life. The following words attest the equal privilege she and fellow prophets enjoyed as they shared the place around the throne of God (cf. Rev. 4–5):

> John thou wilt not offended be
> That handmaids here should sing
> That they should meddle to declare
> The matters of the King.
> John will not be displeased that
> They should sit about the throne,
> And go unto original
> And nothing else will own ...
> And the handmaids were promised,
> Much of that spirit choice,
> And it is, and it shall go forth
> In a rare singing voice.[19]

'[...] words and writings were all nothing, and must die, for action is the life of all'

Winstanley's explanation of the mission of the Diggers is set out in some memorable words which are among the first ones we hear from him in Kevin Brownlow's and Andrew Mollo's film *Winstanley* (1975):[20]

> Not a full yeere since, being quiet at my work, my heart was filled with sweet thoughts, and many things were revealed to me which I never read in books, nor heard from the mouth of any flesh, and when I began to speak of them, some people could not bear my words, and amongst those revelations this was one, *That the earth shall be made*

> *a common Treasury of livelihood to whole mankind, without respect of persons*; and I had a voice within me bad me declare it all abroad, which I did obey, for I declared it by word of mouth wheresoever I came, then I was made to write a little book called, *The new Law of righteousnesse*, and therein I declared it; yet my mind was not at rest, because nothing was acted, and thoughts run in me, that words and writings were all nothing, and must die, for action is the life of all, and if thou dost not act, thou dost nothing. Within a little time I was made obedient to the word in that particular likewise; for I tooke my spade and went and broke the ground upon *George-hill* in Surrey, thereby declaring freedome to the Creation, and that the earth must be set free from intanglements of Lords and Landlords, and that it shall become a common Treasury to all, as it was first made and given to the sonnes of men.[21]

As the words state, the aim is to show at this moment of *kairos* how the earth may be made a 'common treasury' for all, with no lording of one over another but all being equals serving the needs of each other. It was a deliberate attempt to deal with the expression of covetousness in establishing status in society when all are 'equals in Creation'. The oppression caused by the exercise, and the maintenance of the fruits of covetousness in social institutions preserving the privileges of those who have benefited from its exercise, only cease by the spread of divine power, 'the rising of Christ in sons and daughters', not by pulling the tyrannical power out of others' hands. It is when the universal power of righteous laws written on hearts is acted on that the phrase 'Mine and Thine shall be swallowed up in the law of righteous actions one to another'.[22] Incidentally, it is interesting to note that the rhetoric of 'Mine and Thine' was used by followers of the second-century CE heterodox teacher, Carpocrates: 'the idea of Mine and Thine came into existence through the laws so that the earth and money were no longer put to common use'.[23]

Winstanley described his vocation in words from Galatians 1 and Revelation. He wrote of the way in which he was a good Christian man 'but since God was pleased to reveal his son in me (cf. Gal. 1:16) and caused me to speak what I know from an inward light and power within',[24] then he entered into a new phase of his life. Just as Paul had used words of Jeremiah and Isaiah to describe what had happened to him (cf. Gal. 1:15 where Paul alludes to Isa. 49:1 and Jer. 1:5), Paul's own words in their turn offered

Winstanley a language in which to articulate his own prophet-like vocation. Among the revelations to Winstanley that prompted his prophetic witness in 1649 was this, 'That the earth shall be made a common Treasury of livelihood to whole mankind, without respect of persons'. But the revelation included a commission just like those of Ezekiel (Ezek. 2:1–3), Isaiah (Isa. 6:5–9) and Jeremiah (Jer. 1:6–10); he too was sent by the voice which spoke with him to 'declare it all abroad, which I did obey'.[25]

The characteristics of Winstanley's biblical interpretation

There are several key hermeneutical characteristics which are central to Winstanley's work, even in the early material:

- the importance of 'experiment', and with it the protest against the view that visions and revelations are over;[26]
- an emphasis on God within;
- the human person being a site of struggle between flesh and spirit;[27] and
- the 'original' sin being the acquisitive attention on the outward (covetousness), as a consequence of which attention to the promptings of the spirit within is blocked, as covetousness leads to possession and the maintenance of possessions to the exclusion of others.

In Winstanley's writings we find a rejection of the priority of the written text of Scripture and a subordination of it to the inner understanding, which comes through the Spirit. *What use is to be made of the Scriptures,* Winstanley asked. The answer he gave was 'they are, or may be kept as a record of such truths as were writ not from imagination of flesh, but from pure experience, and teachings of the Father. Secondly, we are taught thereby to wait upon the Father with a meek and obedient spirit, till he teach us, and feed us with sincere milk, as he taught them, that wrote these Scriptures.'[28] The task is to discern the spiritual truth lying beneath the 'experimental words' of the writers who set forth the actions of God in the circumstances of their day. Winstanley's ways of reading the Bible resembled the ways of Quakers, women writers, as well as some representatives of spiritual Anabaptism like Hans Denck.[29]

The commitment to political change is the context of the interpretation, which is central for Winstanley's work and so is very much a precursor of Latin American liberation theology.[30] The new heaven and earth is something to be seen here and now, for royal power is the old heaven and earth that must pass away. The New Jerusalem is not some vague hope for the future, 'to be seen only hereafter' but is *within* creation. Christ's second coming is the establishment of a state of community in the present for it is 'the fullness of time'.[31] God is to be found in the lives and experiences of ordinary men and women. As already indicated, the Second Coming of Christ will be the perfect society, when 'the rising up of Christ in sons and daughters, which is his second coming' takes place. Winstanley, like others in his day, had a firm belief that the New Jerusalem might be built 'in this green and pleasant land', to borrow Blake's famous words.[32] His historical perspective may echo Joachim of Fiore's view of history.[33]

It is in two works written within a short time of each other, *The Saints Paradice* and *The New Law of Righteousnes*, that we find enunciated some of Winstanley's most distinctive theological themes.

The Saints Paradice begins with a quotation from Jeremiah 31:34 ('And they shall teach no more every man his neighbour, and every man his brother, saying, Know the Lord: for they shall know me, from the least of them unto the greatest of them, saith the Lord'). Interestingly it is *not* the verse that mentions the law written on the heart, which is in the previous verse. The quotation is put to use as part of Winstanley's challenge to acceptance of 'the tradition from the mouths & pen of others'. Indeed, the treatise is in large part a challenge to those 'professors' who may know the Bible well and its history, but 'who worshipped a God, but neither knew who he was, nor where he was'. What they were unable to see is that what was required was 'a teacher within yourselves (which is Spirit)' who 'will teach you all things, and bring all things to your remembrance, so that you shall not need to run after men for instruction'. In 1 Corinthians 2:9–16, we have the *locus classicus* of the way in which inner promptings of the Spirit might actually work, without resort to any external authority, e.g. 'this second man is the spiritual man, that judges all things according to the law of equity and reason, in moderation and love, he is not a talker but an actour of Righteousnesse. Cor. 2:15' (the reference is explicitly cited by Winstanley).[34] It is not knowledge of the words of the Bible that counts, but experiential understanding of God that is key, for

> It is very possible, that a man may attain to the literal knowledge of the Scriptures of the Prophets and Apostles, and may speak largely of the History thereof, and draw conclusions, and raise many uses for the present support of a troubled soul, or for the restraining of lewd practises [...] and yet [...] may be not only unacquainted with but enimies to that Spirit of truth, by which the Prophets and Apostles writ.
>
> For it is not the Apostles writings, but the spirit that dwelt in them that did inspire their hearts, which gives life, and peace to us all: And therefore when the Prophets, *Jeremiah, Ezekiel* and *Isaiah* spake what they saw from God, they spake, thus saith the Lord, out of experience of what they saw, and felt, and they were called true prophets.
>
> But when others rise up, that spake their words and writings, and so applying them to another age, and generation of men, saying, Thus saith the Lord, as the other did, yet they were called false Prophets, because they had seen nothing themselves from God, but walked by the legs, and saw by the eyes of the true Prophets [...][35]

Winstanley mounted an explicit critique of a transcendent theology which he sees as the religion of the flesh. As we shall see in Blake's writing, a doctrine such as the resurrection is primarily about its meaning for the contemporary Christian. It is the indwelling Christ, and the pattern of his life as set out in the Gospels, which inspired Winstanley, not what might have happened in Jerusalem in the first century CE. That is not 'saving faith'.

In the *Saints Paradice* Winstanley contrasted the language of transcendence in doctrine with the experience of the indwelling Christ:

> And as the body of flesh in his Ascension, so called, went out of the Apostles sight, in a cloud of the Skies, so shall the same mighty man rise up out of the earth, that is, from under the earthy imaginations and lusts of the sons of men; for mankind is the earth that containes him buried, and out this earth he is to arise [...]

And therefore if you expect, or look for the resurrection of Jesus Christ, you must know, that the spirit within the flesh is the Jesus Christ, and you must see, feel and know from himself his own resurrection within you, if you expect life and peace by him.

For he is the life of the world, that is, of every particular son and daughter of the Father, who are every one of them a perfect created world of themselves, and need not to seek abroad after other creatures for teaching, for every one hath the light of the Father within himself, which is the mighty man, Jesus Christ.

And he is now rising and spreading himself in these his sons and daughters, and so rising from one to many persons, till he enlighten the whole creation (man-kind) in every branch of it, and cover this earth with knowledge, as the waters cover the seas.

[....]

So that you do not look for God now, as formerly you did, to be a place of glory beyond the Sun, Moon and Stars, nor imagine a Divine being you know not where, but you see him ruling within you, and not onley in you, but you see and know him to be the spirit and power that dwells in every man and woman, yea, in every creature, according to his orbe, within the globe of Creation [...]

[...] He that looks for a God without himself, and worships God at a distance, he worships he knows not what, but is led away, and deceived by the imagination of his own heart [...]

[...] Now Gods dwelling is not in any locall place above the skies, as men fancie, and say God dwells above the heavens.[36]

In the slightly later *The New Law of Righteousnes,* he took up a similar theme:

Some there are, nay, almost every one, wonders after the Beast, or fleshly man; they seek for new *Jerusalem*, the City of *Sion*, or Heaven, to be above the skies, in a locall place, wherein there is all glory, and the beholding of all excellent beauty, like the seeing of a show or a mask before a man. And this not to be seen neither by the eies of the body till the body be dead: A strange conceit [...]

But when the second *Adam* rises up in the heart, he makes a man to see Heaven within himself, and to judge all things that are below him. He makes many bodies to be declarers of him, who is the one power of righteousnesse that rules therein: And this is Heaven that will not fail us, endurable riches, treasures that shall

> not wax old, and whose moth and rust cannot corrupt, nor thieves break through and steal. This Christ is within you, your everlasting rest and glory.[37]

Two opposing powers are at work in humankind but, significantly, in Winstanley's biblical interpretation, they exist in humanity from the beginning. There is lack of emphasis on a period of innocence at the beginning of creation, more the sense that one power gets the upper hand in the behaviour of the human person. A contemporary of Winstanley, Peter Sterry, explored the contrasting aspects of experience of the divine, distinguishing between the right and left hands of God. God's left hand is about wrath and is found in the letter of the law. The work of the divine right hand is love, joy and glory. God's wrath is the other side of the coin from divine love, hidden from view often enough, when the tragic circumstances of life are, from the divine perspective, 'the Power, Wisdom, Goodness, Glory, working in every Object'. When the work of God's wrath is regarded as part of the divine purpose, it may be seen as the ultimate triumph of divine love.[38]

Winstanley challenged scholarly study which was cut off from experience:

> While a man is burying his head in studying what hath been done in *Moses* time, in the Prophets time, in the Apostles, and in the Son of mans time, called Jesus the Anointed, and doth not wait to find light and power of righteousnesse to arise up within his heart. This man is a piteous, barren creature, though he have all the learning of Arts and Sciences under the Sun.[39]

Winstanley believed that the Scriptures had been written 'by the experimentall hand of Shepherds, Husbandmen, Fishermen and such inferiour men of the world',[40] but the biblical writings had been subject to dark interpretation and glosses of the learned: 'the Universitie public Ministrie runs before he be sent; they take up another mans message, and carries abroad other mens words, or studies or imagines a meaning; and this is their ministrie. This is not to preach the truth, as it was in Jesus, purely and experimentally'.[41] Thereby, 'they engrosse other men's experimentall spiritual teachings to themselves as if it were their owne by University or Schoole learning succession. Pope like. Nay just the Pope'.[42] So, there is a stress on the centrality of 'experimental knowledge': 'he that speaks from the original light within can truly say, I know what I say and I know whom I worship'.[43] It is not book learning that counts, but what one has received, whether by experience or revelation.[44] Winstanley believed that men and women ought to speak no more than they know from experience. In writing thus Winstanley sided with Quaker positions over against the emerging Baptist positions on the Bible.[45]

He criticised preoccupation with the 'letters, words and histories' at the expense of attention to the promptings of the divine Spirit, for the 'plough man' is in as good a position as the university scholar to understand God:

> Nay let me tel you, That the poorest man, that sees his maker, and lives in the light, though he could never read a letter in the book, dares throw the glove to al the humane learning in the world, and declare the deceit of it, how it doth bewitch & delude man-kinde in spiritual things, yet it is that great Dragon, that hath deceived all the world, for it draws men from knowing the Spirit, to own bare letters, words and histories for spirit: The light and life of Christ within the heart, discovers all darknesse and delivers mankind from bondage; *And besides him there is no Saviour.*[46]

The poor and outcast will be the instruments of change, as was the case with the first coming of Christ (cf. Matt. 11:25):

> The Father now is rising up a people to himself out of the dust, that is, out of the lowest and despised sort of people, that are counted the dust of the earth, man-kind, that are trod under foot. In these, and from these shall the Law of Righteousnesse break forth first, for the poor they begin to receive the Gospel, and plentifull discoveries of the Fathers love flows from them, and the waters of the learned and great men of the world, begins to dry up like the brooks in Summer. Math. 11.25. 1 Cor. 1.27.[47]

Unsurprisingly, he criticised clerics who interpret the poor and meek shall inherit the earth by referring it to 'inward satisfaction'. Instead, Christ 'this great Leveller' shall cause men to beat their swords into ploughshares and spears into pruning hooks (Isa. 2:4).[48] But, as in *The New Law*, there is to be no vindictiveness.[49]

Like William Blake after him Winstanley challenged the resort to memory and invoked the power of inspiration:

> The sight of the King of glory within, lies not in the strength of memory, calling to mind what a man hath read and heard, being able by a humane capacity to joyn things together into a method; & through the power of free utterance, to hold it forth before others, as the fashion of Students is in their Sermon work; which a plough man that was never bread in their Universities may do as much [...]
>
> But the sight of the King within, lies in the beholding of light arising up from an inward power of feeling experience, filling the soul with the glory of the Law of Righteousnesse, which doth not vanish like the taking in of words and comfort from the mouth of a hearsay Preacher, or strength of memory.[50]

Apocalypse now

Throughout Winstanley's work there is a sense of the propitious time in which he writes and acts. The *Kairos* is both promise and threat, however, and in a clever use of Revelation 5–6 he uses the Lion/Lamb contrast found there to indicate the judgement on those who do not respond to the 'King of Righteousnesse': 'if you do not the Lamb shall shew himself a Lion [cf. Rev. 5:5] and tear you in pieces for your most abominable dissembling Hypocrisie'.[51]

Winstanley's interpretation of Daniel 7 is a contemporary political application of apocalyptic imagery. According to Winstanley the first Beast is royal power, which by force makes a way for the economically powerful to rule over others, 'making the conquered a slave; giving the earth to some, denying the Earth to others'. The second Beast is the power of laws, which maintains power and privilege in the hands of the few by the threat of imprisonment and punishment. The third Beast is what Winstanley calls the thieving art of buying and selling the earth with the fruits one to another. The fourth Beast is the power of the clergy, which is used to give a religious or ideological gloss to the privileges of the few. According to Winstanley, the Creation will never be at peace, until these four beasts are overthrown. This will be the moment when humankind will be enlightened.[52]

Humankind is the site of a 'battle in our age of the world' which 'grows hotter and sharper than formerly; for we are under the dividing of times, which is the last period of the Beasts reign; And he will strive hardest now'.[53] In that struggle the word of life, Christ the restoring spirit, is to be found within a person: 'The Kingdom of heaven (which is) Christ is within you'. It is only with the restoration and the deliverance from the curse of preoccupation with coveting external objects, making them one's own and ensuring that all means are used to ensure continued possession, that other creatures and the earth will be restored. It is a time when everyone will know the Law; and everyone shall obey the Law, for it shall be written in everyone's heart (cf. Jer. 31:31–3).[54]

The coming of the age of righteousness is not just for life after death, for it has already begun to appear.[55] Universal freedom has never filled earth but has been foretold by prophets.[56] When this happens it will be a new heaven and earth.[57] The great day of judgement is the Righteous Judge sitting upon the throne in every man and woman.[58]

Gerrard Winstanley: ancestor of liberation theology?

We have seen that according to Winstanley salvation does not come by belief that there was a man called Jesus 'that lived, and died at *Jerusalem*', but by feeling 'the power of a meek spirit come into you, and raign King, and tread all your envy, frowardnesse, and bitternesse of spirit under foot'.[59] Winstanley's words are in effect a commentary on the passage found in the Gospel of Matthew: 'Not every one who says to me, "Lord, Lord," will enter the kingdom of heaven, but only the one who does the will of my Father in heaven' (Matt. 7:21), or 1 John 3:18: 'My little children, let us not love in word, neither in tongue; but in deed and in truth' (cf. John 8:31–2). 'In deed and truth' summarises Winstanley's theology, for he asked, 'What is it to walk righteously, or in the sight of reason?' Winstanley's answer echoes some of the themes from the Gospel of Matthew, especially Matt. 25:31–45 (a favourite text of liberation theologians) and 7:12:

> First, When a man lives in all acts of love to his fellow-creatures; feeding the hungry; clothing the naked; relieving the oppressed;

> seeking the preservation of others as well as himself; looking upon himselfe as a fellow-creature (though he be Lord of all creatures) to all other creatures of all kinds; and so doing to them, as he would have them doe to him; to this end, that the Creation may be upheld and kept together by the spirit of love, tenderness and one-nesse, and that no creature may complaine of any act of unrighteousnesse and oppression from him.
>
> Secondly, when a man loves in the knowledge and love of the Father, seeing the Father in every creature, and so loves, delights, obeyes, & honours the Spirit which he sees in the creature, and so acts rightly towards that creature in whom he sees the spirit of the Father for to rest, according to its measure.[60]

Winstanley offered a view of political change which is dependent on transformation in attitudes: what he describes as the 'rising up of Christ in sons and daughters'.[61] His aim, therefore, was not to conquer by force of arms but to enlighten.[62] Christopher Hill appended a note on analogies between liberation theology and radical religion in seventeenth-century England.[63] There is indeed much that is hermeneutically and politically similar, at least in general terms. The appeal to experience as the motor of understanding the Bible is an obvious example. As we shall see, the popular education material from Brazil makes much of the priority of 'the book of life'. Also, both share the political perspective on Scripture and the rejection of a narrowly religious or otherworldly focus and theological agenda. Theology is now about life and the Bible is a witness to the experiences of the people of God at another time and another place.

While the similarities in form and content between what Winstanley wrote and what we find in liberationist exegesis are striking, there are differences. Experience is the motor of Winstanley's exegesis, but how solidarity with the poor and marginal offers a crucial perspective on the Bible and tradition, and whether it determines political and theological preferences, are never explicitly discussed. Winstanley saw as clearly as anyone the ways in which social institutions, indeed theology as the ideological justification of the *status quo*, served the interests of the rich and powerful in his day, no better seen in his critique of ideology inspired by apocalyptic texts like Daniel and Revelation. What we find in liberation theology, influenced by Marxism, led to a discovery of significant strands in the Bible where practice is regarded as fundamental for theological epistemology.[64] Biblical passages like Jeremiah 22:16; Matthew 25:31–45 and 1 John 4:20–1 summarise this, but none does it better than Winstanley's 'Action is the life of all'.[65] Winstanley's experiences led him to a way of reading the Bible, Genesis 2–3, for example, with a keen political edge, coloured by his appreciation of the divisions in society and church and the action necessary to initiate a change in society's structure. What drove his understanding is experience – of poverty, of oppression and of actual injustice. Indeed, we may note John Gurney's judgement that 'Winstanley certainly learnt much from his short time in Cobham, for one of the most telling aspects of the Digger programme was its successful fusion of religious with social radicalism and its skilful appropriation of traditional languages of rural discontent'.[66]

Winstanley came close to articulating what is in effect the peculiar theological perspective of the poor and the outcast when he wrote of 'Fisher-men, Shepherds, Husbandmen, and the Carpenters son',[67] the 'little ones' of Matthew 11:25; 18:5, 10, rather than 'humane learning' as the authors of New Testament texts, and 'the declaration of this righteous law rising out of the poor people that are trod under foot'.[68] Just as in the time of Jesus, shepherds and ordinary people were the witness, not the scholars of their day, the scribes, so, in Winstanley's day, it was not those with 'book learning' who relegated experience to a subordinate place but ordinary people who were the crucial witnesses (see below, Chapter 7).

There are affinities between the Diggers' situation and that of landless people in a country like Brazil, where ownership of the land is a major issue. The Brazilian Landless Workers' Movement (MST, Movimento dos Trabalhadores Rurais Sem Terra) has practised land occupations, supported by the Roman Catholic Church at a time when it was most influenced by liberation theology.[69] Anecdotally, I did pick up some awareness of the Diggers and Winstanley among some I talked to from the churches, who were involved with MST, when I was in the north-east of Brazil 20 years ago.

'And here I end': the experience of defeat

Winstanley's words spoken at the beginning of Kevin Brownlow's and Andrew Mollo's film *Winstanley* have already been quoted. The film ends with the moving words from Winstanley's *A New-Yeers Gift*, which are a fitting testimony to the witness he and many others have borne to the radical gospel of Jesus of Nazareth down the centuries:

> And here I end, having put my Arm as far as my strength will go to advance Righteousness: I have Writ, I have Acted, I have Peace: and now I must wait to see the Spirit do his own work in the hearts of others, and whether *England* shall be the first Land, or some other, wherein Truth shall sit down in triumph.[70]

As already mentioned, the latter end of Winstanley's life remains something of a mystery. He seemingly lived what appears to have been a fairly conventional life in Surrey, though he died a Quaker.[71] The concluding words of his final work *The Law of Freedom in a Platform* hint at a sense of despair at the way in which the moment for change and transformation, political and personal, seemed to have come and gone. The words at the end of *The Law of Freedom* are altogether much more pessimistic than the more upbeat words just quoted. Like many others of his generation, who entertained hopes of a change in society, as their hopes of political transformation evaporated, Winstanley seems to have experienced disappointment. Like so many others, the quest for inner transformation enabled a generation which had hoped for so much but were disappointed to seek for the radical light within and engage in an inner struggle, when the prospects for engaging in it in the world at large seemed to lead only to defeat.[72] The egalitarian spirit of the Quakers, with which Winstanley seems to have identified by the end of his life, kept alive a commitment to the eschewal of hierarchy and force. A silent protest against the *status quo* became the only viable strategy available to those who sought to keep alive the flame of hope, when the opportunities of the 1640s seemed to have disappeared.

Despite the rhetoric of the importance of martyrdom, 'Nicodemism' was a strategy of survival for non-conformists.[73] The term arises from the leader of the Jews, Nicodemus, who comes to

Jesus by night looking for some special divine revelation according to the Gospel of John (John 3), and later, along with another secret disciple, Joseph of Arimathea, arranges the burial of Jesus (cf. John 19:38–9). It is arguably a strategy present in the New Testament itself. Paul's words of advice to his Gentile churches in 1 Thessalonians 4:10–12 and 2 Thessalonians 3:12–13 suggest that the recipients of his letters try to make themselves invisible rather than look for martyrdom. One wonders if a similar strategy was employed by the likes of Gerrard Winstanley. We know he became, at least outwardly, a respected member of Cobham society but died a Quaker, perhaps remaining committed to his non-conformity, but 'secretly' for fear of the dominant power, a typical 'Nicodeman'; but like many others who had to keep parts of their lives 'undercover', practising strategies for resistance and non-conformity in an age when different sets of values dominated.[74]

Winstanley did not die a martyr's death, but in one respect he is like Jesus. According to the Gospel of Mark, Jesus' final words were a cry of despair, quoting Psalm 22: 'At three o'clock Jesus cried out with a loud voice, 'Eloi, Eloi, lema sabachthani?' which means, 'My God, my God, why have you forsaken me?' (Mark 15:34–5). Even further back, the sense of helplessness and despair in the heart-rending words of the radical prophet of the post-exilic period probably contemplated the failure of his political aspirations for a different kind of community: 'O that you would tear open the heavens and come down, so that the mountains would quake at your presence [...] will you restrain yourself, O LORD? Will you keep silent, and punish us so severely? (Isa. 64:1, 12).[75] In similar vein, the words which conclude Gerrard Winstanley's last work echo the words of despair of the Galilean radical prophet, who claimed to inaugurate a new age and summoned his contemporaries to share it and its values, but to no avail:

> Here is the righteous Law, Man, wilt thou it maintain?
> It may be, is, as hath still, in the world been slain.
> Truth appears in Light; Falshood rules in Power;
> To see these things to be, is cause of grief each hour.
> Knowledge, why didst thou come, to wound, and not to cure?
> I sent not for thee; thou didst me inlure.
> Where knowledge does increase, there sorrows multiply,
> *To see the great deceit which in the World doth lie.*

Man saying one thing now, unsaying it anon,
Breaking all's Engagements, when deeds for him are done.
O power where art thou, that must mend things amiss?
Come change the heart of Man, and make him truth to kiss:
O death where art thou? Wilt thou not tidings send?
I fear thee not, thou art my loving friend.
Come take this body, and scatter it in the Four,
That I may dwell in One, and rest in peace once more.[76]

Chapter 6

'From impulse not from rules'

William Blake's Apocalyptic Pedagogy

Despite William Blake (1757–1827) being little involved in activist politics, his ideas are in so many respects quintessentially radical. His espousal of the Bible as an inspiration and his critical challenge to its hegemony is one feature of this radical prophet, mounted in his biblically inspired political challenge. As indicated in the first chapter, what reading Blake brings to our subject is a challenge to dualism, and views of God, which emphasised the transcendent monarch, rather than the incarnate Christ. Meeting God in others, prioritisation of 'inspiration' over 'memory' and the prophetic protest, and hope for a better world, all pervade the rest of this book. Above all, Blake was 'a Holy Ghost Christian, an "enthusiast", like Gerrard Winstanley'.[1] The rescue of the Spirit from the clutches of the Devil and its restoration to the heart of Christianity in *The Marriage of Heaven and Hell*[2] is typical of Blake's quest to recover that which had been lost or eclipsed by dull conformity.

This chapter covers familiar themes in Blake scholarship: prophecy, of course, but also the place of Law, the centrality of 'Contraries', Blake's juxtaposition of texts and images, and how his work fits into the story of Christian radicalism. Together these themes are necessary ingredients to understand his radical prophecy, continuous in many ways with what has gone before, but also distinctive in form and content. It starts with a consideration of what Blake says about prophets and prophecy, and how, in his later work, the understanding deepened. Prophetic protest was necessary because of the hegemony of the 'law of commandants' in Christianity and the preoccupation with a transcendent theology. Blake had a grasp of the 'down to earth' character of the life of

Christ. Incarnation is central theologically, as Plate 17 of Blake's *Illustrations of the Book of Job* (see Figure 3) exemplifies. From his earliest illuminated book onwards the recovery of the Poetic Genius and the Prophetic Character is his life's work.

'From impulse not from rules'

Harold Bloom has written of 'strong poets' that they 'misread one another, so as to clear imaginative space for themselves'.[3] No one does this more determinedly, explicitly and effectively than Blake. His complex understanding of his relationship with the past is allied to a grasp of creativity and autonomy. Nowhere is Blake's understanding of inspiration better seen than in the criticism of Swedenborg, for turning out to be a typical ecclesiastic in his construction of the conventional church, with its orders and hierarchy and the like.[4] For Blake, there is a basic datum of what is learnt and intellectually grasped from the predecessor, but this also means moving beyond it. At times (particularly with regard to Swedenborg) this may sound like rejection, but the reality is rather different, as the complexity of the relationship with Milton makes clear.

In his relationship to his great literary predecessor, John Milton, Blake related less to the writings than to the author himself. Thus, in his understanding of Milton's work, Blake's view of discerning the underlying subject matter is to see himself as relating to the 'spirit' of Milton, and by that mystical identification to redeem the shortcomings of the earlier writer who was 'of the Devil's party without really knowing it'.[5] Blake never does this explicitly with Paul, yet we can see similar approaches to the Pauline material at work. Blake attaches himself to the radical Paul, and it is this Paul whose work he focuses on and reads over and against the conformist and pragmatic (Blake never had to engage in the practical politics of community organisation that beset Paul's later life).

Some words of William Blake from *The Marriage of Heaven and Hell* have hovered around what has already been written and form the title of this section. In one of his most daring statements about Jesus, Blake presents him as a challenger of the *status quo*:

> did he not mock at the sabbath, and so mock the sabbaths God? murder those who were murderd because of him? turn away the law from the

> woman taken in adultery? steal the labor of others to support him? bear false witness when he omitted making a defence before Pilate? covet when he pray'd for his disciples, and when he bid them shake off the dust of their feet against such as refused to lodge them? I tell you, no virtue can exist without breaking these ten commandments: Jesus was all virtue, and acted from impulse: not from rules.[6]

In verses found in Blake's notebook, known as *The Everlasting Gospel*, Jesus' activity is pervaded with a lack of concern for the propriety of custom and law. He did not respect the requirement to 'honour his father and mother'.[7] As dissidents, John and Jesus suffered for their disobedience ('John for disobedience bled').[8] What Jesus did was break the shackles imposed by culture and tradition, what Blake elsewhere calls the 'mind-forg'd manacles' of religion.[9] A theme throughout these fragments is the 'mental fight',[10] which has its echoes in the Gospels, where the 'binding of the strong man' (Mark 3:22) is a figurative way of describing Jesus' struggle with the satanic powers.[11] Jesus broke the 'manacles' of traditional religion and culture because 'he scourg'd the Merchant Canaanite/From out the Temple of His Mind'.[12] In one of the longest sections of 'The Everlasting Gospel' there is a retelling of the story of the Woman taken in Adultery in John 8, reference to which has already been made in the quotation from *The Marriage of Heaven and Hell*. It offers an unequivocal challenge to the Mosaic Law, which is implicit in the story in John 8:2–11. Jesus is a symbol of non-conformity, who wrestled with the principalities and powers, and offers a dynamic, imaginative space for those who can take advantage of that aspect of the human intellect, which is too easily neglected or derided.

Blake was not part of 'the hegemonic Christian tradition'.[13] The criteria of orthodoxy are determined by faith communities and evolve over a period of time during which minority views are incorporated, including those hitherto deemed unpalatable, though shorn of the features which caused most offence. In this way, the wielders of ecclesiastical power embrace the widest form of belief and dissent. In Blake's time, there was no church which offered him a sufficiently capacious umbrella under which to shelter, and it is of no surprise that he found himself, like Jesus, 'outside the gate' (Hebr. 13:12). So, becoming a victim of habit and of tradition was something which had to be questioned, not because habit had to be cast aside, so much as its effects had to be questioned constantly. The problem is the way in which precedent, indoctrination and upbringing can shackle the vocation to be the person one is and the discovery in the process of what inhibits that person from relating well to others around them. The 'apocalyptic' element is prominent, whether it is appeal to the visionary and the prophetic, or the unmasking of the present state of affairs. Although the poetry and the illuminated books demonstrate intense labour and ingenuity, Blake said that some came as the result of inspiration.

Blake in many ways is the consummate radical. His radicalism was not that of a political activist, though some kind of involvement was not for want of trying. Unlike Winstanley, whose Digger experiment was a direct reaction to the aftermath of the end of monarchy in England in 1649, a grasping of the 'propitious moment', or Muentzer's involvement in the Peasants' Revolt in 1525 and before that in actions to overturn the hegemony of Catholicism,[14] Blake seems never to have been closely involved in that kind of active politics. His attempt at gaining a public voice, for example in 1809, met with rejection and derision. His was primarily a 'mental fight', an exercise in 'conscientisation'[15] to build Jerusalem, whatever his sympathies for the radical movements of his day. So, it causes little surprise, given the state of politics at the time of writing and the differences from Blake's own, that he wrote: 'I am really sorry to see my countrymen trouble themselves about politics'.[16] In Blake's day, as in Jesus', the scope of politics was determined by the interests of a wealthy elite. For Blake, as for Jesus, those interests were at odds with all he believed and stood for. No wonder he could speak so derisively of the political process of his day as 'something Else besides Human Life'.[17] So, conventional politics was almost an impossibility, except by the kind of demonstration Jesus acted out in the Temple which brought down upon himself 'the Cruel Rod'.[18] Indeed, Blake just managed to escape that descending on him too, thanks to the support of powerful patrons, when he was put on trial for sedition.

As the years went by, Blake continued to find ways of expressing his deep-seated radical political convictions, and his vocation to disseminate them. His task was *always* educational, with the intention of being transformative, about 'cleansing the doors of perception'.[19] So while Blake's understanding of the relationship of change and order, constraint and subversion, evolved, the dialectic remained the same; from his earliest work to his last,

Blake never retreated from a committed political position, even if the way in which he expressed that political wisdom did evolve.[20] Nevertheless, Blake's obscurity does echo Winstanley's retreat from the political after 1652, but with this major difference: it was his art, skills and insight which were put to use in the interests of a radical politics and religion, or, as he more cogently put it, 'Are not Religion and Politics the same thing',[21] and the contribution to radical prophecy continued to be the very stuff of his literary and artistic expression.

'Every honest man is a prophet'

Blake himself wrote two explicitly titled prophecies about America and Europe in the form of illuminated books, in which, by word and picture, a process of conversion, spiritual and political, is sought in the reader through the effects of the texts. *America a Prophecy* and *Europe a Prophecy* are not prophecies intended to predict exactly what would happen; they are not another form of the sayings of Nostradamus, therefore, for they were written after the events that are described. Rather, they lay bare the inner dynamic of all revolutions, their potential for positive change and their corruption. We catch a glimpse of how the images suggest something of their themes.

For example, at the opening of *Europe* (1794, see Plate 3) is one of Blake's most famous images, known as 'The Ancient of Days'. It is a depiction of a divinity who orders and measures, an image which may have been inspired by Proverbs 8:27 and Milton's words in *Paradise Lost*.[22] On the right is the title page with the serpent (see Plate 4). The divinity's hair in the previous image is blown sideways. Blake probably intended the two images to face each other, so that what stirs the hair of the ordering divinity comes from the direction of the juxtaposed image of the serpent. The wind of change blows from the right, from the east, the direction from which the divine glory comes to the restored Jerusalem in Ezekiel's prophecy (Ezek. 43:2). The juxtaposition of the measuring, bounding and restricting Ancient of Days, and the energetic serpent that brings liberation, sets the scene for the prophecy to come.[23] Whatever ideas may be generated by energy, reason is needed to build upon them:

> Reason is the bound or outward circumference of Energy [...] This is shewn in the Gospel, where [Jesus] prays to the Father to send the comforter or Desire that Reason may have Ideas to build on [...][24]

Blake briefly expounded his views on prophecy in 1798, in the wake of Tom Paine's views on the Bible, which were the subject of an episcopal refutation, to which Blake reacted angrily. His marginal annotations have come down to us, and in one of his notes to Richard Watson's (Bishop of Llandaff) 'Apology' he mentioned prophets:

> Prophets in the modern sense of the word have never existed Jonah was no prophet, in the modern sense for his prophecy of Nineveh failed Every honest man is a Prophet he utters his opinion both of private & public matters Thus If you go on So the result is So He never says such a thing shall happen let you do what you will. a Prophet is a Seer not an Arbitrary Dictator. It is mans fault if God is not able to do him good. for he gives to the just & to the unjust, but the unjust reject his gift.[25]

So, prophecy is not about prediction but the assertion of insight and warning, setting out the situation as it is and getting a response. The distinction between prophecy as 'forth telling' (roughly speaking, pronouncing the divine word about society and individuals) and 'foretelling' (predicting that which is to come in the future) is one which is important and is needed to complement the variety of prophetic activity in Blake's day, and indeed at other times.[26] Blake is to be placed more in the category of a 'forth teller'. Prophecy is the prerogative of every one, for 'every honest man is a Prophet'.[27] Revelation, while apparently being future-orientated, is as much about laying bare the realities of politics and history as offering a map of the end of the world. In its visions, threats and eschatological promises the divine Spirit speaks to the churches about the extent of their self-deception, about their present state, in order to get them to change. It is, to paraphrase Blake's own words, 'cleansing the doors of perception'.[28] Indeed, Blake saw his words as being in continuity with what John saw on Patmos.[29]

In one version of *The Marriage of Heaven and Hell* over the words 'As a new heaven is begun, and it is now thirty-three years since its advent',[30] Blake has written '1790', seemingly drawing attention to the year 1757, the year of Blake's birth and also the age of Jesus at his death (cf. Luke 3:23) and (probably less significantly) the year of the Swedenborgian Last Judgement.[31] The addition seems to confirm that Blake considered that his birth was the moment when 'the return of Adam into Paradise' was opened up,[32] the new creation had begun and the eschatological age was initiated. As we have seen, Jesus, after his call and testing, according to Mark 1:15, said: 'the time (*kairos*) is fulfilled and the kingdom of God is at hand'. Such prophetic actualisation is found elsewhere in the pages of the New Testament (Chapter 3, 'The ultimate 'opportune moment' in the New Testament and the agents who sought to act on it'). For example, John the Baptist was the Elijah who was to come (e.g. Matt. 11:14 and 17:13), Paul was the agent of salvation to the nations in the Last Days, alluding to the prophetic vocation of Jeremiah and Isaiah (Gal. 1:15) and possibly Ezekiel as well.[33] At the start of one of his earliest illuminated works he quoted the classic prophetic words, 'The Voice of One Crying in the Wilderness' (Isa. 40:3),[34] in a work which argues for the necessity of rediscovery of 'the Poetic genius, the Spirit of Prophecy' to fructify the consequences of sense perception. Blake's quotation of Numbers 11:29 at the end of the Preface to *Milton, A Poem*, suggests that being a prophet was not a vocation peculiar to an elite, for he had democratised prophecy: 'Every honest man is a Prophet'. Hence, the complex task of the prophet to cleanse 'the doors of perception' belongs to all.

Blake's theological ancestors lie with the prophets of the Bible. He exemplifies an author who gives priority to the 'prophetic principle' as described by Rosemary Radford Ruether. Throughout his work there is a criticism of priest craft, its separation of life into neat compartments, and its devotion to tradition. Jeanette Winterson reflects this not least because of the quotation from Isaiah 40, which Blake uses at the very start of *All Religions are One*:[35]

> The priest has a book with the words set out. Old words, known words, words of power. Words that are always on the surface. Words for every occasion. The words work. They do what they're supposed to do; comfort and discipline. The prophet has no book. The prophet is a voice that cries in the wilderness, full of sounds that do not always set into meaning. The prophets cry out because they are troubled by demons.[36]

Building Jerusalem: what it means to be a prophet

That said, Blake's work from time to time reveals unease, perhaps even a dissatisfaction and ambivalence, about the role of the prophet–artist. We saw that the end of Winstanley's last extant writing of substance in his Digger period of protest, advocacy and anticipation is marked by words of profound despair. The spiritual and mental effort, the 'mental fight' in which the prophet has to engage is no more graphically portrayed than in Jeremiah's anguish.

There can be few passages more redolent of the revolutionary optimism of biblical prophecy than this plate from Blake's prophecy, *America* 6 (in Erdman's edition, E53. See Figure 1).[37] It reads like an anthology of allusions to biblical passages, which merge to portray the hopeful mood of the young man with eyes raised, looking for the 'redemption' which 'draweth nigh', to quote Luke 21:28. But Blake also reveals ambivalence about prophecy. In versions of *America a Prophecy,* there are the following additional words, which are masked in some versions but present in other copies, suggesting Blake may have been ambivalent about prophecy (cf. 1 Cor. 13:8–9):

> The stern Bard ceas'd, asham'd of his own song; enrag'd he swung
> His harp aloft sounding, then dash'd its shining frame against
> A ruin'd pillar in glittring fragments; silent he turn'd away,
> And wander'd down the vales of Kent in sick & drear lamentings.[38]

In *Vala* (or, as it was entitled later, *The Four Zoas,* reflecting the influence of the prophecy of Ezekiel), we also note Blake's ambivalence about revolutionary energy. By the end of *Vala* the prophetic function is recognised as a distraction, a 'delusive Phantom'.[39] In words which seem to echo 1 Corinthians 13:8–10 about the new age ('Love never ends. But as for prophecies, they will come to an end [...] For we know only in part, and we prophesy only in part; but when the complete comes, the partial will come to an end'), when 'sweet Science reigns', 'dark Religions are departed'. What is 'dark' is an enigma, Tyndale's 'in a darke speakynge' (1 Cor. 13:12 ἐν αἰνίγματι).

The contrasting fortunes of the hero of Blake's mythological system, Los, especially in the later work, *Jerusalem,* indicate the problems for a prophet which Blake teases out in his words and

FIGURE 1: *America a Prophecy*, 6

images. What comes across as this complex poem moves to its conclusion is that, however sincere Los's redemptive intentions may be, they do not always achieve their aim, and, indeed, seem to be misplaced and counterproductive. Prophetic endeavour there may be, but the energy generated can often lead in a direction different from what was intended. Los's activities have little effect,[40] until, that is, Los is 'united with Jesus and casts off Selfhood'.[41]

Two dramatic images from *Jerusalem* make the point (see Plates 5 and 6). *Jerusalem* 75 shows Blake invoking Revelation 17. Babylon as a mermaid is seated upon a sea monster. In the words above, we read about Jesus breaking through death and hell to open eternity in time and space in the face of the aggression of 'Babylon the Great, the Abomination of Desolation, Religion hid in War'. The very next page of *Jerusalem* (76, see Plate 6) shows a figure with arms outstretched towards the crucified Jesus, possibly Los (75:23) or Albion (75:27). The man turns his back on 'Babylon the Great' and looks up at the crucified Christ and seems to embrace Christ's example. It is the adoption of a different frame of mind, and behaviour, in which the human ego, which Blake calls 'Selfhood', is not allowed its sway. It is the kind of thing that Paul seems to enjoin when he talks about being identified with Christ. It is about humility and the diminution of self-importance, recognising the Other rather than putting the self in first place. The pictorial example is summarised in words elsewhere in *Jerusalem*: 'if I die I shall arise again & thou with me This is Friendship & Brotherhood without it Man Is Not'.[42] Los's final struggle with his spectre is told very graphically at the climax of *Jerusalem*, when 'Los alterd his Spectre & every Ratio of his Reason Till he had completely divided him into a separate space'.[43] That had been preceded by a ferocious activity 'of strict severity self-subduing', typified by the hammer on the anvil and the turning of the Spectre to dust. Thus, Los is no longer blighted by Selfhood. The character of the prophet in building and redeeming is crucial.

The ethical dimension of the life of the prophet slowly emerges, obliquely but insistently, in Blake's later works, particularly in *Jerusalem*; the growing realisation of Los that frantic activity is not sufficient for the prophetic task if the issue of Selfhood is not addressed. Similarly, in the *Illustrations of the Book of Job*, while dreams and visions are crucial in enabling Job to say, 'I have heard thee with the hearing of the Ear but now my Eye seeth thee' (in Blake's rendering of Job 42:5), it is the fact that he prays for his friends,

Plate 1: Sandro Botticelli, *Mystic Crucifixion*

Plate 2: Sandro Botticelli, *Mystic Nativity*

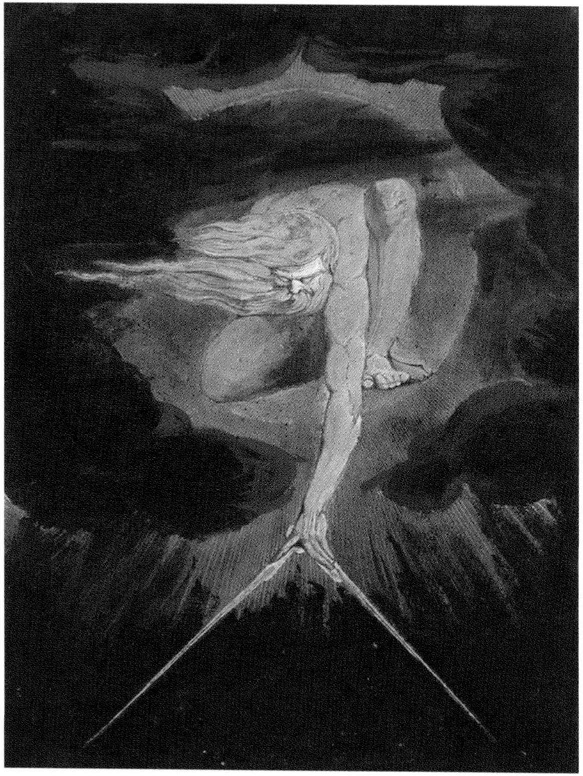

Plate 3: William Blake, *Europe a Prophecy*, Frontispiece

Plate 4: William Blake, *Europe a Prophecy*, Title Page

Plate 5: William Blake, *Jerusalem*, Plate 75

Plate 6: William Blake, *Jerusalem*, Plate 76

Plate 7: William Blake, *Europe a Prophecy*, Plate 12

Plate 8: William Blake, 'Holy Thursday', *Songs of Experience*

Plate 9: Missionary methods

Plate 10: Down to earth

PLATE 11: Reading the book of everyday life

PLATE 12: A twin track approach – life first then the Bible

Plate 13: Looking at the world differently with the help of the Bible

Plate 14: Reading the Bible in the context of everyday life and community

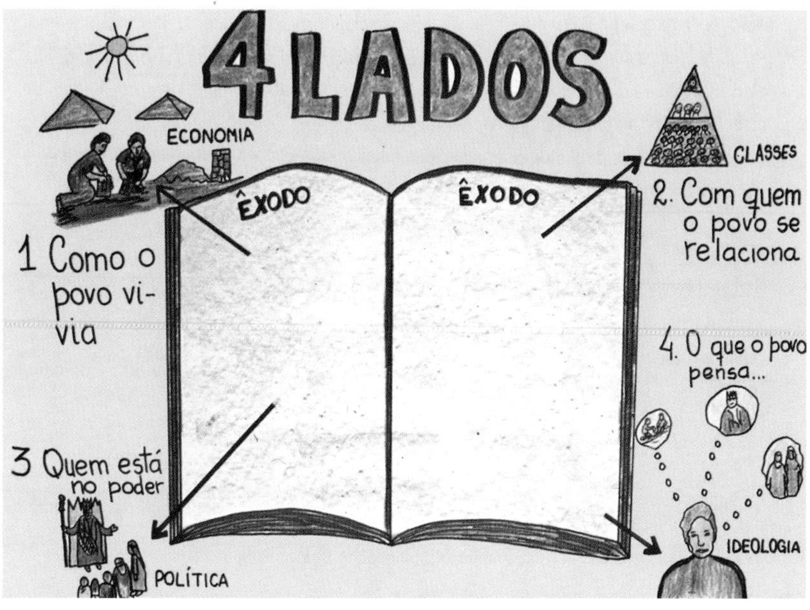

Plate 15: The Bible's witness to the life of the people of God – then and now

Plate 16: Guidelines for reading the Bible

and so practises love for his enemies, that seals his redemption (Job 42:10, *Illustrations* 17 and 18). So building Jerusalem is not just about the exercise of the poetic genius; Blake plumbed the complexities of the human personality, including the prophetic ego and the need to ensure that its potentially counter-productive endeavours were informed by, if not subordinated to, 'Human Brotherhood'.[44]

There is another development, picking up themes within the Bible itself, that it is not just the words of the prophet but how he lives and indeed how he acts, which are important. In the prophecy of Jeremiah, however, we find the exposition of the personal and psychological cost of prophetic activity, both in the accounts of the effects of Jeremiah's controversial activity and in the so-called 'confessions' of Jeremiah, in which the prophet laments the difficulties of his calling (e.g. Jer. 15:10–18; 17:5–8; 20:7–12). The prophecy of Jeremiah in the Bible differs in important respects from the collections of the other prophets. Like the Book of Daniel, in addition to prophetic oracles and visions there are references to the burden of his prophetic activity and a narrative context for the prophet's message. What emerges in both is that being a prophet involves words, actions and life as a whole coming together. Gradually, the medium becomes part of the message.

Complementing the accounts in Jeremiah, which indicate the cost of the prophetic vocation, evident in the narratives, the hostility, which is described, and the anguished outbursts, there is another phenomenon, which emerges in the Book of Ezekiel. In addition to words of woe for his generation, there are dramatic signs as well as visions, something noticed also by Abiezer Coppe (Chapter 5, '"Thy sons and thy daughters shall prophesy": setting the scene'). Indeed, Blake makes mention of Ezekiel's actions, and their prophetic import.[45] Ezekiel eats a scroll and describes the experience, out of which comes an understanding of the nature of the message (Ezek. 3:2). He takes a brick and portrays a city on it and the siege against it and lies on his left side for a number of days indicating that he bears the punishment inflicted on Jerusalem. After that he lies on his right side, bearing the punishment of the house of Judah, and baking bread prepared on human dung (Ezek. 4:12–13). He then takes a sharp sword (Ezek. 5), and an exile's bag and digs through the wall as a sign (Ezek. 12). Most dramatically of all, when tragedy strikes Ezekiel, when God takes away 'the delight of his eyes' and his wife dies, the prophet is instructed not to mourn for her. Once again this experience and his actions have meaning for the situation in which Ezekiel finds himself (Ezek. 24:15–24). 'Ezekiel shall be a sign to you'. The prophet as a sign is echoed by a later prophet, Jesus of Nazareth, who looked back not to Ezekiel but to Jonah who was a sign to the people of Nineveh (Luke 11:30).

The opening words of the Letter to the Hebrews encapsulate this and also typify the form and content of the Gospels: 'Long ago God spoke to our ancestors in many and various ways by the prophets, but in these last days he has spoken to us by a Son' (Hebr. 1:1–2). Prophetic words, visions and their interpretation are by themselves not enough. The demeanour and life of the prophet are the crucial medium of their prophecy. It is no accident, therefore, that when the early Christians collected the words of Jesus, it was not only his words, but the story of his life, which was the way in which they communicated the prophetic word. Similarly the opening verses of John's Gospel are not about creation but about God's plan for humanity,[46] which is not a vision or the words of an angelic communication but a life lived. What Jesus heard and saw with God becomes less important than the revelation of God in himself (John 14:9). The point of mentioning this in the context of elucidating Blake as a prophet is to draw out the fact that, in addition to the words and the images as a medium of the prophetic communication, there is also set forth the importance of the prophet himself as a mode of communication. That sense of prophetic vocation is there in one of Blake's earliest illuminated books, as we have seen.

'The law of commandments'

In the double-page spread which begins The Blake Trust/Tate Gallery edition of Blake's *All Religions are One* there is an image of a young man pointing with both hands towards the image on the following page, with the caption, 'The Voice of one crying in the Wilderness' (Isa. 40:3) underneath the image. On the other page there is an elderly man with a book open on his lap gazing up to heaven and standing behind him at his shoulder is an angel with the stone tablets inscribed with the words 'All Religions are One'. The solitary voice may be the young Blake pointing towards a pattern of religion, based on the holy book, whose interpretation was devoid of the Prophetic Character. Blake saw that 'The five books of the

Decalogue' and 'the law of commandments' had become a form of Christianity, adherence to which was quenching 'the Poetic Genius, the Spirit of Prophecy' (cf. 1 Thess. 5:19).

Central to Blake's work is the attack on the divinely sanctioned Decalogue by the transcendent divinity, and on the Church's quenching of the Spirit in his and indeed every age.

Blake's problems with the Bible concerned the way in which he considered major themes had been co-opted by 'the primeval Priests assum'd power' in the service of a monarchical state. There is 'One King, one God, one Law'.[47] The image from Blake's *Europe a Prophecy* 12 (see Plate 7) demonstrates how Blake saw religion and politics intertwined. The enthroned divinity is depicted with the facial features of the King of England and crowned with a papal tiara and with an open book on his lap. In the caption, Blake wrote: 'Albions Angel rose upon the Stone of Night. He saw Urizen on the Atlantic; And his brazen Book, That Kings & Priests had copied on Earth Expanded from North to South'.[48] Here we see demonstrated his conviction about what he considered the unhappy effects of religion and politics being the same thing. He saw what was believed to be a divinely sanctioned book, the Bible, particularly the Decalogue, and certain political themes serving the interests of a monarchical state. The 'brazen Book' is said to be that of Urizen, the lonely authoritarian divinity in Blake's idiosyncratic mythology.

In Blake's theology is the subtle dialectic between immanence and transcendence: 'All deities reside in the human breast,' wrote the defiant author of *The Marriage of Heaven and Hell*.[49] This was a view which he maintained to the end of his life. This terse statement, which might be taken to be an indication of the death-knell of belief in a transcendent divinity, underlines his conviction that divinity is among humans, 'God with us' (Matt. 1:23). 'The Divine Body' is the environment within which humans live, a divine space. Such ideas, which are no better exemplified than in the aphorism from *Laocoön*, 'The Eternal Body of Man is THE IMAGINATION, that is God himself The Divine Body, JESUS we are his members'.[50] The Divine Body is an environment, in which one lives and moves and has one's being (cf. Acts 17:28).

At the start of the book I quoted Blake's Preface to *Milton* and his hope for 'the New Age' when 'all will be set right: & those Grand Works of the more ancient & consciously & professedly Inspired

Men, will hold their proper rank, & the Daughters of Memory shall become the Daughters of Inspiration'.[51] Writing thus he borrowed John Milton's warning not to invoke 'Dame Memory and her Siren Daughters', and pray 'to that eternal Spirit who can enrich with all utterance & knowledge & sends out his Seraphim with the hallow'd fire of his Altar to touch & purify the lips of whom he pleases'.[52] Indeed, he quotes the passage from Milton in full in his annotations to Joshua Reynolds's writing.[53]

Blake challenged the interpretation of a sacred book based solely, or mainly, on memory rather than inspiration, with no imaginative engagement. The effects of that on the devotion to Scripture as sacred code is summed up in 'The Garden of Love', where the chilling effect of the religion of 'Thou shalt not' is evoked (see Figure 2):

> I went to the Garden of Love,
> And saw what I never had seen:
> A Chapel was built in the midst,
> Where I used to play on the green.
>
> And the gates of the Chapel were shut,
> And Thou shalt not. writ over the door;
> So I turn'd to the Garden of Love,
> That so many sweet flowers bore.
>
> And I saw it was filled with graves,
> And tomb-stones where flowers should be:
> And Priests in black gowns, were walking their rounds,
> And binding with briars, my joys & desires.[54]

The problem with 'Priests in black gowns, were walking their rounds, And binding with briars, my joys & desires' is that they pay scant attention to the minute particulars of life.

Ethical concerns are not ignored by Blake – far from it. The forgiveness of sins, which he outlines brilliantly in his re-reading of Joseph's discovery of Mary's pregnancy in *Jerusalem* 61, does not involve an appeal to what the law required. Indeed, according to Blake, the righteous Joseph moves from enacting what the law requires, via his acceptance of Mary, and his attending to the dream of the angel about God's rejection of a religion based on

FIGURE 2: 'The Garden of Love', *Songs of Innocence and of Experience*

retribution, to an understanding of the heart of divinity as the forgiveness of sins:

> But Jehovahs Salvation Is without Money & without Price, in the Continual Forgiveness of Sins In the Perpetual Mutual Sacrifice in Great Eternity! for behold! There is none that liveth & Sinneth not! And this is the Covenant Of Jehovah: If you Forgive one-another, so shall Jehovah Forgive You: That He Himself may Dwell among You.[55]

The ethical note that Blake sounds is the ongoing task of forgiveness of sins and the rejection of 'Religion Hid in War'. A divine space opens up in which 'Religion & Politics [are] the Same Thing? Brotherhood is Religion'[56] and 'As God is Love: every kindness to another is a little Death In the Divine Image nor can Man exist but by Brotherhood'.[57]

Blake was not much interested in the Bible as a window onto history. For him it was 'the Sentiments & Examples which whether true or Parabolic are Equally useful'.[58] His theology rejected preoccupation with the transcendent and the holy. It was about God with humanity and in humanity. This is what comes out very strongly in Job's dramatic theological transformation, as set out in Blake's *Illustrations of the Book of Job* (1825).

In Illustrations of the Book of Job 17 (see Figure 3) the biblical quotations from the Gospel of John stressed the identification of the divine Christ with humanity.[59]

There is an amusing anecdote told by Henry Crabb Robinson about a meeting with Blake in 1825, when Blake is reported to have said:

> We are all co-existent with God – Members of the Divine body – We are all partakers of the divine nature – On my asking in what light he viewed the great question concerning the Divinity of Jesus Christ he said – 'He is the only God – But then he added – And so am I and so are you'.[60]

Blake's focus on the *effect* of texts, whether the Bible, or his own allusive illuminated texts, beckons a receptive openness to the impact of the Bible, in which the texts are less an object to be explained than a stimulus to the exploration of the imaginative space which biblical texts may offer. We can see the ways in which Blake explored life in that 'space', and the way in which the Bible's particularly rich allusiveness, helped expand the horizons of readers of the Bible, to include the 'minute particulars' of life.[61] If the Bible could help with that, so be it, but it didn't have to be the instrument to do that if other resources were better equipped to do so. If it did not, then it had to be put on one side and seen for what it was, a relic

FIGURE 3: *Illustrations of The Book of Job*

of the past, which no amount of apologetics could possibly justify. But the paradox was that, despite the criticisms he had of the Bible, Blake found in it the resources to create afresh words of hope and insight, which he hoped might galvanise a complacent society to see the folly of 'Religion Hid in War' and take up the practice of forgiveness of sins, with all that this entailed.

'Without Contraries is no progression'

What is distinctive about Blake's writing is his repudiation of dualism. It is not the case that dualistic language is absent from the Blake corpus: far from it. Challenging the hegemony of one pole in the dualistic struggle is crucial, but overcoming it is another. Blake contrasted the need for wrestling with 'contraries' as the very stuff of human existence, as opposed to one contrary negating the other. In writing thus, Blake challenged a central feature of much Christian theology down the centuries. But, Blake took on that kind of understanding and, in 'Shewing the Two Contrary States of the Human Soul' (as the title of *Songs of Innocence and of Experience* indicates),[62] he challenged the language of repression which can be so typical of Christian spirituality and offered instead the importance of glorying in the opposites: 'Without Contraries is no progression', he wrote in *The Marriage of Heaven and Hell.*[63] That was the foundation stone of his work. In other words, a way is found of enabling opposites to be engaged with, which involves the recognition of difference without violence. Contrasts between light and darkness, truth and falsehood and good and evil are typical of most religions and Blake wants us to get away from thinking that one eclipses the other. Instead 'Contraries' are the stuff of existence:

> Man was made for Joy & Woe
> And when this we rightly know
> Thro the World we safely go
> Joy & Woe are woven fine
> A Clothing for the soul divine[64]

Blake as artist and writer emphasised 'contraries', both Energy and Reason.[65] Blake will have none of a dualism that sees any form of negation. This is what principally separates him from the religion of the Bible and its emphasis on holiness:

And this is the manner of the Sons of Albion in their strength
They take the Two Contraries which are calld Qualities, with which
Every Substance is clothed, they name them Good & Evil
From them they make an Abstract, which is a Negation
Not only of the Substance from which it is derived
A murderer of its own Body: but also a murderer
Of every Divine Member: it is the Reasoning Power
An Abstract objecting power, that Negatives every thing
This is the Spectre of Man: the Holy Reasoning Power
And in its Holiness is closed the Abomination of Desolation[66]

The Marriage of Heaven and Hell is a challenge to dualistic errors, explicitly a challenge to biblical traditions of holiness rooted as they are in dualism, between the sacred and the profane, the pure and the impure, the righteous and the unrighteousness. Blake's rhetorical flourish at the end of *The Marriage of Heaven and Hell*, 'For every thing that lives is Holy',[67] tells us everything about his understanding of the Church and the world. The ways in which one participates in the divine life is less about 'going to church' than engaging in actions such as forgiveness of sins, and enjoying the universal presence of Christ in the human imagination. Blake's view is not just a challenge to any ecclesiology, but it makes normal understandings of the Church/world distinction redundant and unhelpful for participation in the divine life. This is one of the points made by the judgement on the experience of Church going on in 'The Little Vagabond' (see Figure 4):

Dear Mother, dear Mother, the Church is cold,
But the Ale-house is healthy & pleasant & warm;
Besides I can tell where I am use'd well,
Such usage in heaven will never do well

But if at the Church they would give us some Ale.
And a pleasant fire, our souls to regale;
We'd sing and we'd pray, all the live-long day;
Nor ever once wish from the Church to stray,

FIGURE 4: 'The Little Vagabond', *Songs of Innocence and of Experience*

Then the Parson might preach & drink & sing.
And we'd be happy as birds in the spring:
And modest dame Lurch, who is always at Church,
Would not have bandy children nor fasting nor birch.

And God like a father rejoicing to see,
His children as pleasant and happy as he:
Would have no more quarrel with the Devil or the Barrel
But kiss him & give him both drink and apparel.[68]

Blake rejected the traditional biblical understanding of holiness as special and separate, applying just as much to persons, place, or matter. For all the polemic against the Law as part of a passing aeon, Christian writers from the New Testament onwards did not make any significant transition from the biblical understanding of holiness and its practice. The means whereby they understood its implementation were different (one was enabled to practice holiness by the divine Spirit, 1 Cor. 3:16; 6:19, or gain it through the effects of the sacrifice of Christ, 1 Peter 1:19; 2:9), but essentially the same dualistic framework persisted, in which the sacred and profane were to be set apart one from another. Blake will have none of this thinking; it is one of the features that make him a radical prophet and stern critic of the tradition he had inherited. It is the way in which 'the priests in black gowns' maintain their power and 'bind with briars' humanity's 'joys and desires'. So, for Blake, the story of Job is about how he has to get out of his system habit, convention and devotion to a religion of the book, so he can appreciate the divine glory of the cosmos as he and the God within.

'Jesus & his Apostles & Disciples were all artists'

This quotation from Blake's *Laocoön*[69] not only indicates the wide range of what Blake understood by art but also its indispensability in the transformative pedagogy which was his life's work. The whole thrust of the Job engravings is to redress the balance between words and pictures, by privileging vision over audition, pictures over words, and thereby to challenge the logocentrism of the post-Reformation world. It is through images, dreams of the night, that Job comes to the realisation that the world of words cannot be allowed the hegemony to quench the spirit of the imagination.

In the medieval period illuminated manuscripts stimulated an affective experience in which an encounter with the divine came about through meditation;[70] visual images aided understanding and facilitated meditation. The exercise of imagination, which involved the visualisation in the mind of scriptural passages, has been an important part of the reading of Scripture. The monastic practice of meditation notably involved making mental images or cognitive 'pictures' for thinking and composing.[71] Ancient readers and hearers of texts sought to 'visualise' what they read (or heard), and that seeing or listening would frequently involve the creation of mental images. So, through meditative recall, biblical texts yielded new meaning by a process of spontaneous interconnections.

Down the centuries, the Apocalypse has evoked a string of visual representations when artists responded to the 'picturely' quality of the text of the Apocalypse, as the words prompted comparison with colours and creatures.[72] But, as with all the visions from antiquity (and indeed most visions ever since), its pictures readily became encapsulated, perhaps, even imprisoned, in words. Blake's composite art, however, exemplifies the struggle of the pictures within a text like the Apocalypse to break out of the words and have a life, if not of their own, at least one which lies alongside the words. Blake's work marks a later stage of the process started by Dürer, in which the apocalyptic visions are given priority over the words that might eclipse them. Blake, of course, needed words as much as any of us to deconstruct the hegemony of words. But in the Job sequence he offered a composite art, in which image and text compete one with another. It is our (sometimes difficult) task as interpreters to make sure that we do not let our propensity for words and language evacuate the images of their heuristic power. Nowhere is this better exemplified than in Blake's illustrated version of the story of Job where apocalyptic visions are the key to the cleansing of Job's theological perception, climaxing with him and his wife seeing God in Christ and in themselves. Blake never uses the word apocalypse or apocalyptic, but Coleridge very appropriately used the latter of him: "A man of Genius – and I apprehend, a Swedenborgian certainly, a mystic emphatically. You perhaps smile at my calling another Poet, a Mystic, but verily I am in the very mire of commonplace common-sense compared with Mr. Blake, apo-, or rather ana-, calyptic Poet, and Painter!".[73]

Blake: radicalism and radicalisation

What the radicals do is to extract from the Bible what they think is a basic underlying message. So Rosemary Radford Ruether's prophetic/messianic thread, the spirit of protest against the *status quo*, non-conformity, or as Blake puts it, writing of contemporary opinion of the Indwelling of the Spirit, 'Pride & Vanity of Imagination That disdains to follow this Worlds Fashion',[74] conditions the way in which the Bible, *and* life, are read. The radical spirit is one that speaks and acts and attracts the opprobrium of those who are the keepers of 'this Worlds Fashion'. This has its analogies in some modern Christian biblical interpretation, where expressing the drift of scriptural writers like Paul better than they did themselves or even correcting them when they do not follow their best intentions is part and parcel of some modern exegesis.[75] Even Karl Barth comes close to sharing Blake's understanding of exegetical engagement as some kind of identity with the original author 'until a distinction between yesterday and today becomes impossible' and the original document 'seems hardly to exist as a document; *till I have almost forgotten that I am not its author; till I know the author so well that I allow him to speak in my name and am even able to speak in his name myself*'.[76] The received wisdom in books, which dominates a culture or religion, is subjected to critique, but not complete rejection. That echoes the New Testament writings themselves, for, when seeking to discern what may be of God and what not, early Christian writers did not primarily appeal to texts, for they never allowed what had been written in the past to determine what God's Spirit was calling people to in the present. The Spirit opens up the meaning of the letters of Scripture to the eye of faith; in the Gospel of John the divine Spirit leads the disciples into all truth (John 16:13).

In Blake's work, whether pictures or texts, the biblical text becomes a catalyst in the exploration of pressing contemporary issues, whether psychological or political. Experience is as important a text as the text of Scripture itself, as in liberation theology. That twofold aspect is well brought out by Carlos Mesters: 'emphasis is not placed on the text's meaning in itself but rather on the meaning the text has for the people reading it'.[77]

People can be rather scornful of the way in which Blake's 'Jerusalem' has been adopted by the Women's Institute, has become one of the favourite hymns at weddings, and is annually sung at the

Last Night of the Proms. But in one very important respect, those who are moved by Blake's wonderful words understand something absolutely fundamental about his work: they have allowed the 'faculties' to be 'rouzed'. As such they are interpreters who may not understand what the words mean in their detail but have been open to their effects. Of course, it is an open question whether those who sing Blake's words to Hubert Parry's music so lustily, any more than the academic poring over the texts and pictures, want to go on from being 'rouzed', to 'acting' and to engage in the 'mental fight' to 'build Jerusalem in this green and pleasant land', but it may be the first step to being reminded of the situation captured in the altogether more sombre and challenging words which open the poem, 'Holy Thursday', from *Songs of Experience* (see Plate 8):

> Is this a holy thing to see,
> In a rich and fruitful land,
> Babes reducd to misery,
> Fed with cold and usurous hand ?
>
> Is that trembling cry a song ?
> Can it be a song of joy ?
> And so many children poor ?
> It is a land of poverty ![78]

These words of the 'Experience' poem quoted here could not be more telling. 'Holiness' is part of the disorder which Blake sought to criticise. It hints at division, hypocrisy, and above all else, a 'holier than thou' attitude. So, there is a biting irony in the opening words 'Is *this* a holy thing to see?' This poem exposes the pervasive poverty in a land that is not only supposed to be 'holy' but also 'rich and fruitful'. Yet in it 'babes' are 'reduced to misery'. Readers are stopped in their tracks, as Blake sought to 'cleanse the doors of perception' of his readers/viewers.[79]

A comparison of the work of Emily Dickinson and William Blake ends with a quotation from the last line of a Dickinson poem (Poem 1545):

> The Bible is an antique Volume –
> Written by faded Men
> At the suggestion of Holy Spectres –

> Subjects – Bethlehem –
> Eden – the ancient Homestead –
> Satan – the Brigadier –
> Judas – the Great Defaulter –
> David – the Troubadour –
> Sin – a distinguished Precipice
> Others must resist –
> Boys that 'believe' are very lonesome –
> Other Boys are 'lost' –
> Had but the Tale a warbling Teller –
> All the Boys would come –
> Orpheus' Sermon captivated –
> It did not condemn –

One senses that Blake rose to being 'a warbling teller' of what is in the 'antique Volume'. Helen McNeil writes:

> Dickinson's uncanny resemblance to William Blake (whose Songs of Innocence and Experience weren't available for her to read) arises from their shared inheritance of radical Protestantism. For Dickinson, doubt and suffering are what 'gave me that precarious Gait/ Some call Experience' (875). For both writers, what Blake calls the 'minute particulars' of the perceived world are hugely important, though of the two Dickinson is more likely to stay with the luminous detail. Both Blake and Dickinson also wrote in the deliberately humble, even childlike tetrameter hymn quatrains of Isaac Watts, meanwhile adapting and playing upon his conventional piety. Dickinson's doubts about religion didn't lead her to construct an alternative mythology, as Blake did, or to turn to classical myth, as Shelley did, although she notes crisply that in contrast to the Bible, 'Orpheus' sermon captivated- /It did not condemn-.[80]

Those last words remind us that there is something *different* from the Bible not only in Dickinson's but also in Blake's work: Blake, like Dickinson, believed in the fundamental goodness of men and women. That was not because he denied the propensity to do things that were destructive of human flourishing, but that the human soul was made of contraries, and because of that he could not accept any notion of utter human depravity. There is in Blake, therefore, something that is not easily found in the Bible and Christian tradition: the worth of humans in themselves, echoing the sentiments of Genesis 1:26–7. Blake's assessment of the humans in their integrity included 'weal & woe', reason and imagination, energy and desire as well as constraint. Nevertheless, within humanity, and in its social organisation, if ever one of the contrary states of the human soul were to gain hegemony, the delicate balance of the soul would be tilted in ways which might cause either humility and subservience, on the one hand, or violence, destruction and oppression, on the other.

Conclusion

Blake was a prophet. He was not in the business of engaging in either abstract criticism or dispassionate study of the Bible, or anything else, for that matter. His marginal notes on books he read and annotated reveal a passionate man with strong opinions, who read, not for the sake of what he might get out of it for academic study, but as part of a political and theological struggle.

We misunderstand Blake if we think that for him it was either law or inspiration, constraint or revolutionary freedom. *It was both/and.* In a revealing passage in his *Descriptive Catalogue* Blake described his artistic method:

> The great and golden rule of art, as well as of life, is this: That the more distinct, sharp, and wirey the bounding line, the more perfect the work of art [...]. Leave out this l[i]ne and you leave out life itself; all is chaos again, and the line of the almighty must be drawn out upon it before man or beast can exist.[81]

In other words, in his art the 'bounding line' enabled the channelling of creative energy into images and words. His creative engagement with a diverse literary and artistic inheritance involved stimulation, aware of its shortcomings and resistance. That mix of inspiration and resistance enabled him to open up a creative, imaginative space for his own poetic genius and was the heart of his prophetic radicalism.

Seers and artists like Blake explore hidden dimensions of life. That means being prepared to see things from another, unusual, point of view and being open to the possibility that difference of perspective will enrich our view and lead to difference of insight. Arguably Blake was one of the most biblically based and prophetic poets. Mere repetition of what is in the Bible is unable to loosen the Bible from the bands of ecclesiastical power and dogma, wedded to conservative political and economic power. A new myth was needed to tell the story in language which would subvert the Bible and enable a different perspective. His interpretative radicalism is in a sense licensed by the Apocalypse itself. It is not a biblical interpretation but itself Scripture commissioned by Christ. As such it presents the symbols and myths of that which was Scripture in a new visionary guise.

Blake's early illuminated books make great play of undermining their authority by the difference in order and design (perhaps imitating the complex history of the textual tradition of the Bible itself, especially the New Testament). That textual instability and uncertainty should make us wary of elevating Blake's own work to an authoritative status. The legacy that Blake passed on is not a corpus which requires exegesis so much as one which 'rouzes the faculties to act' and empowers us, as interpreters, in our time and place, to understand and be inspired by the flame of criticism, protest and hope that he lit. The Bible, like other texts, is a gateway, a catalyst, in order to indicate that engagement with the Bible is more about its effects than its ancient meaning, more about how it might grasp and inspire a reader than be an object of minute and detailed exposition. Blake's work, therefore, potentially revolutionises exegesis, beckoning us to a different kind of engagement with texts from the past, in which the interplay of the reader's situation, imagination and patient engagement provides a frame of reference and remedial space for human flourishing.

Blake's was a dialectical method, which never saw revolution as the sole principle, for it was in constant tension with that which enabled creative energy to function effectively and humanely. Blake saw the energetic force of revolution at work in the French Revolution and the death and destruction which ensued, when revolution became an end in itself. That did not mean that revolutionary energy was bad. It was what happened when one principle became hegemonic and either paralysed or destroyed rather than promoted human flourishing.

How reading Blake's works and viewing his images engage and transform us will be a story of apocalypse taking place with every reading, every 'digesting' of the text. A new moment of unveiling occurs through the images and texts that Blake has bequeathed to us. We may be curious about the meaning of symbols, or distracted by historical reference, but the fundamental task is reading, hearing, appropriating, in whatever way our faculties allow us, and having our imaginations engaged and our perspectives transformed. What we are offered in Blake's work, and also John's Apocalypse, is not a manual of eschatology, ethics or theology and yet it enables all of these by its disturbing and destabilising effects (that applies just as much if our reaction to what we read is rejection or distaste). By refusing the predictable and immediately readable, and demanding that suspension of what counts for normality, we may perceive where the Beast and Babylon are to be found, discover resources 'for intellectual War' and discover how 'the dark Religions are departed and sweet Science reigns'.[82]

In the context of a perceptive review of Thomas Altizer's book on Blake[83] and its contribution to the 'Death of God' debate, Thomas Merton agreed that Blake was talking a language similar to the radical theologians.[84] For Merton, doing full justice to the apocalyptic and prophetic character of Blake's vision is essential, as is the recognition that Blake repudiated the Antichrist of inhuman authority, whether ecclesiastical or secular – 'the Abomination which maketh desolate, i.e. State Religion which is the source of all cruelty'.[85] For Merton, Blake's vision is an integration of mysticism and prophecy, 'a return to apocalyptic faith which arises from an intuitive protest against Christianity's estrangement from its own eschatological background'. Rightly did Merton point out that Blake saw official Christendom as *narrowing* of vision, 'a foreclosure of experience and of future expansion, a locking up and securing of the doors of perception'.[86] For Merton, Blake turns out to be a radical Christian, believing that Churches had perverted Christian truth by creating an idol whom humans set up, which was nothing but a cloak for the things of Caesar:

> we can certainly agree that Blake was a radical Christian in his belief that Churches had perverted Christian truth and that the God of the Christian Churches was really Urizen, Nobodaddy, and even Satan – not the lover of man who empties himself to become identified with Man, but a spectre whom man sets up against himself, investing him with the trappings of power which are not 'the things of God' but really 'the things that are Caesar's'. There is indeed much in Blake that anticipates – with far more powerful poetic effect and human authenticity – the ideas of religious alienation in Feuerbach, Marx, and Freud.

> Blake's vision is then – and here we can agree perfectly with Dr Altizer – a total integration of mysticism and prophecy, a return to apocalyptic faith which arises from an intuitive protest against Christianity's estrangement from its own eschatological ground. Blake saw official Christendom as a *narrowing* of vision, a foreclosure of experience and of future expansion, a locking up and securing of the doors of perception. He substituted for it a Christianity of openness, not seeking to establish order in life by shutting off a little corner of chaos and subjecting it to laws and to police, but moving freely between dialectical poles in a wild chaos, integrating sacred vision, in and through the experience of fallenness, as the only locus of creativity and redemption. Blake, in other words, calls for 'a whole new form of theological understanding'.[87]

The two images at the start of *Europe a Prophecy* (see Plates 3 and 4) illustrate a theme, which is central to Blake's art, his theology and his understanding of humanity: his advocacy of living with 'Contraries'. Blake's artistic work involved great precision as the 'bounding line' enabled the channelling of creative energy into images and words. In the process of wrestling with texts like those of Milton and the Bible, Blake pioneered an interpretative method for any who sought a more creative and contemporary relationship with the tradition they received, acknowledging the influence of authoritative predecessors and isolating what was most important but at the same time pointing out their shortcomings. We see him taking major themes from the Bible, like prophecy, forgiveness of sins and 'human brotherhood'. Together they informed his critique of contemporary church and politics and enabled him to criticise other, to him, less palatable, biblical themes.

Part 4

Christian Radicalism in Modernity
An Example and a Neglected Perspective

At first sight this section fits rather uneasily in a book about mystics, subversives and visionaries. But each chapter in their different ways concerns issues of central importance for the subject matter of this book.

The Book of Revelation resonates with the hopes and fears of many poor people and its hope for a better world, though liberation theology does not seem particularly 'apocalyptic', if one supposes that 'apocalyptic' is just about visionary claims. The way experience opened up new perspectives on life and received wisdom, however, is reminiscent of the way in which visionary experience too throws this age into sharp relief in the light of a world where sorrow and sighing have departed. In liberation theology priority is given to 'life', and the way it becomes the key to understanding, and criticising, what has been received, as well as society more generally. That means a challenge to, and a departure from, current practices, conditions or institutions. This has led to a critical perspective on the present, prompting a different kind of practice in anticipation of the Kingdom of God. So, where it fits into this book is that it offers a contemporary version of the challenge arising from experience to 'revelation only in preserved form'.[1]

The second chapter is not primarily about the radical prophets or those engaged in what may be thought of as radical prophetic activity, but more about those who appreciated the importance of that radical messianic impulse in the Christian and the Jewish tradition. As such, it forms a fitting retrospective on the contents of the book as a whole. Ernst Bloch and Jacob Taubes in different, though related, ways trace the importance of the apocalyptic and eschatological strand as a central intellectual dynamic in Christianity, and Benjamin's final work is one of the most radical and salutary testimonies to the nature of messianism and its effects in the twentieth, or indeed any, century. We consider writers who took apocalyptic and messianism seriously, in the case of two of them, for the history of Christian thought. Benjamin may not have thought of himself as a radical prophet but his 'Theses on the Philosophy of History', in my view, counts as one of the most searching examples of radical prophecy there is.

Chapter 7

Liberation Theology

How to Proclaim God in a World that is Inhumane

Diego Velázquez's 'The Kitchen Maid and the Supper at Emmaus'[1] depicts a young woman, who is at work in the kitchen and appears to look behind her out of the corner of her eye at a scene, in which one can see two figures, one of them with a halo. This is almost certainly Christ at the supper after the meeting on the road to Emmaus in Luke 24. The sombre foreground of kitchen and servitude, which dominates the picture, contrasts with the scene in the background. Here we have the juxtaposition of everyday life with a biblical scene. In the story of the journey to Emmaus there is an *apocalyptic* moment when Jesus' companions recognise who Jesus is. As Luke 24:31 puts it, 'their eyes were opened, and they knew him'. The apocalyptic moment comes for Jesus' companions as connections are made and 'the penny drops'.

In the Velázquez picture the halo on Christ's head suggests the apocalyptic moment when he was recognised. It is the moment, to borrow Blake's words, when the doors of perception are opened. In the foreground the woman looks at the Emmaus supper scene and possibly also sees that in the midst of her experience of a life of drudgery Jesus, too, is with her. The juxtaposition perfectly encapsulates liberation theology as the Bible opens up new perspectives on life, and beckons the viewers to recognise for themselves what the juxtaposition of the two scenes might mean.

The Dublin picture, 'Christ in the House of Martha and Mary', is less well known, and more ambiguous, than the more familiar one of the servant girl, by the same artist, with a similarly positioned image of Jesus with Martha and Mary (Luke 10:38–42).[2]

In the latter an older woman in the foreground is pointing, probably at the younger woman ('Martha') in the foreground and indirectly at the biblical scene in the background. In the other picture there is a simple contrast between the young black woman bent over the kitchen table and the white men in the background, enjoying their meal, the kind of thing she might herself have prepared day after day.

At the heart of this chapter is an outline of the way some popular education material from Brazil enables this kind of engagement to take place, so that what is in the background of everyday life, the text of the Bible, can illuminate, though not eclipse, 'the text of life', one's context, and offer new perspectives on it and see it in a new light. That is the heart of the subversive visionary co-operative exercise which typifies this way of doing theology and which this chapter seeks to elucidate.

Explaining liberation theology

Liberation theology has its origins in the reality of the lives of millions of people, their poverty, their experiences of injustice and oppression, and the conditions in which they live and work. However sophisticated the books and articles from the liberation theologians may seem to be, it is their experience, and that of those with whom they work, that is the motor which drives their theology. In so doing, theologians testify to the way they have learnt afresh from the poor as they have lived and worked with them, and this has been an indispensable lens through which to view the Bible and tradition, and so to articulate what theology is about. There is nothing new in this challenge posed to theology. In the very earliest years of Christianity's presence in South America, priests like Bartolomé de Las Casas in the sixteenth century took up the cause of indigenous people.[3] As the young priest prepared a homily on Ecclesiasticus 34:21–7, the words 'Like one who kills before his father's eyes is a person who offers a sacrifice from the property of the poor' crystallised a sense of the injustice of the religious and economic system, of which he was a part, which exploited indigenous peoples. The rest of his life was devoted to obtaining rights for indigenous peoples from the Spanish crown (see Plate 9).

The theology of liberation arises out of the specific needs and concerns of the poor. It is no surprise that in a country like Brazil, where the struggle for access to the land is such a potent political issue, especially in rural areas, the story of the Exodus and the Promised Land enable a direct link between the present circumstances of many peasants and the biblical narrative.[4] In this correlation, however, there is no expectation that there will be a blueprint from the Bible, the tradition, the theologians or the bishops. It is the circumstances in which the people of God find themselves that is crucial. Theology does not come from outside that situation but is to be found there *within the struggle* for justice and survival ('struggle', *luta*, is a word that one often hears). The unjust world and the suffering of millions is the starting point. It is life in the shanty towns, with the lack of basic amenities, the carelessness about the welfare of human persons, the shattered lives of refugees, in a subcontinent, and in the land struggles. It is, as the image (see Plate 10) suggests, about pulling the Church down to earth. Gustavo Gutiérrez characterises it thus: 'the question in Latin America will not be how to speak of God in a world come of age, but rather how to proclaim God as Father in a world that is inhumane. What can it mean to tell a non-person that he or she is God's child?'.[5] In contrast to much theology in the Northern Hemisphere liberation theologians' faith is in dialectical relationship with life, so understanding matters of faith is illuminated in the process of solidarity with the poor, and their condition is analysed and alleviated.

The well-known dictum of Helder Câmara, Archbishop of Recife and Olinda, 'When I give to the poor, they call me a saint. When I ask why the poor have no food, they call me a communist', captures the refusal to be satisfied with the practice of charity. 'Contemplation and commitment'[6] leads to social critique, political and indeed theological analysis, of which the apocalyptic tradition, as found in Revelation, offers a prime example. Like Winstanley (Chapter 5, 'The characteristics of Winstanley's biblical interpretation'),[7] liberation theologians consider that the poor have a peculiar capacity to understand the ways of God and can grasp the immediate impact of biblical themes, and find a message which can so easily elude those who are not poor: 'the kingdom of God comes first and foremost for those who by virtue of their situation have most need of it: the poor, the afflicted, the hungry of the world'.[8] Matthew 25:31–45 suggests that the poor, vulnerable and marginalised 'are the latent presence of the coming Saviour and Judge in the world, the touchstone which determines salvation and damnation'.[9] That is a significant role. The mark of the true Church is going to be its acceptance of the perspective of the poor.[10]

Liberation theology contrasts with a theology centred in university or seminary, with the priority increasingly placed on intellectual discourse detached from life and the practice of prayer and charity. So, in many respects, liberation theology harks back to the method of an earlier age when worship, service to humanity and theological reflection were more closely integrated. What has been rediscovered, in particular, is the commitment to the poor and marginalised as a *necessary* context for theology. In liberation theology, faith, reflection and real life are in dialectical relationship with each other.[11] As we shall see, the first step of the theology of liberation is to grasp the reality of the context in which one finds oneself, assisted with a variety of socio-analytic tools to assist the understanding of the causes of injustice and a contextually appropriate strategy for remedying the situation. A parallel step is theological, so that experience enables light to be shed on the meaning of biblical texts. Finally, there is an orienting action in the light of reflection. It is an ongoing process of action and reflection. Crucially, the initial move is not the result of detached reflection but comes in the midst of commitment and action.

The priority given to human experience echoes important aspects of theology over the last 200 years. This has been, in part, an exercise in opening a space for the experience of the interpreter. Liberation theology is in continuity with that demand. The difference is that it is being worked in shanty towns, land struggles, oppressed and humiliated groups, areas of deprivation in the Southern Hemisphere, where the rebuilding of shattered lives takes place.

Of course, because of its deep-rooted connection with particular contexts and experiences, liberation theology presents peculiar problems for those who seek to write *about* it. A proper understanding of it demands something more than an intellectual appreciation alone. Understanding involves the move from a previous position of detachment, to be open to that transformation of perspective, which comes either at the margins or in social estrangement. To paraphrase the dialogue of Jesus with Nicodemus in John 3, it is only by changing sides and identifying with the Christ who meets and challenges men and women in the persons of the poor, the hungry and the naked that one may enable them to 'see the Kingdom of God'.[12] What is required here, as the liberation theologians of contemporary Latin America and elsewhere put it, is an 'epistemological rupture'. The theological presupposition reflects an oft-quoted passage in Jeremiah 22:16 where the prophet asserts that knowing God is doing justice.[13]

Experiencing biblical study in the comunidades eclesais de base *(CEBs)*

Liberation theologians have been at pains to stress the deep roots that the *comunidades eclesais de base* (Basic Ecclesial Communities; CEBs) have within the life of the Church. Certainly they may offer a new perspective and are a sign of hope for the renewal of the Church.[14] Frequently, I heard those working with CEBs talk about the ways in which their eyes had been opened to look at the world differently through involvement with them, often with the help of the Bible. One woman talked about reading the Bible independently of the struggle for change, when she found it boring. Now she read and discovered ways in which biblical words came alive as life experience enabled engagement with the biblical text. Many spoke of the way in which a sense of resignation had been replaced by a faith leading to active involvement. Poverty was not something decreed by God but an evil which they could have a role in changing. To that end they would read the Bible and walk miles in pursuit of the practice of justice.

One remarkable story among many I heard was of the group O Movimento do Dia do Senhor, in the Sobral region, near Fortaleza, in the far north-east of Brazil. Because of the huge distances separating them, communication, solidarity and the exchange of ideas were difficult. In addition to regular radio programmes, which publicised human rights abuses, there were various projects taking place in the region and news related to community development. Like the Apostle Paul, for whom letters were an essential means of keeping in touch with communities, using them as a vehicle of his presence, sharing emerging common practice and ideas, and a common sense of purpose, the communities in O Movimento do Dia do Senhor used letters in a similar way. It enabled communities to feel part of a bigger social and theological process rooted in the hope for the coming of God's Kingdom. Like Paul and his companions, *campesinos* travelled miles, often on foot, in the hot and arid wastes of the rural north-eastern Brazil, encouraging, maintaining a common vision and sharing their struggles.

In the light of the last paragraph it will come as no surprise that, among the CEBs, the Bible has offered a different perspective on life and a language so that the voice of the voiceless may be heard. To enable the poor to read the Bible has involved a programme of education in the contents of the biblical material. In such popular education programmes full recognition is taken of the value of life.[15]

The essential features of liberationist reading are best illustrated visually. The sequence of pictures and diagrams which follows was prepared for use in grassroots communities in Valença, Bahia, in the north-east of Brazil.[16] Their origin comes from a chance meeting I had in 1990 with a group of catechists, who were preparing material for use in the local communities surrounding the fishing town of Valença. It gave me an opportunity to see the genesis of material, which is typical of the way liberationist reading has evolved. The parish in Valença had been served by Salesian Fathers for the previous 25 years. Their visits to an enormous parish of a million people were few (two or three times a year), which placed enormous responsibility on lay people to organise for the local community. The priests were part of a popular education group, serving the area as a whole not just the parish, called CEMEP (Centro Missionário de Evangelização e Educação Popular). There were 20 pastoral agents, with an 'animator' in each area supported by executive teams with workers from the centre. They had six main areas of work: popular education, work with rural unions, political education, a theological correspondence course for animators, which involved basic literacy if needed, solidarity and human rights, and published material. They explicitly identified themselves with Carlos Mesters' work through the organisation Centro de Estudos Bíblicos.

The images explain and challenge the way of being Church. All too often focus is on the individual and personal piety. Here there is a very different emphasis on the Church as a 'down-to-earth' engagement with the everyday needs of ordinary people (see Plate 10), rather than being about otherworldliness. In this the Bible functioned as an important catalyst in contributing to the struggle for human rights. They compared their model of theological reflection to a wheel, with the Bible at the centre and the spokes of the wheel being the various kinds of participation and various experiences.

The wheel moves when the struggle is entered into ('action is the life of all', to quote Gerrard Winstanley's words). They gave attention to the process of small group workings, including the question of leadership. As we see from the slide sequence, there is an emphasis on the importance of the life of the people and their context. The priests said that what they saw the CEBs offering was hope in a situation which seemed devoid of it. Poor people were enabled to do things for themselves and with others, which could be a sign to themselves that things need not always remain the same. They also offered space for analysis of society which may not be represented elsewhere, so that the reality need not be accepted as a given, and the understanding of it, offered in the media, could be challenged. The impression was of a movement not waiting for structural change globally but starting to bring about change in its own social context and forging new ways of being together in community, in ways which offered a model for society as a whole. They saw the practice of Jesus, challenging the middle class to look at life and the world afresh, and enabling solidarity with the poor and marginalised.

The first image (see Plate 11) describes the principal objective, which is to 'read' the world. In other words it is 'the book of life' which is primary and so what is required are the skills to read that. This initial move is fundamental and explains the heart of liberation theology, which prioritises the act of solidarity, identification with the poor and vulnerable. This itself, of course, resonates with biblical themes, but the inspiration comes from actual experience. The following words from the popular educator Carlos Mesters indicate the importance of both poles, even though in this formulation (reflected in the priority given to the 'book of life' in this Brazilian sequence of pictures) the Bible's role is an essential, though ancillary, one:

> emphasis is not placed on the text's meaning in itself but rather on the meaning the text has for the people reading it. At the start the people tend to draw any and every sort of meaning, however well or ill founded, from the text [...] the common people are also eliminating the alleged 'neutrality' of scholarly exegesis [...] the common people are putting the Bible in its proper place, the place where God intended it to be. They are putting it in second place. Life takes first place! In so doing, the people are showing us the enormous importance of the Bible, and at the same time, its relative value – relative to life.[17]

As we have noted, the experience of poverty and oppression, 'life' or 'reality' for many, represents another text to be studied alongside that contained between the covers of the Bible. God's 'word' is to be found in the dialectic between the literary memory of the people of God in the Bible and the continuing story to be discerned in the contemporary world.

The 'twin-track' approach (see Plate 12), in which the Bible and life together provide the tracks on which the vehicle of the process of interpretation moves, encapsulates two issues, which in theory and practice are important for liberation theology. First of all, there is the necessity of *both* tracks preventing one pole in the interpretative process from gaining the ascendancy. The Bible offers a language with which one might interpret the world (*A Bíblia ajuda a decifrar o mundo* – the heading in the picture, Plate 13). Here we see the juxtaposition of biblical narrative and the social situation so that the one interprets the other. The Janus-headed man is looking two ways. On the left he looks at the Bible, which talks about the land belonging to God and the land being for all (a theme of Leviticus 25). On the right is the situation of enclosure in which large ranches leave millions of landless peasants dependent on subsistence farming or, worse, subject to the fate of being an occasional labourer on a large estate (a constant theme of the politics of the highly influential 'Sem Terra' movement – a movement for and of the landless in Brazilian rural life and a live issue in rural north-east Brazil).

A central component of liberationist interpretation is what Gustavo Gutiérrez summarises as the fruit of 'Contemplation and commitment within history, in which the mystery reveals itself through prayer and solidarity with the poor'.[18] So, what liberationist interpretation requires is the ability to 'read' life and to do so with that degree of contemplation which allows awareness of the extent to which prejudice and generalisation can reduce what it is one sees (*A Bíblia nos devolve o olhar da contemplação*).

The community context emphasises the importance of social engagement (see Plate 14). The checks and balances of the communal setting are an important antidote to individual reading. The triangular character of the interpretative process stresses that the sense of attending to others as a necessary complement to one's own understanding represents a basic feature of ecclesial life.

In an important respect Plate 15, illustrating four different 'aspects' of the understanding of the life of the people of God, to which the Bible bears witness, represents a significant feature of the pedagogical process. Here, immediate engagement, in which text and contemporary situation merge, is replaced by a model in which the two discrete historical moments are kept separate and the integrity of both Bible and contemporary context are maintained. This is done by the way in which a diachronic perspective is stressed, which for the first time in the picture series begins to relate the whole reading project to what is most familiar about the reading of the Bible in the contemporary academy. What we see at the centre of the image is the Book of Exodus and around it four sides *(lados)* of how it might be interpreted outlined: firstly, how the people (of Israel) lived (*como o povo vivia*); secondly, with whom the people related, that is, where they were in the structure of society (*com quem o pove se relaçiona*); thirdly, who had political power (*quem está no poder*); and, finally, what was it that people thought (*o que o povo pensa*). This last is a question of ideology: how is it that people who were slaves took on board ways of thinking which were conditioned by the interests of those in power? – hence the comments such as we find in Exodus 16:3 ('If only we had died by the hand of the LORD in the land of Egypt, when we sat by the fleshpots and ate our fill of bread').

Here the meaning of the text in its original context is explored, thereby underlining the importance of the integrity of the text as a witness to the life of the people of God at another time and in another place. But the perspectives on its meaning are not primarily about religion and piety but about the dynamics of life. In this picture the biblical text (in this case the Book of Exodus) is understood as a witness to the situation of a people who were once oppressed. The questions which are asked here are not those typically asked about the biblical text in mainstream textbooks of the so-called First World (When was the passage written? What does it tell us about God and religion?). Rather, the concerns here are: What does the passage tell us about the sort of people who are the subjects of the text's concern, their relationship to political and economic power? How may their views have been formed by the culture of their day? How far did they imbibe ideas which meant that they felt inferior to the rich and powerful? The Book of Exodus thus becomes a witness to a story of the liberation of a people from a subaltern status and its struggle through the action of leaving this situation of slavery, to be freed from the bondage which a sense of inferiority and marginality imposes and to learn to adopt a new way of thinking and behaving.

Here, complementing the communal orientation inserted into the third picture of the series, the sense of relating to the life of a people of God lived at another time is stressed, with a tacit assumption that the Bible is in large part a witness to the story of a people who, like the poor in modern Brazil, find themselves dealing with poverty, marginalisation and homelessness, both spiritual and physical.

The relationship between text and reader is maintained by insisting that there is a dialectical relationship between the understanding of the text and the experience of the reader. The sense of distance between, on the one hand, the readers and their experience and, on the other hand, the text as a witness to the people of God at another time and place (however many affinities there may be in terms of the issues and experience) is to some degree emphasised. In this kind of engagement with the text, the role of the 'expert' will be crucial, even if that expert is working alongside the poor as what Antonio Gramsci called an 'organic intellectual', that is, one with intellectual expertise committed to the struggle of the poor and marginalised, and not seeking to impose particular solutions on the poor.[19] Where this method differs from the kind of historical study that has been typical in European and North American exegesis of the Bible is that the engagement with the text does not bracket-out contemporary questions and experience in favour of a detached investigation of the ancient historical context of the biblical book and its origins. The motor of the exegesis is the present experience of the poor as a way of asking questions of the biblical book. There is a two-way process involving reading life through the Scriptures and the Scriptures through life. Of course, liberationist readings are intensely historical, but the Bible is part of the interpretation of life lived in community (*leitura ecumênica*), rather than offering a blueprint for life irrespective of context.

As the image *Mandamentos* indicates (see Plate 16), the emphasis is on reading in community (*ler em comum*), attentiveness in reading (*escutar a palavra de deus*), and the rejection of biblical literalism; getting behind the words (*ler por tras das palavras*) to grasp the essential subject matter of a biblical text and not being overly preoccupied with its details, grasping its essential subject matter concerning the struggles (*luta*) of the life of the people of God in another time and place. Thus, the quest for meaning is one that is never reduced to a simple obedience to 'what the Bible says', for what the Bible means is inevitably contingent on the particular

FIGURE 5: Popular education from Brazil: how everyday experience enables revelation

circumstances. But the key to the whole sequence of pictures is the way in which epistemology and practice coincide in the words *saber é server* ('knowledge is service'; see Plate 16). Here we find the central component of liberationist hermeneutics summarised concisely, in that Christian practice which Gustavo Gutiérrez describes as the fruit of 'contemplation and commitment within history, in which the mystery reveals itself through prayer and solidarity with the poor'.[20]

The method expands the horizon of the understanding of divine revelation beyond the usual ecclesial channels of Bible, teaching and sacraments and embraces the many different experiences of creation (see Figure 5) and, crucially, to include the experience of the political, which together point to the knowledge of God. As such, it offers a more comprehensive form of theology. This involves not only the Bible and Church teaching, but also the created world, 'life', and its struggles, past and present (*história*), all illuminated by the social sciences and the Bible, as well as the ability to interpret 'the present time' (Luke 12:56), in an apocalyptic process, a *revelação de Deus*, to enable a different understanding and perspective on life and opens up new ways of acting.

This echoes a central theme of a key document of the Second Vatican Council, *Gaudium et Spes*, the Pastoral Constitution on the Church in the Modern World, which affirms the place of humans in the struggle of the less advantaged as central to Christian solidarity:

> The joys and the hopes, the griefs and the anxieties of the men [sic] of this age, especially those who are poor or in any way afflicted, these are the joys and hopes, the griefs and anxieties of the followers of Christ. Indeed, nothing genuinely human fails to raise an echo in their hearts. For theirs is a community composed of men. United in Christ, they are led by the Holy Spirit in their journey to the Kingdom of their Father and they have welcomed the news of salvation which is meant for every man. That is why this community realizes that it is truly linked with mankind and its history by the deepest of bonds.[21]

Parábolas de Hoje

Popular education influenced by liberation theology has been a key component of pastoral programmes in many Brazilian dioceses. Knowing and action are the basis for a concept of education. Many have contributed to this work, but it was particularly inspired by the distinguished Brazilian educator, Paulo Freire (1921–97). In his pedagogical writings, Freire emphasises the link between knowing and doing, experience and learning. He criticises a view of education in which students become accumulators, storing material away as if in a banking process,[22] in particular the roles played by teacher and student within a 'banking' concept of education, in which the all-knowing teacher fills the grateful, ignorant and inert student with deposits of 'knowledge' concerning the roles of oppressor and oppressed. What Freire promotes instead is a process whereby human beings engage in active, yet critical, forms of education through which they embrace both their world and each other. The 'how' of education is inseparable from questions of politics and also of the nature of theology. Learners have much to bring to the learning process, and their experience is not only valued but becomes the raw material for the learning that takes place. Freire believed that education must be the site of transformation, in which the traditional teacher–student relationship is examined. This relationship maintains and mirrors other forms of oppression within society. The student-centred education is central to the understanding of power relations, both in a local community and especially in the reading group. Engagement with those power relations is an integral part

FIGURE 6: *Parábolas de Hoje, A Ovelha Perdida,* São Paulo, 1982

of the educational process, and is crucial for the understanding of, and participation in, a wider societal transformation. Liberation pedagogy is not 'top-down', in which the thoughts of a liberal intelligentsia allow some kind of Olympian perspective on the doings of fellow men and women.[23]

In one of the most original interpretations of the parables of Jesus in the sequence *Parábolas de Hoje,*[24] a way of looking at the Parable of the Lost Sheep (Matt. 18:10–14) starts with the story of a young man from a *favela* (shanty town) getting ready for priestly ordination within the community. The preparations for the celebration of the ordination were complete. The time came for the service, and the festivities began, with children taught to sing and refreshments prepared. When the moment came, the bishop did not turn up. A phone message came through to say that he would not be able to attend the church service because he was accompanying a political activist who had been arrested. The ordination was postponed, but in the end the activist was released to his family (see Figure 6). This story brilliantly exemplifies the ecumenical character of the interpretation: searching for the lost sheep is not about getting people into church. Indeed, those who are in church are not the main concern of the pastor of the church, but rather those who are on the sharp end of (as it was in the 1970s) a repressive police state.

In the process of engaging with life and the Bible, participants are asked to consider that the community of God's people does not exist for itself. It was called by God to serve those who are lost, because they have no land, no job or no home, because they are hungry, sick or suffering persecution. So the parable shows that the model of the Church is not preserving the 99 sheep who at the moment are gathered together. The model of the Church is to search unendingly for the needy. Mercy is at the centre of daily life. Jesus tells us that the Church that acts this way is imitating his ministry. Jesus was always criticised by the religious people of his time who thought that he should always be with Church people. But whenever Jesus met anyone who needed help, he always went to the needy and the poor. Jesus used parables to make us think, to revise our way of seeing the world and to change our lives to give priority to the needy and others who are lost and who most need the community's support (to summarise the notes of guidance which accompanied the slide sequence).

Groups might well start with a short slide sequence of the pictures, which puts them in touch with the familiar scenes of everyday life in Brazil. After viewing the slides, groups are asked to discuss the story and encouraged to recall similar experiences, identify with various members of the story, and share what their own feelings might be. This would lead to a focus on familiar scenes of everyday life, partly because many participants feel that the biblical text is far too sacred for them to interact with, whether critically or in relating it to everyday life. At another, later, meeting the relevant biblical text (like the Parable of the Lost Sheep) is read and discussed and a comparison is made with the story in the slides in order to provoke discussion. Life comes first then the Bible. It is only at the end of the process that a commentary is read and discussed, along with the group's own insights (drawn from the experience), on the present call to discipleship in the community. If there is a fundamental theological dictum in liberationist biblical interpretation it is that the understanding of the Bible is not a clerical or elite activity but is one in which all participate, an inclusive 'grassroots' phenomenon in a realistic sense.

Correspondence of Terms and Correspondence of Relationships: teasing out how the Bible is read

$$\frac{\text{scripture}}{\text{its political context}} = \frac{\text{theology of the political}}{\text{our political context}}$$

FIGURE 7: Correspondence of Terms[25]

A helpful introduction to the nature of biblical interpretation, influenced by liberation theology in the CEBs, has been set out by Clodovis Boff.[26] Boff raises problems with the notion of the Gospel as a code of norms to be applied, which ignores both the complexity of the biblical texts and the historical situation in which the application takes place and is lived out. He contrasts two ways of engaging with the Bible in biblical interpretation influenced by liberation theology. One of these he calls 'correspondence of terms' and the other 'correspondence of relationships'. The first is the more immediate; here the similarities between the biblical stories closely overlap with those of the people of God in the modern world. The '=' sign is crucial! Readers identify with a person or event in the Bible and see the biblical situation being re-enacted in the modern world. This first approach involves insertion of oneself and one's life experiences into the biblical narrative so that the Bible offers a way of speaking about and indeed understanding, for example, displacement and homelessness, and the experience of being an oppressed people. Thus, the biblical stories are seen to express *directly* the modern experiences, for example, of displacement, poverty and powerlessness. They correspond roughly with the first three slides from the Brazilian sequence (1. *Objetivo*, 2. *Trilhos* and 3. *Ângulos*, see Plates 11, 12 and 14).

The first 'correspondence of terms' approach has many similarities with the kind of interpretation we find in a passage such as 1 Corinthians 10, where Paul tells the Corinthians that what was written in the Bible was directed to *them*: 'These things happened to them to serve as an example, and they were written down to instruct us, on whom the ends of the ages have come' (1 Cor. 10:11). Like Paul's addressees, the peasants of Latin America probably did not think of their struggle for life and health in biblical terms all the time, but in the process of reflection the Bible functioned as a resource, which gave meaning and hope. In this kind of engagement with the Bible, the words become the catalyst for discernment of an immediate application of Scripture in the present.

Boff sees a similarity between the way in which biblical figures and movements are directly related to contemporary equivalents, so Roman power is equivalent to imperialism, and the Zealots are revolutionaries. Boff rightly points out that too often positions, say with regard to Jesus and pacifism and Jesus and revolutionaries, have been too much conditioned by the historical moment in which they have been worked out. Rightly, Boff raises important questions about the particularity of each situation and the way in which biblical examples can all too easily be seen as offering a model in all circumstances. Boff insists on the importance of the analytical tools available to us to understand our context better than a simple application can achieve.

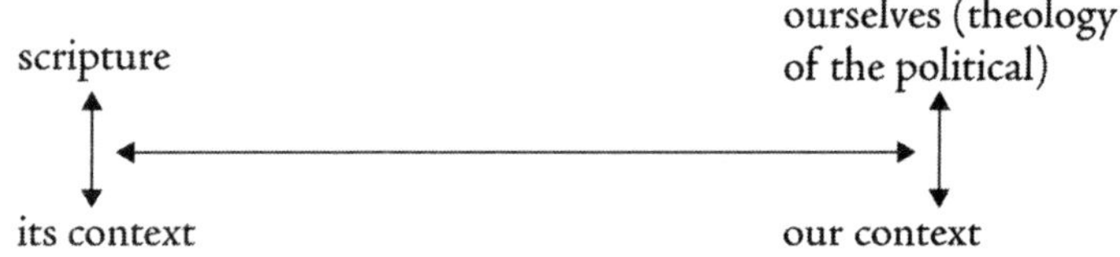

FIGURE 8: Correspondence of Relationships[27]

Unsurprisingly, Boff favours a different kind of model, which introduces a distance between texts and readers and even more between the events to which the texts bear witness via their textual form and the contemporary reader. What Boff seeks is the adoption of an attitude analogous to the earliest Christians with regard to the words and actions of Jesus, namely, creative fidelity. What is important for Boff is that texts, and the situations to which they are to be 'applied', are taken *in their respective autonomy*.[28] In this exercise of creative fidelity, 'meaning transpires, "comes to light", in historical currency, through and beyond the letter of the text of the past'.[29] The other main way of engaging with the Bible is also influenced by historical study of the Bible. So, one must look at the correspondences between the relationship of text to context in the case of both the biblical text, which bears witness to the life and struggles of the people of God at a particular time and place, and the modern 'text of life'. There is no direct co-relation. Rather, the relation of the contemporary situation of the people of God, properly understood, sociologically and politically, may be illuminated by the situation to which the Bible bears witness, and may inform, inspire and challenge modern readers of the Bible. This method corresponds with the fourth slide in the Brazilian sequence (4. *Lados*, see Plate 15).

In turn, the modern situation may be a lens to shed light on the understanding of the Bible. There is some ambiguity about the relative priority between text and experience in what Boff writes. According to Boff, the inspiration comes from Scripture.[30] In his diagrammatical encapsulation of this method, Boff suggests that in the dialectical relationship between experience and text the former may be a heuristic device to help illuminate the ancient situation to which the Bible bears witness: 'the hermeneutical equation I have drawn does not "travel a one-way street", or "read from left to right", from scripture to ourselves. The relationship is circular, like any genuine hermeneutic relationship. I might speak of a "dialectical hermeneutic"'.[31]

So, the meaning emerges in particular historical contexts as the text leads to new insights and new perspectives. It is not a case of replicating the letter of the text but allowing the text to fructify insight into the present context.[32] The method he offers is not a quest for formulas to 'copy' or techniques to 'apply' from Scripture. It does not presuppose the application of a set of principles of a theological programme or pattern to modern situations. Rather Scripture offers orientations, models, types and inspirations – elements permitting us to acquire, on our own initiative, what Boff calls a 'hermeneutic competency', that is, an ability to begin to understand the Bible for ourselves without being all the time dependent on the priest, minister or scholar. It is a theme already anticipated in the writings of Gerrard Winstanley, as already indicated (Chapter 5, 'The characteristics of Winstanley's biblical interpretation'). This then offers the capacity to judge – on one's own initiative – 'according to the mind of Christ', or 'according to the Spirit', the new unpredictable situations with which we are continually confronted. The Bible, therefore, offers us not a *what*, but a *how* – a manner, a style, a spirit.[33] What is important is 'what the Spirit says to the churches' rather than apprehending what the Spirit said 'once upon a time'. To quote Boff's words, what is needed is 'the intent to decipher the historical present, to read *kata tas graphas*, and not the *graphai* as such'.[34] In other words, it is context informed by the Scriptures rather than the determination of the meaning of the Scriptures defining what should be done in one's context. For Boff, the movement of the Spirit emerges from practice and not primarily from theological research. Attention to context with the tools of social analysis is an indispensable part of the search for meaning.

Priority is accorded to the value of practice over any theoretical elaboration. It is that priority we see in the Brazilian illustrations. Indeed, what we find in that sequence is an integration of a 'correspondence of terms' model with a 'correspondence of relationships' model in a pattern of developing interpretative awareness. What Boff commends is a twin cultivation of an interpretative skill alongside the socio-analytic. The socio-analytic element enables a better understanding of that on which we are reflecting.

The ideological character of all theology

One of liberation theology's challenges to theology has come from the recognition of the 'ideological' character of all theology and its role within a complicated political struggle in the churches to maintain the ascendancy of certain positions. The emphasis on the contextual nature of all theology has led liberation theologians to question the absolute character of theological pronouncements from the past as well as the present and to a theological unmasking of the reality.[35] Leonardo Boff, for example, challenges theologians to be aware of the socio-economic context in which they practise their theology:

> Theologians do not live in clouds. They are social actors with a particular place in society. They produce knowledge, data, and meanings by using instruments that the situation offers them and permits them to utilise [...] The themes and emphases of a given christology flow from what seems relevant to the theologian on the basis of his or her social standpoint [...] In that sense we must maintain that no christology is or can be neutral [...] Willingly or unwillingly christological discourse is voiced in a given social setting with all the conflicting interests that pervade it. That holds true as

> well for theological discourse that claims to be 'purely' theological, historical, traditional, ecclesial and apolitical.[36]

Resort to such ideas is the consequence of the pre-existing commitments to the poor and the disadvantaged on the part of the writers concerned. Indeed, the social engagement of those involved in higher education has become a widespread feature of Brazilian intellectual life, with many university institutions requiring that a significant part of the syllabus in which their students should engage, and the research their staff should undertake, should involve social engagement as well as relevance to the lives of the communities in which the universities are located.

Interpretation, finding meaning in texts (with all that this involves in terms of 'reading in' via illustrative parallels or the insight of experience) is always going to be experimental and cannot be a detached affair, though critical reflection is always necessary. But we need to keep in mind the ideological character of our study, in particular not imagining that we are extracting from the text simply what it contains.

Conclusion

The funeral rites for liberation theology have been conducted by the wielders of ecclesiastical and political power for the last 20 years, especially since the fall of the communist regimes of Eastern Europe. But, as the veteran liberation theologian Jon Sobrino has suggested, if liberation theology has had its day, there is still the need for which the protest and articulation of that perspective first arose. In Brazil the impact of grassroots groups, inspired by a liberation theology model, have had a widespread impact on politics in that country. The election of the Workers' Party, Partido dos Trabalhadores, in 2003, under their president Luiz Inácio Lula da Silva ('Lula'), owed much to the work of the Basic Ecclesial Communities and their liberation theology practice and vision, especially in the mighty conurbation of São Paulo. Arguably, it is a parallel example to the point made by Jacob Taubes about the effects of a movement of people informed by a messianic vision and apocalyptic hopes, who settled in the so-called 'New World' in the seventeenth century: 'Consider the millenarian expectations of the Puritan community in New England. Arriving in the Bay of Massachusetts to create a New Zion, they founded in the end the United States of America'.[37]

At the time of the writing of this book when the fortunes of liberation theology and its advocates have been embraced by the present pope, Francis I, it now seems incredible that the previous pope, Benedict XVI, as Cardinal Ratzinger, condemned liberation theology in what, in retrospect, seem intemperate terms, as a violent, fanatical movement, comparing it with a text from the Dead Sea Scrolls which imagined a holy war in which humans and angels would together engage in a struggle against the forces of darkness:

> It is astounding how the mixture of an almost abstruse military exactitude with wild-eyed theological expectations, which we encountered in the Qumran War Scroll [dating probably from just before the beginning of the Common Era], is to be found in the literature of liberation theology. [...] theology's only contribution here has been to connect irrational goals and grounds with political reasoning in such a way as to give rise to a course of political action that is carefully planned in detail but as a whole is profoundly irrational. There is no real connection between the promise and the approaches to it; particular projects are meaningful, but the scheme as a whole must be branded a delusion.[38]

What is so striking about this assessment to anyone who knows anything about liberation theology is how misguided it is. One possible response to Josef Ratzinger's words is the contrasting stories of Camilo Torres on the one hand and Gustavo Gutiérrez on the other. The working out of what love of neighbour meant led Torres to take up arms against the Colombian government and to his death. His actions made him an example of the practice Ratzinger condemned. Gustavo Gutiérrez, a contemporary of Torres, has become one of the most remarkable figures in late twentieth-century Roman Catholicism. His work among poor people, and his reflection upon it, led to a form of Christian radicalism whose impact has been enormous worldwide.

Ratzinger has not been alone in his views. Even Britain's leading left-of-centre newspaper talked of the Islamic movement which inspired the bombings in London and its antecedents as 'a violent brand of Islamic liberation theology that eventually spawned al-Qaeda'.[39] In the light of the deeds of Camilo Torres, and other

Christians down the centuries who have turned to armed struggle through history, one can see why that link might have been made. But it is not the story of Camilo Torres, but that of Gustavo Gutiérrez, which enables us best to see the character of modern faith-based radicalism. So, while there may have been the odd exceptions, in the main the radicalisation initiated by liberation theology and its practitioners has not been militant in the sense of engaging in armed struggle, but changing hearts and minds and enabling solidarity with the poor, marginalised and vulnerable. 'Conscientisation' is after all the watchword of the educationalist, Paulo Freire, whose work was so important for pedagogy influenced by liberation theology.[40]

In his analysis of the predicament of liberation theology, Ivan Petrella has demonstrated that liberation theology's genius is its commitment to the emergence of a theology originating within specific social and political projects, both reflecting its contextual character and its roots in action for social change.[41] This, not the various theoretical and culturally aware developments that have emerged in the last decade, is crucial and takes us straight back to Winstanley's 'action is the life of all'. Petrella not only grasped what is central in liberation theology but also what is necessary for any theology, which is related to the project of the coming of God's Kingdom on earth. Implicit within the argument is the conviction of Vatican II (of course echoing Acts 2 and the prophecy of Joel) that the Spirit is poured out on *all* flesh, and that change is neither ecclesial nor apolitical, or for that matter merely inward or psychological. The practitioners of liberation theology have put their fingers on the pulse of historical change, which is the work of the Holy Spirit, who makes all things new. It did this by realising that theological understanding comes through the commitment and action and discernment that are a complement to that activity, not a replacement for it. All these together are part of the reading of 'the signs of the times' and the possibility of working for change, which discernment within the context of commitment to the poor and marginalised can offer. Perhaps this is the most disturbing thing about the theological tradition, which liberation theology represents: that there exists a hermeneutical privilege for the poor and marginalised, and a consequent loss of privilege and status in academy or Church. As one English ancestor of liberation theology, Gerrard Winstanley, put it: 'Nay let me tell you, that the poorest man, that sees his maker, and lives in the light, though he could never read a letter in a book, dares throw the glove to all the humane learning in the world, and declare the deceit of it.'[42] A contemporary voice stresses that the message of liberation theology is as relevant as it ever was:

> As climate change racks up inequalities around the world, and populations struggle to defend what they have, Gutierrez's message to both church and world remains absolutely as relevant as it ever was. The theology Gutierrez seeks is one which is open to the gift of the kingdom of God 'in the protest against trampled human dignity, in the struggle against the plunder of the vast majority of people, in liberating love, and in the building of a new, just, and fraternal society'. All of this remains to be done.[43]

Chapter 8

Apocalypticism and Millenarian Eschatology

Recovering Neglected Strands

The importance of the intellectual history sketched in this book has been appreciated by scholars from outside the Christian tradition. Norman Cohn's epoch-making book, *The Pursuit of the Millennium* (1957), in particular, put these features firmly on the scholarly map, and since its publication all of us who have been interested in the history of eschatology and apocalypticism have been in his debt, even if in key ways we may have dissented from him. Indeed, 'the pursuit of the millennium' emerges as a particularly lethal part of the pathology of religion. What Cohn's book opens up is a rich seam of radicalism, which, far from being incoherent or not worth theological attention, represents, if not a tradition of interpretation, at least a corpus of material with sufficient intellectual coherence to warrant a more comprehensive study. One can glibly talk of a 'radical tradition', but there is a strong sense in many of these writings that the inspiration of the present moment trumps tradition, though that does not, of course, absolve the commentator of the responsibility to note the connections with antecedent ideas and writings, whether or not a prophet consciously drew on them. Nevertheless, there are similar sets of experience and conviction which emerge at different times and in different places.

Ernst Bloch was a Marxist philosopher, but one with a difference.[1] One of Bloch's earliest books was on Thomas Muentzer and he also pointed to strands within the Bible which are very much akin to the 'prophetic-messianic principle'. His influential work on utopianism demonstrates the fundamental importance of the horizon of hope for human flourishing and his work has understandably been influential on the study of Christian eschatology, as is exemplified by the pioneering work by Jürgen Moltmann, which is indebted to Bloch's ideas.

If Cohn's work evinces little sympathy with apocalyptic radicalism, Jacob Taubes is different. Like Bloch, he traced the importance of the apocalyptic and eschatological strand as a central intellectual dynamic in Christianity. Walter Benjamin's inspiration is similar but from the Jewish messianic inheritance. His friendship with the great historian of Jewish mysticism and messianism, Gershom Scholem, illuminates his last work, though hints of it can be found much earlier. His writing evinces radical criticism of culture and received wisdom that we find elsewhere and which Bloch and Taubes themselves charted. But there is also, alongside, a profoundly pessimistic strand, probably reflecting his sense of despair at the end of his life as he fled Nazi persecution in France. Others in the Frankfurt School, like Theodor Adorno, also appreciated the intellectual potency of the messianic, as we shall see.

Ernst Bloch (1885–1977)

Bloch understood what made primitive Christianity tick. As with the New Testament writers, for him utopia is not primarily a cause for fantasising about a different world. It is primarily about this world and the discernment of a different kind of world and society latent within it. Throughout his work, Bloch appreciated the political significance of the eschatological and utopian.[2] He had a special interest from his earliest days in the religious manifestations of this. So Bloch picked out the revolutionary theology of Thomas Muentzer, and to Muentzer he returned again in later writing.

Bloch found in Judaism and Christianity anticipations of that which is to come, which involved moments of ecstasy, 'standing outside oneself', thereby getting a glimpse of what we could become, not just as fantasy but as practised anticipation. Such looking, and moving forward on a journey to something new, may assist the ultimate liberation. The desire to become, to be on a forward journey to an as yet not fully known destination is central to Bloch's work. In stressing this, Bloch echoes a more sympathetic understanding towards experiments in this age, found also in Engels' study of American communalism. For example, Engels wrote that communism 'is not only possible but has actually already been realized in many communities in America [...] with the greatest success'[3] so different from the pungent criticism of 'the anticipation of communism by fantasy' he used of earlier radical movements in 'The Peasant War in Germany' (quoted above in Chapter 3, 'The Sermon before the Princes').[4]

In the most succinct statement of his position with regard to Christianity, in *Atheism in Christianity* (1972), Bloch sought to trace its 'messianic/utopian' thread. It is rather a pity that the title of Bloch's statement of the centrality of hope in the Bible should have the rather provocative if somewhat misleading title, *Atheism in Christianity*. The sub-title, 'the religion of the Exodus and Kingdom', aptly summarises a challenge to the marginalisation of eschatology in Christian doctrine by an exposition of biblical themes, which look forward to the moment when 'God will be all in all' from both parts of the Christian canon. This is far from being a systematic theology – Bloch does not write like that – but it is a determined attempt to place this-worldly eschatology at the centre of Christian belief and practice. Bloch teases out the contradictory threads in the Christian tradition, not least in respect of Christology. It is a sustained exposition of an alternative 'Exodus' pattern in the Bible, one that is not nostalgic but determined to pursue the winding quest for full human potential for all. He picked on the liberative potential of the Exodus and explored the ways in which early Christians developed their understanding of Christ from the eschatologically orientated figure, the Son of Man, to the divine Kyrios, who, as celestial despot, validated human monarchy. Such a critique has many similarities with the theology of William Blake, whom Bloch approvingly called a 'chiliastic mystic',[5] though without recognising the way Blake had anticipated his ideological critique. In language which is reminiscent of New Testament inaugurated eschatology, Bloch stresses the importance of the 'not yet' and the process of becoming, which is not an individual journey but includes a wider social group. For Bloch, utopia is not just a matter of speculation but is also a potent impulse challenging and inspiring here and now, albeit only available in fragmentary and difficult-to-interpret glimpses. What is true of the present moment in this age is its inadequacy and hope for a better world. It only impels one on the ongoing journey towards true human flourishing.[6]

Few have better understood the deeply unsettling, subversive call of hope, and the consequences of living by and in it, than Ernst

Bloch. He manages to capture the sheer precariousness of it, the temptation to be satisfied with the 'ease of the ready-made' option, the kind of struggles which one can find throughout the New Testament and more widely in Christian tradition. His words 'the only thing one can really hold on to is the search for a handhold – the constant feeling that one is on the way to finding it, and the faithful following of the signs' capture that sense of living on a rock face. The discontent with not having arrived 'is in itself a handhold for the hoper'. Filling in precipitately the gap that lies ahead is false comfort, 'a treacherous handhold that will lead to an even greater fall'. What is needed is the 'determination to stay, despite everything, in open ferment; its determination to remain in an open traversable Way, foreshadowing the future', for 'out of the future shadows on this Way there comes a continuous call; but no more faith is needed than faith in discontented hope'.[7]

Jacob Taubes (1923–87) and Walter Benjamin (1892–1940)

A voice which has been more widely heard in New Testament circles in the last decade has been that of Jacob Taubes.[8] I had been aware for many years of a brilliant short article by Taubes, which I had come across in the early 1980s, in which he rightly challenged Gershom Scholem's claim that while in Judaism redemption takes place in the political realm and in history, in Christianity it takes place only in the individual. In so doing Taubes makes an interesting comparison between Paul and Sabbatai Sevi,[9] a subject to which W.D. Davies also devoted an important essay in 1975.[10]

In *Occidental Eschatology*, as the title suggests, Taubes argued that deep within the Bible are the seeds of modern thought, whether individual or social, with the key being apocalyptic thinking. This is the theological heart of Western culture, the rise of apocalypticism, its importance for a Christian understanding of history and its contribution to modern thought. The Taubes thesis is far-reaching. Taubes considered apocalyptic thought to be 'not in some indeterminate future but entirely proximate'.[11] Whereas Taubes was working with an understanding of apocalypticism which focused almost entirely on eschatology, he also pointed out the ways in which this way of thinking has a strong interior, as well as exterior dimension, the inner light which sets the 'world on fire'.[12]

Here Taubes could well have been writing about the early Christian movement as evidenced in the pages of the New Testament.

Taubes noted the demise of chiliasm in the early Church, the rediscovery of Revelation and its contribution to an understanding of history in the writings of Joachim of Fiore on to the Radical Reformation, particularly Thomas Muentzer. Augustine's brilliant theological treatise, *The City of God*, by its use of Tyconius' apocalyptic hermeneutics, not only infused Christian theology with a key apocalyptic element, but also succeeded in taming its chiliastic elements. Nevertheless, even this theological *tour de force* never quite succeeded. The chiliastic prophecy of the Apocalypse of John, which, as a vision of future events, threatened time and again the foundation of the Church, was integrated by Augustine into the context of the Church. Christ's Kingdom on earth should not be expected in the future, and the 'thousand years' describe in fact the reign of Christ and the saints in the Church. Since Christ, the history of the world has become irrelevant. Christian eschatology does not wait for an event in history, and its interest shifts to the destiny of the soul at the end of its earthly journey. According to Taubes, with Augustine, the eschatology of history was relegated to heresy.[13]

> The theology of Joachim of Fiore contained the dynamite that was to explode the foundations of medieval religion and society that had been drawn in the light of Augustine's theology of history. In Joachim's theology of history there emerges a principle that will challenge the 'chiliastic' reign of the Catholic Church. He envisages a new era in human history that shall supersede the era of the church [...] [it] marks a change in the theological pattern itself. Joachim's theology denies the 'central' position of Jesus Christ [...] the goal of Joachim's theology is not in Christ but in the Holy Ghost, which supersedes Christ.[14]

That is brilliantly put and grasps the intellectual prophetic power of Joachim's ideas. Taubes then works out an ambitious thesis suggestively characterising the debt of aspects of modernity to patterns of apocalyptic thought rooted in the Bible. Taubes' historical survey supports the view of Rosemary Radford Ruether that a 'prophetic' or 'messianic' principle is central to the Bible as a whole.[15] He argued that it is apocalypticism and eschatology which have inspired key figures in the history of

Christianity from Joachim of Fiore, via Muentzer to Kierkegaard and Marx. In some ways the Taubes thesis both echoes and anticipates later studies by Ernst Bloch, such as *Principle of Hope* and *Atheism in Christianity*.[16] Taubes argued that the imminence of the future fulfilment lends an aura of urgency and ultimate significance to the apocalyptic mind-set. It is akin to the points made by Karl Mannheim about the 'chiliastic mentality'.[17] Like Mannheim, and later Cohn, Taubes focused on instances where the epistemological potential of apocalypse, as well as its imagery, has been particularly prominent. It is that underworld of eschatology fed by the apocalyptic conviction that knowledge of the divine purposes came to the favoured individual, man or woman, by means of visions and revelations, licensed as they are by the Scriptures themselves.

Taubes' philosophical discussion is often subtle and complex, but the basic thesis of his sweeping intellectual history about the centrality of apocalyptic and eschatology in Christian thought is compelling, even if, in relation to apocalyptic, I would put things somewhat differently from him! My perhaps too simplistic view of apocalyptic is primarily much more about epistemology than eschatology, the revelatory mode through which ancients came to comprehend, among other things, their eschatological convictions. But, as we have seen, Taubes, too, recognised this dimension, when he rightly noted the similarity of outlook between apocalyptic and gnosis.

What Taubes offered is a wider contextualising and construal of the effects of the rediscovery of eschatology in New Testament scholarship, so helping us better to understand the intellectual threads with which commentators like Johannes Weiss, Franz Overbeck and Albert Schweitzer have struggled to integrate into New Testament theology. Taubes' work does offer a way of comprehending how the central eschatological elements might be worked out in contemporary theological terms, as Jürgen Moltmann, inspired as he was by the thought of Ernst Bloch, was to explore.

I am not entirely sure that Taubes fully grasps that sense of the anticipation of the messianic which is there in Bloch's work. In his *Minima Moralia*, Theodor Adorno (1903–69) expresses a similar view to Ernst Bloch when he writes:

> The only philosophy that can be responsibly practised in the face of despair is the attempt to contemplate all things, as they would present themselves from the standpoint of redemption. Knowledge has no light but that shed on the world by redemption: all else is reconstruction, mere technique. Perspectives must be fashioned that displace and estrange the world, reveal it to be, with its rifts and crevices, as indigent and distorted as it will appear one day in the messianic light'.[18]

Taubes was scathing about these words of Adorno, dismissing them as the 'aestheticization' of the problem.[19] He preferred instead Walter Benjamin's 'Theologico-Political Fragment', probably an early piece, which at first sight at least, does not allow any impact of the messianic on the history of this age. Indeed, Taubes believes that 'Romans 8 has its closest parallel' with this text:[20]

> Only the Messiah himself consummates all history, in the sense that he alone redeems, completes, creates its relation to the Messianic.
>
> For this reason nothing historical can relate itself on its own account to anything Messianic. Therefore the Kingdom of God is not the *telos* of the historical dynamic; it cannot be set as a goal. From the standpoint of history it is not a goal, but [an] end.[21]

One can understand why Taubes wrote what he did about some of Benjamin's last extant written words, for, similar to Paul's words, they were forged in the midst of the terrible experiences that Benjamin endured at the end of his life.[22] Also, they probably resonated with the dying Taubes, and in comparison, Adorno's words, written in the comfort of academic detachment, seemed to him nothing more than an 'aestheticization of the problem'. But this ignores the fact that the fragment by Benjamin was probably not written in his last months but dates from 20 years earlier. *At first sight*, it suggests a view of the relationship between the messiah and history which Taubes himself had rightly criticised in Scholem's work.[23] The clear-cut contrast between history and the messianic time does not do justice either to Benjamin's words or even to the New Testament. Indeed, this contrast is reminiscent of a view of early Christian and Jewish apocalyptic texts, that 'apocalyptic eschatology' involves 'the end of history'. It is a widespread opinion which has dominated New Testament scholarship since the nineteenth century (see Chapter 4, 'Apocalypse'). Benjamin's words and the New Testament writings suggest, like Bloch's view, that elements of messianic latency contribute to the future and are found in history: 'the order of the profane assists, through being profane, the coming of the Messianic kingdom'.[24] In Benjamin's 'Theologico-Political Fragment', 'activity in this world which may seem commonplace [...] is simultaneously the cornerstone from which the *next* world is itself built'.[25] What Benjamin writes is very nuanced (e.g. the words 'all history' and the addition of the phrase 'on its own account'). Of course, Pauline passages do not have any idea of human agency *independent of the messiah*, but human agency inspired and informed by the messiah are part of Paul's self-understanding as a divine agent ('Christ in me' from Galatians 2:20 springs to mind). It is that element from the New Testament, wrestling with the notion of the messianic era as in some sense already present and active, which is lacking in Taubes' exposition.

Benjamin's 'Theses on the Philosophy of History' is one of the great prophetic texts of the twentieth, or indeed any other, century, probably written shortly before his death. The 'Theses' certainly problematise optimism in the light of catastrophe and the loneliness of the task of the historical materialist in seeking to wrest history from the victors. If it does not qualify the lofty sentiments of Ernst Bloch and the deeply problematic character of hope, whether Jewish, Christian or Marxist on which it is based, Benjamin's words evince the ambiguous impact of the advent of the messiah on the cultures and societies of the present age. Nowhere is this better exemplified than in Thesis IX:

> My wing is ready for flight
> *I would like to turn back*
> If I stayed timeless time
> *I would have luck. – Gerhard Scholem, 'Angelic Greetings'*

> A Klee painting named 'Angelus Novus' shows an angel looking as though he is about to move away from something he is fixedly contemplating. His eyes are staring, his mouth is open, his wings are spread. This is how one pictures the angel of history. His face is turned toward the past. Where we perceive a chain of events, he sees one single catastrophe which keeps piling wreckage upon wreckage and hurls it in front of his feet. The angel would like to stay, awaken the dead, and make whole what has been smashed. But a storm is blowing

> from Paradise; it has got caught in his wings with such violence that the Angel can no longer close them. This storm irresistibly propels him into the future, to which his back is turned, while the pile of debris before him grows skyward. The storm is what we call progress.[26]

In Thesis IX, Benjamin wrote of the angel of history whose face is turned towards the past, but a storm blowing from Paradise drives him irresistibly into the future. Here is a messianism of an ominous kind, perhaps tinged with a note of despair. These are not the words of one who believed that the divine was at work in and through humans. The storm from Paradise is the impact of the future not the past, where the victors have always been in control and where hope in progress is naively optimistic. The way of the messiah is open, but it is a narrow gate (cf. Matthew 7:13–14). It is the future which is where Jews and Christians believe Paradise is located. Thence comes the storm which blows away the pretensions of those who would organise history and call it progress.

Elsewhere in 'Theses', Benjamin writes that a 'historical materialist [...] brushes history against the grain' (Thesis VII). It prompts the recollection of the African proverb, which gained wide circulation as a result of its use on an Oxfam poster and which stated pointedly, '*Until lions have their own historians, tales of the hunt will always glorify the hunter*'. Brushing against the grain is the task of reviving the stories of those who in the words of Ecclesiasticus 44:9 'have no memorial, who have become as though they had never been born'. Messianic/utopian hopes offer a corrective to the cycle of repetition when the same returns in ever new guises, as Blake put it, the 'Poetic or Prophetic character' preventing the same dull round over again.[27] Benjamin saw that discerning truth about empire can enable us to see, perhaps to our discomfort and sadness, that the cultural monuments celebrated by official, establishment history could not be understood outside the context of their origins, a context of oppression and exploitation: 'there is no document of civilization which is not at the same time a document of barbarism' (Thesis VII). Benjamin's *Theses* resemble Blake's 'Holy Thursday' in *Songs of Experience*, where the bleak historical situation is illuminated briefly by 'the messianic light':

> For where-e'er the sun does shine,
> And where-e'er the rain does fall:

> Babe can never hunger there,
> Nor poverty the mind appall.[28]

This final stanza sits uneasily with the dark despair about society, politics and the effects on the vulnerable of the rest of the poem.

Apocalypse may offer a fleeting glimpse of an alternative, the 'involuntary memory of a redeemed humanity', which contrasts with convention and false tradition. What is required is that 'in every era the attempt must be made to wrest tradition from a conformism that is about to overpower it' (Thesis VI). No more eloquent description of the hermeneutics of apocalypse could be offered. Here are the words of prophecy.

'Theses' is one of the most insightful social commentaries of any age, which in its terse, elusive aphorisms captures the contradictions of life for a stranger and exile in an alien land, as Benjamin surely was, particularly at the end of his life. It stands as a witness to hope, albeit one that manifests its fragility and is utterly realistic in its pessimism about the consequences of the fallibility of humanity. It is in its brevity a fitting memorial there to be seized 'as it flashes up at a moment of danger' (Thesis VI).

To return briefly to Taubes: in *Occidental Eschatology* he captured something of the contraries of the dialectic of apocalyptic and eschatology, its potential for creativity and renewal on the one hand and its possibilities for leading to chaos on the other. Indeed, what Taubes writes about here reminds me very much of what Blake writes about the 'Prolific' and 'the Devourer' in *The Marriage of Heaven and Hell.*[29]

> Apocalypticism is revolutionary because it beholds the turning point not in some indeterminate future but entirely proximate. Apocalyptic prophecy thus focuses on the future and yet is fully set in the present. The telos of the revolution binds the forces of chaos, which otherwise would burst all forms and overreach established boundaries. Even revolution has its forms and is 'formalized', particularly when it shatters the rigid structures of the positivity of the world. The apocalyptic principle combines within it a form-destroying [*gestalt-zerstörend*] and a forming [*gestaltend*] power. Depending on the situation and the task, only one of the two components emerges, but neither can be absent. If the demonic, destructive element is missing, the petrified order, the prevailing positivity of the world

> cannot be overcome. But if the 'new covenant' fails to shine through in this destructive element, the revolution inevitably sinks into empty nothingness [*leere Nichts*].
>
> If the telos of the revolution collapses, so that the revolution is no longer the means but the sole creative principle, then the destructive desire becomes a creative desire. If the revolution points to nothing beyond itself, it will end in a movement, dynamic in nature but leading into the abyss [*ins leere Nichts*]. A 'nihilistic revolution' does not pursue any goal [telos], but takes its aim from the 'movement' itself and, in so doing, comes close to satanic practice.[30]

This is a complex summary of the radical character of apocalypticism, but it succeeds in capturing features which are essential to the thesis of this book. The stress on the indispensability of the form-destroying and a forming power, and the constant danger of one eclipsing the other, leading to petrification on the one hand or the chaos of the abyss on the other, is a recognition of the ever-present risk of the chaos which lurks in the destructive forces that are unleashed and the repressive reaction set in train to manage those forces by a form which can petrify. It is the kind of thing that Blake was struggling to articulate in his insistence on the importance of the bounding line ('Leave out this l[i]ne and you leave out life itself; all is chaos again', (Chapter 6, 'Conclusion') and the juxtaposition of the subversive serpent with the bounding divinity at the beginning of *Europe a Prophecy* (see Plates 3 and 4). It touches on hermeneutical and practical problems, which run through Christian texts. Paul is engaged in negotiating the tension between the disruptive effects of the messianic impulse, and the constraints of community, which prompt much of Paul's advice, particularly in a text like 1 Corinthians, where arguably he sought to 'bind the forces of chaos'. The genius of Paul lies in the fact that he sought a way of incorporating the messianic enthusiasm in a communitarian framework, which promised some kind of stability.[31] We shall never know for certain how successful he was. 2 Corinthians suggests that he may not have been successful with regard to the church in Corinth. A text like 2 Corinthians (along with the Collection for the Saints in Jerusalem) represented a last throw of the dice to save his own eschatologically significant activity.

No one can read Paul's letters without having a strong sense of a writer desperately trying to bring what appears to be an enthusiastic messianic community under some control. Indeed, the Pauline corpus is replete with those attempts to rein in such enthusiasm, culminating in the straitjacketing rigour and sobriety of the Pastoral Epistles, which have characterised much of mainstream Christianity ever since. In the Pastoral Epistles the charisma of prophecy was regulated by laying on of hands and the claim to prophetic inspiration both suspected and restricted. But such sobriety conceals the reality of the apocalyptic enthusiasm, which was the energy that brought Christianity to birth and inspired its founding figures. Early Christians came to read apocalyptic images in an otherworldly way, which encouraged adherents to set their minds on things above where Christ is seated (to quote the Letter to the Colossians). The Book of Revelation may be the only visionary text in the New Testament, but, I have suggested, its sentiments are those of early Christianity generally, including Jesus, Paul and the Synoptic Gospels, even if the Gospel of John represents an initial stage of a process in which focus on the age to come became focus on the world above, utilising the 'vertical' dimension inherent in apocalypticism. That apocalyptic legacy was non-negotiable; it could not be easily sloughed off. It needed the genius of Augustine, inspired by Tyconius, to offer a mutation.

Taubes' critique of Scholem's view, that the price which the Jewish people have had to pay for messianism is the 'endless powerlessness of the Jews during all the centuries of exile', is important for the subject matter of this book:

> It is not the messianic idea that subjugated us to a 'life in deferment'. Every endeavour to actualize the messianic idea was an attempt to jump into history, however mythically derailed the attempt may have been. It is simply not the case that messianic fantasy and the formation of historical reality stand at opposite poles. Consider the millenarian expectations of the Puritan community in New England. Arriving in the Bay of Massachusetts to create a New Zion, they founded in the end the United States of America. If Jewish history in exile was 'a life lived in deferment', this life in suspension was due to rabbinic hegemony. Retreat from history was rather the rabbinic stance, the outlook that set itself against all messianic lay movements and cursed all messianic discharge *a priori* with the stigma of 'pseudo messianic'. [...] Only those who jumped on messianic bandwagons, religious or

> secular, giving themselves entirely to their cause burned themselves out taking the messianic risk.[32]

What Taubes wrote here about the retreat from history of the Jewish people under rabbinic hegemony, as he recognised, equally applies, *mutatis mutandis*, to Christianity under ecclesial hegemony. The solution to the messianism and apocalypticism, which are integral to Christian identity, was solved by the Church in a way similar to the Rabbis. Or put another way, the Church picked out the authoritarian, rabbinic strand in Paul at the expense of communal participation in the messianic/apocalyptic element and set itself against all messianic lay movements and cursed all messianic democratisation *a priori* with the stigma of being 'pseudo messianic'. The major difference is that post-Constantine imperial power allied with an ecclesial hegemony, shorn of its messianism, readily dominated Christianity in succeeding centuries.

Conclusion

The perspectives of Bloch and Taubes indicate differing, but complementary, aspects of the practice of a religion of hope, particularly where hope is in the process of realisation. For Bloch it is the fragility and uncertainty of negotiating the path, the possibility of following false trails, but the necessity of the recognition of the indispensability of discontent while avoiding the temptation to anticipate too much too quickly. For Taubes there is the recognition of the ever-present risk of the chaos which lurks in the destructive forces, which are unleashed, and the repressive reaction which manages their forces by a form which can petrify. In their different ways they touch on hermeneutical and practical problems, which run through Christian texts. Bloch concentrates on the *hypomone* necessary to remain 'in an open traversable Way with discontented hope and without resorting to a precipitate solution'.[33] Taubes stresses the indispensability of the form-destroying and a forming power and the constant danger of one eclipsing the other, leading to petrification on the one hand or the chaos of the abyss on the other.

Taubes' historical survey corroborates Rosemary Radford Ruether's 'prophetic' or 'messianic' principle as a basic pattern by indicating that it is apocalypticism and eschatology, history and life and the mystical understanding of them which are a barely audible, but crucial, counterpoint to mainstream theology. Taubes grasped the nature of the radical epistemology which apocalypticism may engender and the way in which it has inspired key figures in the history of Christianity.

Epilogue

... *'And here I end'*

Concluding Reflections

> And here I end, having put my Arm as far as my strength will go to advance Righteousness: I have Writ, I have Acted, I have Peace: and now I must wait to see the Spirit do his own work in the hearts of others ...[1]

There is something wistful and sad about Winstanley's words 'having put my Arm as far as my strength will go to advance Righteousness' (quoted in full above in Chapter 5, '"And here I end": the experience of defeat') still hopeful that change would come, and willing to wait for it patiently; 'Patience take the Crown', Winstanley wrote in lines at the start of *A New-Yeers Gift*.[2] The sentiments in *A New-Yeers Gift* contrast starkly with the angry, desperate words with which Winstanley closed his final extant writing. Winstanley's project of digging the common land in 1649 was not 'communism by fantasy' but a sign of what could happen to initiate a true commonwealth in England, with a change of hearts and minds. His words in *A New-Yeers Gift* are a testimony to a longing for a different way of human relating which would point to the peaceable kingdom of the Lamb, heralding the coming of which required much 'patient ferment'.[3] Knowledge of God comes in such endeavour. Gustavo Gutiérrez put it that 'to be followers of Jesus requires that [we] walk with and be committed to the poor; when [we] do, [we] experience an encounter with the Lord who is simultaneously revealed and hidden in the faces of the poor',[4] and in the words of Hans Denck: 'No one may truly know Christ except one who follows Him in life'.[5] Such ideas are deeply rooted in the Bible itself (Jer. 22:16; John 8:31, 32).

Ronald Paulson summarised brilliantly the thesis of this book when he wrote:

> While establishment Christianity, founded on the Bible of the Church Fathers, was content with an ordered status quo in this life, revolutionary Christianity, which harked back to the 'true' reading of the New Testament – called for change. 'How long, O Lord, how long!' was their cry, and their expectation was the reign of Christ upon this earth in the near future. They stood for, or easily were made to stand for, the desire for an imminent and total overthrow of the existing order and the substitution of a 'new heaven and a new earth' in which would dwell 'righteousness'. Sometimes, as with the sixteenth-century Thomas Münzer and the seventeenth-century radical protestants in England, the result had been directly political and bloody. More often it remained only religious and involved a patient waiting for divine intervention. But the desire was always discernible to such conservatives as Burke; and it was always lurking in the minds of such radicals as Blake – to be entertained or acted upon.[6]

The opening chapter started with Blake's Preface to *Milton, A Poem* which offered such an apt summary of the book and so an explication of its title. It is a radical appeal to prophesy, in which all can, and must, participate. It is a struggle, though not with force of arms, but a war of intellect to share in the task of bringing heaven on earth and in the meantime sharing the horizon of hope. 'It does not yet appear what we shall be,' wrote the author of the First Letter of John (1 John 3:2). In these few words is encapsulated a fundamental feature of Christianity. There is something inadequate about the present state of things and about the way we understand things: 'For now we see in a mirror dimly, but then face to face' (1 Cor. 13:12).[7] Christianity includes a positive, and hopefully healthy, rather than pathological, dissatisfaction, with oneself, with society and the world. Its foundational texts demand a forward-looking view, to a better life, more often than not, more's the pity, beyond this world, but also in the New Testament, in this world. Christianity is about living with grit in the shoe of life, being restless, never content with things as they are. There is a constant struggle to come to terms with a cosmos, viewed as the organisation of the world, or the created world, where things seem out of joint. One reason for this is the consequence of apocalyptic and eschatology. That arises from the apocalyptic unmasking, resulting in a deep-seated discontent with that which is seen and the way things are, and the longing for something unseen, which casts into sharp relief the inadequacies and injustices of this world. But it also acts as a spur to action, to change, to ameliorate the personal and social ills.

So one aim of this book has been to bring to the fore an element which has been on the agenda of all New Testament scholars for nearly 150 years, but whose implications for understanding the identity of emerging Christianity, and indeed the character of the religion it became, have all too easily been ignored. As Jürgen Moltmann and Heikki Räisänen rightly point out, the implications for exegesis and theology still need further exploration.[8]

We have seen that the coming, indeed bringing in, of the kingdom of God, initiated by radical prophets, is key to understanding the New Testament and is one of the major contributions of modern historical study of the New Testament texts. While there may not be much dispute about that, there will be more disagreement about whether humans just have to wait for some divine intervention to come about or are active agents in its coming. The radical prophets mentioned in this book, in their different ways, demonstrated their conviction in the latter route. Blake shared the hope for the New Jerusalem on earth, as every participant in singing 'Jerusalem' knows, but it was the Book of Revelation, not the Jesus portrayed in the Gospels, which inspired him. Blake grasped as well as anyone Jesus' visionary non-conformity, but the gospel of hope for a new age on earth is *not* part of his picture of Jesus.

'I appeal to you to contend for the faith that was once for all entrusted to the saints' (Epistle of Jude 3) is a theme which has echoed down the centuries. It is the cornerstone of all those who look back to the Apostles, to the Bible, to the teaching of the Church as an infallible guide to Christian life. It is in short what Blake would term 'memory'. It is dependence on this from which Blake believed Job had to be weaned away, and through experience he recognised that 'the Daughters of Memory shall become the Daughters of Inspiration'.[9] The determination to preserve the faith handed down from the Apostles, and to do what the Bible says, is not only boring and unadventurous but is contrary to a major strand of the New Testament, found in what is written about both Jesus and Paul. Visionary radicals like Jesus are always going to be at odds with society, institutions or the intellectual elite. They are not safe – not even Paul, pioneer contextual theologian that he was. Paul was just as motivated by eschatology as these pages have suggested. But, and this is crucial, he was also a pragmatist, and the mix of visionary and community organiser meant that there were compromises to be made. We saw that finding a way to live eschatologically in the present age meant compromises, which owed much to beliefs he had inherited from his upbringing. That is not to deny that Paul gave mixed messages, at one time emphasising 'Inspiration' (1 Cor. 2:8–14; 1 Thess. 4:9) and at other times stressing 'Memory' (1 Cor. 11:2; 15:3) or 'catholic' practice (1 Cor. 14:33). It says everything about the difference between conservative and radical, that safety too often snuffs out adventure because it might rock the boat of familiarity and adherence to the past, not to mention challenge the gatekeepers who claim to allow access to the past and its meaning. But adventure is exactly what is there in the New Testament and for that matter in the Hebrew Bible too.

Mutatis mutandis, liberation theology picks up a crucial theme of the New Testament. It may not stress recourse to dreams and visions (though the influence of that aspect in a culture saturated by the Afro-Brazilian religions should not be discounted). In liberation theology, as we have seen, the emphasis is on 'the text of life' as central interpretative perspective. That is equally true of the New Testament as well. *Experience* is crucial. Whether it is of the Spirit, of the life in the charismatic community, or of what it means to be sharing the life of messiah, experience is primary. They are the ones who have tasted of the age to come and are the ones who have seen fulfilment. Experience turns on a spotlight which illuminates what Rosemary Radford Ruether calls the 'shiny bits' of a heterogeneous tradition.[10] These fragments of tradition endorse and inspire. Experience is the lens through which the past, and indeed the present world, should be viewed.

The heart of the Christian faith is that the Word became flesh (cf. John 1:14). God spoke (and continues to speak) not in prophetic words but in a human being (Hebr. 1:1–2). What Blake came to see was the character of prophetic embodiment which involved learning to live with all those other embodied people, standing up for those who get a raw deal and tending to those who feel lost and hurt by the vagaries of life. The emphasis is on the perception of the divine in others. The first step is to see the divine in every human. Therein lies the possibility of human flourishing rather than 'Religion hid in War', for which religions (not least mainstream Christianity) have all too often been ready to offer ideological justification. Blake's promotion of contraries makes that kind of adversarial religion redundant. The images in the early part of the 'Job' series suggest a view of God 'in a place of glory beyond the Sun, Moon and Stars' as Winstanley put it,[11] but he came to understand that divinity was with and in us all.

The disconcerting impression offered by the New Testament Gospels is that Jesus did not come to die but to proclaim and inaugurate the Kingdom of God on earth open to all, irrespective of status and education. As a result, he experienced hostility and responded to that by going to Jerusalem to give the elite one last chance to discern what made for their peace (Luke 19:42), but he perished in so doing. But his story lived on, and it continues to catch people's imaginations, as it did Albert Schweitzer's:

> He comes to us as One unknown, without a name, as of old, by the lake-side, He came to those men who knew Him not. He speaks to us the same word: 'Follow thou me!' and sets us to the tasks, which He has to fulfil *for our time*. He commands. And to those who obey Him, whether they be wise or simple, *He will reveal Himself in the toils, the conflicts, the sufferings which they shall pass through in His fellowship*, and, as an ineffable mystery, they shall learn *in their own experience* Who He is.[12]

Whatever Jesus of Nazareth, the paradigmatic Christian radical prophet, who died at the hand of the Roman colonial power, may have said shortly before his death, within a few decades it was thought that he had asked to be commemorated in a shared meal (1 Cor. 11:23–5 cf. Mark 14:22–5). So his story lives on. Jesus is unlike the millions down the centuries who, in the words of Ecclesiasticus 44:9, 'have no memorial, who have become as though they had never been born; but these too were merciful people, whose righteousness hath not been forgotten'. If this book does nothing else, it brings to mind those whose names may not be included in the official lists of the great cloud of witnesses; their witness should not be forgotten.

I often think of a moment 30 years ago when I was chatting with a distinguished colleague of mine over the photocopying machine. Out of the blue he said to me, 'I do not know how anyone who holds beliefs like yours can live in the world as it is, continue in the church, or remain on an even keel'. At the time I was taken aback but have come to see that he perceived something profoundly true, not only about the beliefs I hold and the contradictions in which I find myself, but also what I take to be the problem, as well as the possibility which is offered in the New Testament and the remarkable social movement to which it bears witness. I am not the first, and will not be the last, to struggle to come to terms with that pervasive apocalyptic and eschatological inheritance, and to find myself at odds with institutional Christianity. What the colleague rightly perceived is that if one takes the fundamental eschatological and apocalyptic ethos of the New Testament seriously, the struggle to live in this age is, and always will be, a challenge. That applied equally in antiquity as it does in modernity as men and women and children seek to understand what it means to take up their cross and follow. Arguably, the history of Christian theology arises as a complex series of responses to that fundamental datum and its companion, the discrepancy between what is and what might be, and how that vision may inform the present.

Notes

Preface

1 S. Makdisi, *William Blake and the Impossible History of the 1790s* (Chicago: University of Chicago Press, 2003).
2 G. Scholem, *Sabbatai Sevi: The Mystical Messiah, 1626–1676*, Littman Library of Jewish Civilization (London: Routledge & Kegan Paul, 1973), and M. Idel, *Messianic Mystics* (New Haven: Yale University Press, 1998).
3 J. Shaw, *Octavia, Daughter of God: The Story of a Female Messiah and Her Followers* (London: Jonathan Cape, 2011); P. Lockley, *Visionary Religion and Radicalism in Early Industrial England: From Southcott to Socialism* (Oxford: Oxford University Press, 2013).
4 W. Brueggemann, *The Prophetic Imagination* (Minneapolis: Fortress Press, 1978).

Chapter 1: 'Would to God that all the Lords people were Prophets'

1 William Blake, *Milton a Poem* Preface, E95–6 in David V. Erdman (ed.), *The Complete Poetry and Prose of William Blake* (Berkeley, CA: University of California Press, 1988), henceforth abbreviated as 'E', followed by the page number.
2 For example, *Jerusalem* 75:20, E231.
3 G.E. Bentley, *The Stranger from Paradise: A Biography of William Blake* (New Haven: Yale University Press, 2001), pp. 251–65.
4 William Blake, 'The Garden of Love', E26.
5 Department of Education, *The Prevent duty: Departmental advice for schools and childcare providers* (London, June 2015), p. 4, note 4.
6 J. Shaw, *Octavia, Daughter of God: The Story of a Female Messiah and Her Followers* (London: Jonathan Cape, 2011).

7 G.E. Aylmer, 'Collective mentalities in mid seventeenth-century England: III. Varieties of radicalism', *Transactions of the Royal Historical Society* 5th ser., 38 (1988), pp. 1–25.

8 R. Radford Ruether, 'Feminist interpretation: a method of correlation', in Letty M. Russell (ed.), *Feminist Interpretation of Scripture* (Philadelphia, PA: Westminster Press, 1985), pp. 111–24; R. Radford Ruether, *Sexism and God-Talk* (Boston, MA: Beacon, 1983); D. Hampson, *Theology and Feminism* (Oxford: Blackwell, 1990), pp. 25–9; and D. Hampson and R. Radford Ruether, 'Is there a place for feminists in the Christian Church?', *New Blackfriars* 68 (1987), pp. 7–24.

9 *All Religions Are One*, Principle 5, E1.

10 Radford Ruether, *Sexism*, pp. 12–13.

11 Radford Ruether, 'Feminist interpretation', p. 117.

12 Ibid., p. 118.

13 *Pirke Aboth* 1:1.

14 Hampson and Radford Ruether, 'Is there a place', p. 15.

15 M. Kishlansky, *A Monarchy Transformed: Britain 1603–1714* (London: Penguin, 1996), p. 196.

16 Gerrard Winstanley, 'A declaration to the powers of England', in T.N. Corns, A. Hughes and D. Loewenstein (eds), *The Complete Works of Gerrard Winstanley*, 2 vols (Oxford: Oxford University Press, 2009), ii.11.

17 K. Wengst, *Pax Romana and the Peace of Jesus Christ* (London: SCM, 1987).

18 William Blake, *There Is No Natural Religion*, Conclusion, E3. Available at http://www.blakearchive.org/blake/indexworks.htm.

19 C. Rowland, 'The Temple in the New Testament', in J. Day (ed.), *Temple and Worship in Biblical Israel* (London: Continuum, 2005), pp. 469–83 and C. Rowland, 'Friends of Albion? The dangers of cathedrals', in S. Platten and C. Lewis (eds), *Flagships of the Spirit* (London: Darton, Longman and Todd, 1998), pp. 18–34.

Chapter 2: Heaven on Earth

1 G. Caird, *The Language and Imagery of the Bible* (London: Duckworth, 1980).

2 See J. Richard Middleton, *A New Heaven and a New Earth: Reclaiming Biblical Eschatology* (Grand Rapids, MN: Baker, 2014).

3 J.D.G. Dunn, *Jesus and the Spirit* (London: SCM, 1975).

4 D.E. Aune, *Prophecy in Early Christianity and the Ancient Mediterranean World* (Grand Rapids, MN: Eerdmans, 1983).

5 G. Scholem, *The Messianic Idea in Judaism: And Other Essays on Jewish Spirituality* (London: Allen and Unwin, 1971) and M. Idel, *Messianic Mystics* (New Haven, CN: Yale University Press, 1998; cf. J. Taubes, 'The price of messianism', in M. Saperstein (ed.), *Essential Papers on Messianic Movements and Personalities in Jewish History* (New York: New York University Press, 1992), pp. 551–8.

6 J. Weiss, *Jesus' Proclamation of the Kingdom of God* (London: SCM, 1971; first published 1892).

7 For example, Syriac Apocalypse of Baruch 25–30, 4 Ezra 5:20–8 and Rev. 6, 8–9, 16.

8 J. Jeremias, *The Eucharistic Words of Jesus* (London: SCM, 1966).

9 C.f. 1 Enoch 62:4; Syriac Apocalypse of Baruch 29:5.

10 Eusebius, *Ecclesiastical History* iii.28.

11 Papias, in Irenaeus, *Against the Heresies* v.33.3–4.

12 J. Ashton, *Understanding the Fourth Gospel* (New edn, Oxford: Oxford University Press, 2007).

13 C. Williams and C. Rowland, *John's Gospel and Intimations of Apocalyptic* (London: Bloomsbury, 2013); C.B. Kaiser, *Seeing the Lord's Glory: Kyriocentric Visions and the Dilemma of Early Christology* (Minneapolis: Fortress, 2014).

14 See also Ashton, *Understanding*, p. 329.

15 C. Rowland, *Blake and the Bible* (London and New Haven, CN: Yale University Press, 2010).

16 E. Käsemann, *On Being a Disciple of the Crucified Nazarene* (Grand Rapids, MI: Eerdmans, 2010), pp. 138–9.

17 G. Vermes, *Jesus the Jew* (London: Collins, 1973).

18 Flavius Josephus, e.g. *Antiquities* xx. 97–9, 167–72, 185–8; *Jewish War* vi. 281. See also R. Gray, *Prophetic Figures in Late Second Temple Jewish Palestine* (Oxford: Oxford University Press, 1993).

19 Flavius Josephus, *Jewish War* vi.300.

20 William Blake, *The Marriage of Heaven and Hell*, in David V. Erdman (ed.), *The Complete Poetry and Prose of William Blake* (Berkeley, CA: University of California Press, 1988), 23–4, p. 43, henceforth abbreviated as 'E', followed by the page number.

21 William Blake, *Annotations to Watson's 'Apology'*, 5; E614.

22 Friedrich Engels, 'The Peasant War in Germany', in *Marx and Engels on Religion* (Moscow: Progress, 1957), p. 91.

23 D. Allison, 'Acts 9:1–9, 22:6–11, 26:12–18: Paul and Ezekiel', *Journal of Biblical Literature* 135 (2016), pp. 824–5.

24 J.L. Martyn, *Galatians: A New Translation with Introduction and Commentary* (New York: Doubleday, 1997).

25 See also L. Welborn, *Paul's Summons to Messianic Life: Political Theology and the Coming Awakening* (New York: Columbia University Press, 2015).

26 S. Barton, 'Sanctification and oneness in 1 Corinthians with implications for the case of "mixed marriages" (1 Corinthians 7.12–16)', *New Testament Studies* (2017), pp. 63, 38–55.

27 E.P. Sanders, *Paul and Palestinian Judaism* (London: SCM, 1977) and E.P. Sanders, *Paul, the Law, and the Jewish People* (London: SCM, 1985b).

28 C. Rowland, *The New Interpreters' Bible, Vol. 12: Revelation* (Nashville, TN: Abingdon, 1998).

29 William Blake, *Annotations to Watson's 'Apology'*, E611.

30 See also A. Lincoln, *Paradise Now and Not Yet* (Cambridge: Cambridge University Press, 1981); H.W. Kuhn, *Enderwartung und gegenwärtiges Heil* (Göttingen: Vandenhoeck & Ruprecht, 1966).

31 Engels, 'The Book of Revelation', in *Marx and Engels on Religion* (Moscow: Progress, 1957), p.189.

32 B. Daley, *The Hope of the Early Church: A Handbook of Patristic Eschatology* (Cambridge: Cambridge University Press, 1991).

33 *Adversus Haereses* v.33.3–4.

34 E.P. Sanders, *Jesus and Judaism* (London: SCM, 1985a); Weiss, *Jesus' Proclamation*; A. Schweitzer, *The Quest of the Historical Jesus* (London: A & C Black, 1931a).

35 J.D. Crossan, *The Historical Jesus: The Life of a Mediterranean Jewish Peasant* (San Francisco, CA: Harper, 1992); J.D. Crossan, *The Birth of Christianity: Discovering What Happened in the Years Immediately After the Death of Jesus* (Edinburgh: T&T Clark, 1999); B. Mack, *A Myth of Innocence: Mark and Christian Origins* (Philadelphia: Fortress Press, 1988).

36 A. Schweitzer, *The Mysticism of Paul the Apostle* (London: A & C Black, 1931b); M. Werner, *The Formation of Christian Dogma: An Historical Study of Its Problem* (London: Black, 1957).

37 W.D. Davies, 'From Schweitzer to Scholem: reflections on Sabbatai Sevi', in M. Saperstein (ed.), *Essential Papers on Messianic Movements and Personalities in Jewish History* (New York and London: New York University Press, 1992), pp. 335–76.

38 Ibid., p. 357.

Part 2: Kairos: *The Unique Moment and Apocalyptic Discernment*

1 J. Rose, *The Woman Who Claimed to Be Christ': The Millennial Belief of Mary Ann Girling and Her Disciples 1860–1886*, DPhil dissertation, University of Oxford, 2007.

Chapter 3: Human Actors in the Divine Drama

1 Flavius Josephus, *Jewish War* vi. 301–9; *Jewish Antiquities* xx. 97–9; 164–72 cf. Acts 21:38; xx. 185ff; *Antiquities* xviii. 63–4.
2 K. Mannheim, *Ideology and Utopia: An Introduction to the Sociology of Knowledge* (London: Routledge and Kegan Paul, 1936; repr. 1960), pp. 192–202.
3 See also B. McGinn, *Apocalyptic Spirituality* (London: SPCK, 1980), p. 151.
4 P. Matheson, *The Imaginative World of the Reformation* (Edinburgh: T&T Clark, 2000), pp. 19, 9.
5 P. Matheson, *The Collected Works of Thomas Müntzer* (Edinburgh: T&T Clark, 1988) and Matheson, *The Imaginative World*.
6 G.H. Williams, *The Radical Reformation* (Philadelphia: Westminster Press, 1962); G. Baylor, *The Radical Reformation* (Cambridge: Cambridge University Press, 1991).
7 G. Rupp, *Patterns of Reformation* (London: Epworth, 1969), p. 328.
8 Matheson, *Collected Works*, p. 358.
9 Ibid., pp. 359–60.
10 Ibid., pp. 226–52.
11 Matheson, *The Imaginative World*, p. 134.
12 Matheson, *Collected Works*, p. 203; Rupp, *Patterns*, p. 293.
13 'Letter to Frederick the Wise', in Matheson, *Collected Works*, p. 111.
14 Rupp, *Patterns*, pp. 267–75.
15 Matheson, *Collected Works*, p. 199.
16 Rupp, *Patterns*, pp. 200–1.
17 Matheson, *Collected Works*, pp. 226–52.
18 B.S. Capp, *The Fifth Monarchy Men* (London: Faber, 1972).
19 Matheson, *Collected Works*, p. 246.
20 *Recantation* 1, in C. Bauman, *The Spiritual Legacy of Hans Denck: Interpretation and Translation of Key Texts* (Leiden: Brill, 1991), p. 251.
21 N. Cohn, *The Pursuit of the Millennium* (London: Paladin, 1957); Williams, *The Radical*; J. Stayer, *Anabaptists and the Sword* (Lawrence, KN: Coronado, 1972); J. Stayer, *The German Peasants' War and Anabaptist Community of Goods* (Montreal: McGill-Queen's University Press, 1991); K. Deppermann, *Melchior Hoffmann* (Edinburgh: T&T Clark, 1987).
22 Flavius Josephus, *Jewish War* vi.285.
23 J.H. Yoder, *The Politics of Jesus: Vicit Agnus Noster* (Grand Rapids, MI: Eerdmans, 1972).

24 Friedrich Engels, 'The Peasant War in Germany', in *Marx and Engels on Religion* (Moscow: Progress, 1957).
25 *Marx and Engels on Religion*, p. 91.
26 J. Taubes, *Occidental Eschatology* (Stanford, CA: Stanford University Press, 2009), pp. 10–11, quoted in full in Chapter 8, 'Jacob Taubes and Walter Benjamin'.
27 M. Niblett, *Prophecy and the Politics of Salvation in Late Georgian England: The Theology and Apocalyptic Vision of Joanna Southcott* (London: I.B.Tauris, 2015).
28 D. Madden, *The Paddington Prophet: Richard Brothers's Journey to Jerusalem* (Manchester: Manchester University Press, 2010); J. Shaw, *Octavia, Daughter of God: The Story of a Female Messiah and Her Followers* (London: Jonathan Cape, 2011); P. Lockley, *Visionary Religion and Radicalism in Early Industrial England: From Southcott to Socialism* (Oxford: Oxford University Press, 2013); J. Shaw and P. Lockley, *The History of a Modern Millennial Movement: The Southcottians* (London: I.B.Tauris, 2017).
29 Niblett, *Prophecy*, pp. 128–60.
30 Shaw, *Octavia*.

Chapter 4: Subversive Apocalypse

1 J.J. Collins, B. McGinn and S. Stein (eds), *The Encyclopedia of Apocalypticism*, 3 vols (New York: Continuum, 2000); M. Stone, *Ancient Judaism: New Visions and Views* (Grand Rapids, MI: Eerdmans, 2011).
2 M. Hengel, *Judaism and Hellenism: Studies in Their Encounter in Palestine During the Early Hellenistic Period* (London: SCM, 1974).
3 F. Flannery-Dailey, *Dreamers, Scribes, and Priests: Jewish Dreams in the Hellenistic and Roman Eras* (Leiden: Brill, 2004); Stone, *Ancient Judaism*.
4 Also cf. Stone, *Ancient Judaism*, pp. 105–20.
5 C. Rowland, 'Blake, Enoch, and Emerging Biblical Criticism', in J. Baden, H. Najman, and E. Tigchelaar (eds), *Sibyls, Scriptures, and Scrolls* (Leiden: Brill, 2017), pp. 1145–65.
6 C. Rowland, *The Open Heaven: A Study of Apocalyptic in Judaism and Early Christianity* (London: SPCK, 1982); J.J. Collins, *The Apocalyptic Imagination: An Introduction to Jewish Apocalyptic Literature*, 2nd edn (Grand Rapids, MI: Eerdmans 1998); Flannery-Dailey, *Dreamers*; Stone, *Ancient Judaism*.
7 C. Trevett, *Montanism: Gender, Authority and the New Prophecy* (Cambridge: Cambridge University Press, 1996), pp. 95–104; see also Eusebius, *Ecclesiastical History* v.18.1.

8 S.T. Coleridge, *Aids to Reflection*, ed. John Beer (London: Routledge; Princeton, NJ: Princeton University Press, 1993).

9 D. Hall, *The Antinomian Controversy, 1636–1638: A Documentary History* (Middletown, CN: Wesleyan University Press, 1968), pp. 337, 341; 'Antinomianism', in *Encyclopedia of the Bible and Its Reception, 2 Anim-Atheism* (Berlin: de Gruyter, 2009), p. 245; M. Ditmore, 'A prophetess in her own country: an exegesis of Anne Hutchinson's "Immediate Revelation"', *The William and Mary Quarterly* 57 (2000), pp. 349–92, and on the general background in English Calvinism, D. Wallace, *Shapers of English Calvinism, 1660–1714: Variety, Persistence, and Transformation* (New York and Oxford: Oxford University Press, 2011).

10 *The Illuminated Books of William Blake*, Vol. 5: *Milton, A Poem*, ed. Robert N. Essick and Joseph Viscomi (Princeton, NJ: Princeton University Press, 1995), Preface, p. 95.

11 M. Winship, *The Times and Trials of Anne Hutchinson: Puritans Divided* (Lawrence, KN: University of Kansas Press, 2005), pp. 111–12.

12 Ditmore, 'A prophetess', pp. 386–8.

13 Gerrard Winstanley, 'Truth lifting his head', in T.N. Corns, A. Hughes and D. Loewenstein (eds), *The Complete Works of Gerrard Winstanley*, 2 vols (Oxford: Oxford University Press, 2009), i.410, henceforth abbreviated as 'CHL', followed by the volume and page number.

14 Gerrard Winstanley, 'A declaration to the powers of England', CHL ii. 11.

15 William Blake, *The Marriage of Heaven and Hell*, in David V. Erdman (ed.), *The Complete Poetry and Prose of William Blake* (Berkeley, CA: University of California Press, 1988), 23–4, p. 43.

16 See also Z. Bennett and C. Rowland, *In a Glass Darkly: The Bible, Reflection and Everyday Life* (London: SCM, 2016).

17 B. McGinn, *The Calabrian Abbot: Joachim of Fiore in the History of Western Thought* (New York: Macmillan, 1985), p. 21. Also, *Expositio* 39, in B. McGinn, *Visions of the End: Apocalyptic Traditions in the Middle Ages* (New York, 1998: Columbia University Press) and B. McGinn, *Apocalyptic Spirituality* (London: SPCK, 1980), p. 99; also B. McGinn, 'The Concordist imagination: a theme in the history of eschatology', in J. Ashton (eds), *Revealed Wisdom: Studies in Apocalyptic in Honour of Christopher Rowland* (Leiden: Brill, 2014), pp. 217–31 and B. McGinn, 'Image as insight in Joachim of Fiore's Figurae', in G. de Nie and T. Noble (eds), *Envisioning Experience in Late Antiquity and the Middle Ages: Dynamic Patterns in Texts and Images* (London: Routledge, 2016), pp. 93–118.

18 *Ten Stringed Psaltery* 10 in B. McGinn, *Apocalyptic Spirituality* (London: SPCK, 1980), pp. 99–100; McGinn, *Visions*, p. 130.
19 McGinn, *The Calabrian Abbot*, p. 21.
20 Habakkuk Commentary, 1QpHab 7.
21 M. Niblett, *Prophecy and the Politics of Salvation in Late Georgian England: The Theology and Apocalyptic Vision of Joanna Southcott* (London: I.B.Tauris, 2015).
22 Niblett, *Prophecy*, p. 95.
23 M. Reeves, *The Influence of Prophecy in the Later Middle Ages* (Oxford: Clarendon Press, 1969).
24 P. Fredriksen, 'Tyconius and Augustine on the Apocalypse', in R. Emmerson and B. McGinn (eds), *The Apocalypse in the Middle Ages* (Ithaca, NY: Cornell University Press, 1992), pp. 20–37. Augustine, *City of God* xx.9.
25 W. Gould and M. Reeves, *Joachim of Fiore and the Myth of the Eternal Evangel in the Nineteenth and Twentieth Centuries* (Oxford: Oxford University Press, 2001).
26 Translated in McGinn, *Apocalyptic*, pp. 136–7; L. Tondelli, M. Reeves and B. Hirsch-Reich, *Il libro delle figure dell'Abate Gioachino da Fiore*, 2 vols (Turin: SEI, 1953), plate 14; B. McGinn, 'Apocalypticism in Western history and culture', *Encyclopedia of Apocalypticism*, 3 vols (New York, 2000).
27 *Dispositio novi ordinis pertinens ad tercium status*, Corpus Christi College, Oxford, late twelfth century.
28 Tondelli, Reeves and Hirsch-Reich, *Il libro*, plate 31 and M. Reeves and B. Hirsch-Reich, *The Figurae of Joachim of Fiore* (Oxford: Clarendon Press, 1972), pp. 232–48.
29 D. Burr, *Olivi's Peaceable Kingdom: A Reading of the Apocalypse Commentary* (Philadelphia: University of Pennsylvania Press, 1993).
30 P. Garnsey, 'Peter Olivi on the Community of the First Christians in Jerusalem', in Z. Bennett and D. Gowler (eds), *Radical Christian Voices and Practice: Essays in Honour of Christopher Rowland* (Oxford: Oxford University Press, 2012), pp. 35–50.
31 Burr, *Olivi's Peaceable Kingdom*, p. 176.
32 Ibid.
33 Potestà in J.J. Collins, B. McGinn and S. Stein (eds), *The Encyclopedia of Apocalypticism*, 3 vols (New York: Continuum, 2000), ii, p. 110.
34 N. Cohn, *The Pursuit of the Millennium* (London: Paladin, 1957).
35 A.L. Morton, *The Everlasting Gospel: A Study in the Sources of William Blake* (London: Lawrence & Wishart, 1958).
36 L. Martines, *Fire in the City: Savonarola and the Struggle for the Soul of Renaissance Florence* (Oxford: Oxford University Press, 2006);

D. Weinstein, *Savonarola and Florence: Prophecy and Patriotism in the Renaissance* (Princeton: Princeton University Press, 1970).

37 McGinn, *Apocalyptic*, pp. 191, 198–200.

38 D. Weinstein, *Savonarola and Florence: Prophecy and Patriotism in the Renaissance* (Princeton, NJ: Princeton University Press, 1970), p. 336.

39 C. Rowland, 'Imagining the Apocalypse', *New Testament Studies* 51 (2005), pp. 303–27.

40 Sandro Botticelli, 'Ode on the Morning of Christ's Nativity' xviii.168: 'The Old Dragon under ground, in straiter limits bound'.

41 A. Dancer, *William Stringfellow in Anglo-American Perspective* (Aldershot: Ashgate, 2005).

42 W. Stringfellow, *An Ethic for Christians and Other Aliens in a Strange Land* (Waco, TX: Word Books, 1973), p. 13.

43 Ibid., p. 34.

44 Ibid., pp. 21, 152.

45 W. Stringfellow, *Conscience and Obedience: the Politics of Romans 13 and Revelation 13 in Light of the Second Coming* (Waco, TX: Word, 1977), p. 24.

46 Stringfellow, *Ethic*, p. 55.

47 M. Idel, *Messianic Mystics* (New Haven: Yale University Press, 1998); G. Scholem, *Sabbatai Sevi: The Mystical Messiah, 1626–1676* (Littman Library of Jewish Civilization, London: Routledge & Kegan Paul, 1973) and W.D. Davies, 'From Schweitzer to Scholem: reflections on Sabbatai Sevi', in *Jewish and Pauline Studies* (London: SPCK, 1984). (Repr. in M. Saperstein (ed.), *Essential Papers on Messianic Movements and Personalities in Jewish History* [New York and London: New York University Press, 1992], pp. 335–76.)

Part 3: Contrasting Radical Prophets: Gerrard Winstanley and William Blake

1 Cf. J. Welby, *Dethroning Mammon: Making Money Serve Grace: The Archbishop of Canterbury's Lent Book 2017* (London: Bloomsbury Continuum, 2016), pp. 132 and 161 note 1.

2 T.N. Corns, A. Hughes and D. Loewenstein (eds), *The Complete Works of Gerrard Winstanley*, 2 vols (Oxford: Oxford University Press, 2009), pp. 65–6.

Chapter 5: Gerrard Winstanley

1 Gerrard Winstanley, *A New-Yeers Gift*, in T.N. Corns, A. Hughes and D. Loewenstein (eds), *The Complete Works of Gerrard Winstanley*, 2 vols (Oxford: Oxford University Press, 2009), ii.120, henceforth abbreviated as 'CHL', followed by the volume and page number.

2 M. Kishlansky, *A Monarchy Transformed: Britain 1603–1714* (London: Penguin, 1996), p. 196.

3 Gerrard Winstanley, *New Law of Righteousnes*, CHL i.493, 506.

4 Gerrard Winstanley, *True Levellers Standard or Declaration to the Powers of England*, CHL ii.13–15.

5 C. Hill, *The World Turned Upside Down* (London: Penguin, 1972); A. Bradstock, *Radical Religion in Cromwell's England: A Concise History from the English Civil War to the End of the Commonwealth* (London: I.B.Tauris, 2011); C. Rowland, '*To see the great deceit which in the world doth lie*', *Christopher Hill's* 'The World Turned Upside Down', *Caught Reading Again: Scholars and Their Books* (London: SCM, 2009), pp. 54–67.

6 Abiezer Coppe, *A Fiery Flying Roll: A Word from the Lord to All the Great Ones of the Earth* (London, 1649; University of Exeter: Rota 1973); Hill, *The World*, pp. 184–230; S. Makdisi, *William Blake and the Impossible History of the 1790s* (Chicago: University of Chicago Press, 2003), pp. 291–3; 309.

7 C. Hawes, *Mania and Literary Style: The Rhetoric of Enthusiasm from the Ranters to Christopher Smart* (Cambridge: Cambridge University Press, 1996); on Coppe, pp. 77–100.

8 Abiezer Coppe, *Some Sweet Sips, of some Spirituall Wine* (1649), C. Hawes, *Mania and Literary Style*, p. 79, and N. Smith, A *Collection of Ranter Writings* (London: Junction Books, 1982), p. 71. Cf. Winstanley's *A New-Yeers Gift*, CHL ii.131, where the 'Son of universal Love' … makes him, who all the dark time past was a Chaos of confusion, lying under Types, Shadows, Ceremonies, Forms, Customes, Ordinances, and heaps of waste words, under which the Spirit of Truth lay buried, now to enlighten, to worship in Spirit and Truth, and to bring forth fruit of Righteousness in action'.

9 Coppe, *Some Sweet Sips*, 1649, quoted in Hawes, *Mania and Literary Style*, p. 60; N. Smith, *Perfection Proclaimed: Language and Literature in English Radical Religion, 1640–1660* (Oxford: Clarendon Press, 1989).

10 Coppe, *A Fiery Flying Roll*, p. 4.

11 Abiezer Coppe, *A Second Fiery Flying Roule to All the Inhabitants of the earth; specially to the rich ones*, chap. 4 (1649–50).
12 Ibid., chap. 2.
13 P. Mack, *Visionary Women: Ecstatic Prophecy in Seventeenth Century England* (Berkeley, CA: University of California Press, 1992); H. Hinds, *God's Englishwomen: Seventeenth-Century Radical Sectarian Writing and Feminist Criticism* (Manchester: Manchester University Press, 1996) and H. Hinds, *Anna Trapnel: The Cry of a Stone* (Tempe: Arizona University Press, 2000).
14 Mack, *Visionary Women*, p. 119.
15 Also cf. Mack, *Visionary Women*, p. 102.
16 Hinds, *Anna Trapnel*.
17 Ibid., p. 54.
18 Ibid., p. 72.
19 Anna Trapnel, *Voice of the King of Saints*, pp. 37, 54, quoted in E. Hobby, *Virtue of Necessity: English Women's Writing* 1649–88 (Ann Arbor: University of Michigan Press, 1988), p. 33.
20 K. Brownlow, *Winstanley: Warts and All* (London: UKA, 2009).
21 Gerrard Winstanley, *A Watch-Word to the City of London*, CHL ii.80 cf. *A Declaration to the Powers of England*, CHL ii.10–11.
22 Winstanley, *New Law*, CHL i.484.
23 Clement of Alexandria, *Stromata* translation, in J. Baillie, J. McNeill, H. Van Dusen, *The Library of Christian Classics: Volume II, Alexandrian Christianity* (London: SCM Press, 2006), iii.7.
24 Winstanley, *New Law*, CHL i.567.
25 Gerrard Winstanley, *A Watch-Word*, CHL ii.80.
26 Gerrard Winstanley, *Truth Lifting up his Head*, CHL i.410.
27 Ibid., i.409.
28 Ibid., i.435.
29 C. Bauman, *The Spiritual Legacy of Hans Denck: Interpretation and Translation of Key Texts* (Leiden: Brill, 1991); C. Rowland, *Blake and the Bible* (London and New Haven, CN: Yale University Press, 2010), pp. 157–80; S. Apetrei, *Women, Feminism and Religion in Early Enlightenment England* (Cambridge: Cambridge University Press, 2010).
30 J. Holstun, *Ehud's Dagger: Class Struggle in the English Revolution* (London: Verso, 2002), pp. 41–111; C. Hill, *The English Bible and the Seventeenth-Century Revolution* (Harmondsworth: Penguin, 1993), pp. 447–52; A. Bradstock and C. Rowland, *Radical Christian Writings: A Reader* (Oxford: Blackwell, 2002); C. Rowland and M. Corner, *Liberating Exegesis: The Challenge of Liberation Theology to Biblical Studies* (London: SPCK, 1990).

31 Winstanley, *New Law*, CHL i.506; C. Hill, *Winstanley: The Law of Freedom and Other Writings* (Cambridge: Cambridge University Press, 1973), pp. 86–7.
32 Rowland, *Blake*, pp. 120–1.
33 Winstanley, *New Law*, CHL i.486, 504–6, 517, 527, cf. *True Levellers Standard*, CHL ii.14.
34 Winstanley, *New Law*, CHL i.502; *Truth Lifting up his Head*, CHL i.435.
35 Gerrard Winstanley, *Saints Paradice* 1, CHL i.322.
36 Ibid., i.356–63.
37 Winstanley, *New Law*, CHL i.550.
38 D. Wallace, *Shapers of English Calvinism, 1660–1714: Variety, Persistence, and Transformation* (New York and Oxford: Oxford University Press, 2011), p. 64; V. de Sola Pinto, *Peter Sterry: Platonist and Puritan* (Cambridge: Cambridge University Press, 1934).
39 Winstanley, *New Law*, CHL i.547.
40 Gerrard Winstanley, *Fire in the Bush*, CHL ii.200.
41 Ibid.
42 Ibid., ii.200–1.
43 Winstanley, *New Law*, CHL i.548.
44 Hill, *The English Bible*, pp. 223–4 and note the similar presupposition in early Anabaptism, see C.A. Snyder, *Biblical Concordance of the Swiss Brethren, 1540* (Kitchener, Ontario: Pandora, 2001) and C.A. Snyder, *Following in the Footsteps of Christ: the Anabaptist Tradition* (London: Darton, Longman and Todd, 2004), pp. 116–22.
45 T.L. Underwood, *Primitivism, Radicalism, and the Lamb's War: The Baptist–Quaker Conflict in Seventeenth-Century England* (Oxford: Clarendon Press, 1997), pp. 20–33.
46 Winstanley, *New Law*, CHL i.537.
47 Ibid., i.508; text citations in original.
48 See also Winstanley, *New-Years Gift*, CHL ii.144.
49 Ibid., ii.145.
50 Winstanley, *New Law*, CHL i.557, cf. *Saints Paradice*, 'I my self have known nothing but what I received by tradition from the mouth & pen of others', CHL i.313; Rowland, *Blake*, pp. 5–14.
51 Winstanley, *New-Yeers Gift*, CHL ii.141.
52 Winstanley, *Fire*, CHL ii.192.
53 Ibid., ii.182.
54 Winstanley, *New Law*, CHL i.484.
55 Ibid., i.493.
56 Ibid., i.506–7.
57 Ibid., i.550.

58 Ibid., i.506.
59 Winstanley, *Saints*, CHL i.357.
60 Winstanley, *Truth*, CHL i.418–19.
61 Winstanley, *New Law*, CHL i.485.
62 Winstanley, 'A Declaration', CHL ii.10.
63 Hill, *The English Bible*, pp. 447–51; C. Rowland, 'Gerrard Winstanley: man for all seasons', *Prose Studies: History, Theory, Criticism* 36 (2014), pp. 77–89.
64 E. Graham, *Transforming Practice: Pastoral Theology in an Age of Uncertainty* (London: Mowbray, 1996).
65 Gerrard Winstanley, 'Action is the life of all', CHL ii.80, cf. CHL i.508, 516; J. Gurney, *Gerrard Winstanley: The Digger's Life and Legacy* (London: Pluto, 2013), p. 43.
66 Gurney, *Gerrard Winstanley*, p. 21.
67 Winstanley, *New Law*, CHL i.562.
68 Ibid., CHL i.508, 528.
69 J. Burdick, *Looking for God in Brazil: The Progressive Catholic Church in Urban Brazil's Religious Arena* (Berkeley, CA and London: University of California Press, 1993) and J. Burdick, *Legacies of Liberation: The Progressive Catholic Church in Brazil at the Start of a New Millennium* (Aldershot: Ashgate, 2004); and on the impact of Winstanley on The Land Is Ours movement in the UK see Gurney, *Gerrard Winstanley*, pp. 111 and 113; and A. Bradstock, *Radical Religion in Cromwell's England: A Concise History from the English Civil War to the End of the Commonwealth* (London: I.B.Tauris, 2011), pp. xi, 161.
70 Winstanley, *New-Yeers*, CHL ii.149.
71 Gurney, *Gerrard Winstanley*, pp. 109–10.
72 C. Hill, *The Experience of Defeat: Milton and Some Contemporaries* (London: Bookmarks, 1994).
73 D. MacCulloch, *Silence: A Christian History* (London: Allen Lane, 2013); C.W. Marsh, *The Family of Love in English Society, 1550–1630* (Cambridge: Cambridge University Press, 2005).
74 J. Scott, *Domination and the Arts of Resistance: Hidden Transcripts* (New Haven, CN: Yale University Press, 1990).
75 P. Hanson, *The Dawn of Apocalyptic: The Historical and Sociological Roots of Jewish Apocalyptic Eschatology*, rev. edn (Philadelphia: Fortress, 1979).
76 Gerrard Winstanley, *The Law of Freedom in a Platform*, CHL ii.378–9.

Chapter 6: 'From impulse not from rules'

1 M. Ferber, *The Social Vision of William Blake* (Princeton, NJ: Princeton University Press, 1985), p. 70.
2 William Blake, *The Marriage of Heaven and Hell*, in David V. Erdman (ed.), *The Complete Poetry and Prose of William Blake* (Berkeley, CA: University of California Press, 1988), 5, henceforth abbreviated as 'E', followed by the page number.
3 H. Bloom, *The Anxiety of Influence*, 2nd edn (New York and Oxford: Oxford University Press, 1997), p. 5.
4 Blake, *The Marriage*, 22, E43.
5 Ibid., 5, E35.
6 Ibid., 23–4, E43.
7 William Blake, *The Everlasting Gospel*, E518; cf. Luke 2:49.
8 Ibid., E523.
9 William Blake, 'London', E27.
10 William Blake, Preface to *Milton, A Poem*, E95.
11 C. Myers, *Binding the Strong Man: A Political Reading of Mark's Story of Jesus* (20th anniversary edn, Maryknoll, NY: Orbis, 2008).
12 Blake, *Everlasting Gospel*, E524.
13 J. Mee, *Dangerous Enthusiasm: William Blake and the Culture of Radicalism in the 1790s* (Oxford: Clarendon Press, 1992), p. 83.
14 For a comparison of Winstanley and Muentzer, see A. Bradstock, *Faith in the Revolution: The Political Theologies of Müntzer and Winstanley* (London: SPCK, 1997).
15 P. Freire, *Pedagogy of the Oppressed* (London: Penguin, 1972).
16 William Blake, *Public Address*, E580.
17 Ibid.
18 Ibid., E520.
19 To paraphrase Blake's own words from *The Marriage of Heaven and Hell*, 14, E39.
20 Cf. L. Damrosch, Jr., *Symbol and Truth in Blake's Myth* (Princeton, NJ: Princeton University Press, 1980), p. 118.
21 William Blake, *Jerusalem*, 57:19, E207.
22 John Milton, *Paradise Lost* vii.224–31.
23 *The Illuminated Books of William Blake*, Vol. 4: *The Continental Prophecies*, ed. D.W. Dörrbecker (Princeton, NJ: Princeton University Press, 1995), p. 169.
24 Blake, *The Marriage* 4; E34; 6; E35.
25 William Blake, *Annotations to Watson's 'Apology'*, E617.

26 S. Juster, *Doomsayers: Anglo-American Prophecy in the Age of Revolution* (Philadelphia: University of Pennsylvania Press, 2003), p. 4.
27 Blake, *Annotations*, E617; cf. *The Marriage of Heaven and Hell*, 12, E38, 'the voice of honest indignation is the voice of God'.
28 Blake, *The Marriage* 14, E39.
29 William Blake, *The Four Zoas*, Night 8:115; E385.
30 Blake, *The Marriage* 3, E34, Copy F, Pierpont Morgan Library, 1794.
31 *The Illuminated Books of William Blake*, Vol 3: *The Early Illuminated Books*, ed. Morris Eaves, Robert N. Essick and Joseph Viscomi (Princeton, NJ: Princeton University Press, 1993), p. 209.
32 Blake, *The Marriage* 3, E34.
33 D. Allison, 'Acts 9:1–9, 22:6–11, 26:12–18: Paul and Ezekiel', *Journal of Biblical Literature* 135 (2016), pp. 807–26, noting the similarities between Acts 26:13–17 and Ezekiel 1–2.
34 William Blake, *All Religions are One*, E1.
35 See also ibid.
36 J. Winterson, *Oranges Are Not the Only Fruit* (London: Pandora, 1985), p. 161.
37 William Blake, *America a Prophecy* 8 Copy M, 6 in Erdman's edition, E53.
38 Ibid., 2 in Erdman's edition, E52.
39 William Blake, *Four Zoas* ix.850–5, E407.
40 Blake, *Jerusalem* 93 and 94, E253–4; S. Sklar, *Blake's Jerusalem as Visionary Theatre: Entering the Divine Body* (Oxford: Oxford University Press, 2011), pp. 240–50.
41 Blake, *Jerusalem* 96.
42 Blake, *Jerusalem* 96:16; E255; G.A. Rosso, *The Religion of Empire: Political Theology in Blake's Prophetic Symbolism* (Columbus: Ohio State University Press, 2016).
43 Blake, *Jerusalem* 91:50, E252; Sklar, *Blake's Jerusalem*, pp. 57–8.
44 Blake, *Jerusalem* 96:16, 21, 28, E255–6.
45 Blake, *The Marriage* 11, E39.
46 J. Ashton, *The Gospel of John and Christian Origins* (Minneapolis, MN: Fortress, 2014), pp. 145–52.
47 William Blake, *First Book of Urizen* 2:2; E70; 4:40; E72.
48 Blake, *Europe* 12 Copy A, Erdman's edition 11:4–5; E64.
49 Blake, *The Marriage* 11, E38.
50 William Blake, *Laocoön*, E273.
51 Blake, Preface to *Milton*, E95.
52 John Milton, *Reason of Church Government*, Preface to Book II.
53 William Blake, *Annotations to Joshua Reynolds' 'Discourse III'*, E646.

54 Blake, 'The Garden of Love', E26.
55 Blake, *Jerusalem* 61:21–4, E212.
56 Ibid., 57:10, E207.
57 Ibid., 96:28, E256.
58 Blake, *Annotations*, E618.
59 C. Rowland, *Blake and the Bible* (London and New Haven, CN: Yale University Press, 2010), pp. 58–62.
60 Quoted in G.E. Bentley, *The Stranger from Paradise: A Biography of William Blake* (New Haven, CN: Yale University Press, 2001), p. 412.
61 Blake, *Jerusalem* 55:47–66, E205.
62 William Blake, *Songs of Innocence and of Experience*, E7.
63 Blake, *The Marriage*, 3, E34.
64 Blake, 'Auguries of Innocence', E491.
65 As he does in *The Marriage of Heaven and Hell* 16, E40; R.D. Williams, 'The human form divine: radicalism and orthodoxy in William Blake', in Z. Bennett and D.B. Gowler (eds), *Radical Christian Voices and Practice* (Oxford: Oxford University Press, 2012), pp. 151–64.
66 Blake, *Jerusalem* 10:7–16, E152–3.
67 Blake, *The Marriage* 27, E45.
68 Blake, 'The Little Vagabond', E26.
69 Blake, *Laocoön*, E274.
70 M.J. Carruthers, *The Craft of Thought: Meditation, Rhetoric and the Making of Images 400–1200*, Cambridge Studies in Medieval Literature 34 (Cambridge: Cambridge University Press, 1998; repr. Cambridge: Cambridge University Press, 2003).
71 Ibid., p. 304.
72 J. Hagstrum, 'Blake and the sister – arts tradition', in D. Erdman and J. Grant, *Blake's Visionary Forms Dramatic* (Princeton: Princeton University Press, 1970), pp. 85, 88–9.
73 Rowland, *Blake*, p. 241; M. Ferber, 'Coleridge's "anacalyptic" Blake: an exegesis', *Modern Philology* 76 (1978), pp. 189–93.
74 Blake, *Everlasting Gospel*, E519.
75 R. Morgan, '*Sachkritik* in reception history', *JSNT* 33.2 (2010), pp. 175–90.
76 My italics; K. Barth, *The Epistle to the Romans* (Oxford: Clarendon Press, 1933), pp. 6–8.
77 C. Mesters, 'The use of the Bible in Christian Communities of the Common People', in Norman Gottwald (ed.), *The Bible and Liberation* (Maryknoll, NY: Orbis, 1993), p. 122 and C. Mesters, *Defenseless Flower* (London: Catholic Institute for International Relations, 1989), quoted in

full in Chapter 7, 'Experiencing biblical study in the *comunidades eclesais de base* (CEBs)'.

78 Blake, *Songs of Experience*, E19.
79 Blake, *The Marriage* 14, E39.
80 1545, H. McNeil, *Emily Dickinson* (London: Virago, 1986), p. xxi.
81 William Blake, *Descriptive Catalogue* 64, E550.
82 William Blake, *The Four Zoas*, Night 9, 139:10; E407.
83 T. Altizer, *The Radical Christian Vision of William Blake* (Ann Arbor: Michigan State University Press, 1967); also L. Freedman, 'Tom Altizer and William Blake: the Apocalypse of Belief', *Literature and Theology* 25 (2011), pp. 20–31.
84 P. Hart, *The Literary Essays of Thomas Merton* (New York: New Directions, 1981), p. 11.
85 Ibid., p. 8.
86 Ibid., p. 6, cf. *The Marriage of Heaven and Hell* 14, E39.
87 Hart, *The Literary*, pp. 5–6; T. Merton, 'Blake and the New Theology', *Sewanee Review* 76 (1968), pp. 675–6.

Part 4: Christian Radicalism in Modernity: An Example and a Neglected Perspective

1 E. Käsemann, *On Being a Disciple of the Crucified Nazarene* (Grand Rapids, MI: Eerdmans, 2010), p. 138.

Chapter 7: Liberation Theology

1 National Gallery of Ireland, Dublin, available at http://www.nationalgallery.ie/en/Collection/Irelands_Favourite_Painting/Vermeer_Final/Final_Velazquez.aspx. Further Z. Bennett and C. Rowland, *In a Glass Darkly: The Bible, Reflection and Everyday Life* (London: SCM, 2016), pp. 103, 201.
2 National Gallery, London, available at https://www.nationalgallery.org.uk/paintings/diego-velazquez-christ-in-the-house-of-martha-and-mary; J. Boyd and P. Esler, *Visuality and Biblical Text: Interpreting Velázquez' 'Christ with Martha and Mary' as a Test Case* (Florence: Olschki, 2004).
3 G. Gutiérrez, *Las Casas: In Search of the Poor of Jesus Christ* (Maryknoll, NY: Orbis, 1993).

4 M. de Barros Souza, *A Biblia e a Luta pela Terra* (Petropolis: Commissão Pastoral da Terra, 1983).
5 G. Gutiérrez, *The Power of the Poor in History* (London: SCM, 1983), p. 57.
6 G. Gutiérrez, *The Truth Shall Make You Free: Confrontations* (Maryknoll, NY: Orbis, 1990), p. 3.
7 Gerrard Winstanley, *Fire in the Bush*, in T.N. Corns, A. Hughes and D. Loewenstein (eds), *The Complete Works of Gerrard Winstanley*, 2 vols (Oxford: Oxford University Press, 2009), ii.200, henceforth abbreviated as 'CHL', followed by the volume and page number.
8 J.L. Segundo, *Jesus of Nazareth Yesterday and Today*, Vol. 2: *The Historical Jesus of the Synoptic Gospels* (London: Sheed and Ward, 1985), p. 62.
9 J. Moltmann, *The Church in the Power of the Spirit: A Contribution to Messianic Ecclesiology* (London: SCM Press, 1977), p. 127.
10 J. Sobrino, *The True Church and the Church of the Poor* (London: SCM, 1984), pp. 93, 95.
11 Boff in I. Ellacuría and J. Sobrino, *Mysterium Liberationis: Fundamental Concepts of Liberation Theology* (Maryknoll, NY: Orbis, 1993), pp. 57–84; E. Graham, *Transforming Practice: Pastoral Theology in an Age of Uncertainty* (London: Mowbray, 1996).
12 Cf. John 3:3; D. Rensberger, *Overcoming the World: Politics and Community in the Gospel of John* (London: SPCK, 1989).
13 J.P. Miranda, *Marx and the Bible* (London: SCM, 1977), pp. 47–50.
14 L. Boff, *Ecclesiogenesis: The Base Communities Reinvent the Church* (London: Collins, 1986), p. 63 and L. Boff, *Church, Charism and Power* (London: SCM, 1985).
15 Examples of material produced by the Archdiocese of São Paulo may be found in C. Rowland and M. Corner, *Liberating Exegesis: The Challenge of Liberation Theology to Biblical Studies* (London: SPCK, 1990), pp. 7–34 and see Chapter 7, '*Parábolas de Hoje*'.
16 For an earlier version of this section see C. Rowland, 'Liberationist reading: popular interpretation of the Bible in Brazil', in K. Dell and P. Joyce (eds), *Biblical Interpretation and Method: Essays in Honour of John Barton* (Oxford: Oxford University Press, 2013), pp. 133–48.
17 C. Mesters, 'The use of the Bible in Christian Communities of the Common People', in Norman Gottwald (ed.), *The Bible and Liberation* (Maryknoll, NY: Orbis, 2nd rev. edn, 1993), pp. 3–16; C. Mesters, *Defenseless Flower* (London: Catholic Institute for International Relations, 1989), pp. 8–9.
18 Gutiérrez, *The Truth*, p. 3.

19 Q. Hoare and G. Smith (eds), *Selections from the Prison Notebooks of Antonio Gramsci* (London: Lawrence and Wishart, 1971), pp. 10, 60, 330; G. West, *The Academy of the Poor: Towards a Dialogical Reading of the Bible* (Sheffield: Sheffield Academic Press, 1999).
20 Gutiérrez, *The Truth*, p. 3.
21 M. Walsh and B. Davies (eds), *Proclaiming Justice and Peace* (London: CIIR and CAFOD, 1984), p. 81.
22 P. Freire, *Pedagogy of the Oppressed* (London: Penguin, 1972).
23 For Anabaptist antecedents to contemporary popular pedagogy, see C.A. Snyder, *Biblical Concordance of the Swiss Brethren, 1540* (Kitchener: Pandora, 2001).
24 *Parábolas de Hoje* (São Paulo: Edições Paulinas, 1982), produced for use in the Archdiocese of São Paulo, reproduced in Rowland and Corner, *Liberating Exegesis*, p. 8 and C. Rowland and J. Roberts, *The Bible for Sinners: Interpretation in the Present Time* (London: SPCK, 2008), p. 52.
25 C. Boff, *Theology and Praxis* (Maryknoll, NY: Orbis 1987), p. 143.
26 Ibid., pp. 142–50; cf. R.S. Sugirtharajah, *Voices from the Margins: Interpreting the Bible in the Third World* (London: SPCK, 1991), pp. 9–35. Z. Bennett, '"Action is the life of all": the praxis-based epistemology of liberation theology', in C. Rowland (ed.), *The Cambridge Companion to Liberation Theology*, 2nd edn (Cambridge: Cambridge University Press, 2007), pp. 39–54.
27 Boff, *Theology*, p. 149.
28 Boff's italics, ibid., p. 148.
29 Ibid., p. 148.
30 Ibid., pp. 150–1, noted in Z. Bennett and C. Rowland, *In a Glass Darkly: The Bible, Reflection and Everyday Life* (London, SCM, 2016), pp. 149–50.
31 Boff, *Theology*, p. 149.
32 Ibid., p. 148.
33 Ibid., p. 149.
34 Ibid., p. 151.
35 D. Nicholls, *Deity and Domination: Images of God and the State in the Nineteenth and Twentieth Centuries* (London: Routledge, 1994).
36 L. Boff, *Jesus Christ Liberator: A Critical Christology of our Time* (London: SPCK, 1979), p. 265, words which echo Marx's words, 'Philosophy does not reside outside this world', quoted in S. Avineri, *The Social and Political Thought of Karl Marx* (Cambridge: Cambridge University Press, 1968), p. 135.

37 J. Taubes, 'The price of Messianism', in M. Saperstein (ed.), *Essential Papers on Messianic Movements and Personalities in Jewish History* (New York: New York University Press, 1992), p. 556, quoted below, Chapter 8, 'Jacob Taubes and Walter Benjamin'.

38 J. Ratzinger (Pope Benedict XVI), *Church Ecumenism and Politics* (San Francisco: Ignatius Press, 2008), p. 229. The wording has been slightly changed as compared with the 1988 version of this essay, where we read 'the fanatical expectations of the War Scroll [...] can be found again in an astonishing way in the literature of liberation theology'.

39 *Guardian*, 24 July 2005, but see now an authoritative treatment of Islamic liberation theology, S. Rahemtulla, *Qur'an of the Oppressed: Liberation Theology and Gender Justice in Islam* (Oxford: Oxford University Press, 2017).

40 Freire, *Pedagogy*.

41 I. Petrella, *The Future of Liberation Theology: An Argument and a Manifesto* (Farnham: Ashgate, 2004).

42 Gerrard Winstanley, *New Law of Righteousnes*, chap. x, CHL i.537.

43 T. Gorringe, 'Gustavo Gutiérrez's *A Theology of Liberation*', *Theology* 120 (2017), p. 252.

Chapter 8: Apocalypticism and Millenarian Eschatology

1 D. McLellan, *Marxism and Religion: A Description and Assessment of the Marxist Critique of Christianity* (Basingstoke: Macmillan, 1987), pp. 132–3.

2 V. Geoghegan, *Ernst Bloch* (London and New York: Routledge, 1996; P. Thompson and S. Žižek (eds), *The Privatization of Hope: Ernst Bloch and the Future of Utopia* (Durham, NC: Duke University Press, 2013); I. Boldyrev, *Ernst Bloch and His Contemporaries: Locating Utopian Messianism* (London: Bloomsbury, 2014).

3 *Marx and Engels, Collected Works* (Charlottesville: InteLex, 2001), 4:214–22, 1844.

4 See also D. Turner, *Marxism and Christianity* (Oxford: Blackwell, 1983), p. 167.

5 E. Bloch, *Atheism in Christianity: The Religion of the Exodus and the Kingdom*, with an introduction by Peter Thompson (London: Verso, 2009), p. 44.

6 A.N. Chester, *Future Hope and Present Reality* (Tübingen: Mohr Siebeck, 2012).

7 Bloch, *Atheism in Christianity*, p. 220.

8 E.g., D. Harink (ed.), *Paul, Philosophy, and the Theopolitical Vision: Critical Engagements with Agamben, Badiou, Žižek, and Others* (Eugene, OR: Cascade, 2010).

9 J. Taubes, 'The Price of Messianism', in M. Saperstein (ed.), *Essential Papers on Messianic Movements and Personalities in Jewish History* (New York: New York University Press, 1992), pp. 551–8, also in J. Taubes, *From Cult to Culture: Fragments towards a Critique of Historical Reason* (Stanford, CA: Stanford University Press, 2010), pp. 3–9.
10 M. Saperstein (ed.), *Essential Papers on Messianic Movements and Personalities in Jewish History* (New York and London: New York University Press, 1992), pp. 335–76.
11 J. Taubes, *Occidental Eschatology* (Stanford, CA: Stanford University Press, 2009), p. 10.
12 Ibid., p. 85.
13 Ibid., p. 80.
14 Taubes, *From Cult*, pp. 167–8.
15 R. Radford Ruether, *Sexism and God-Talk* (Boston: Beacon, 1983); R. Radford Ruether, 'Ecofeminism and healing ourselves, healing the earth', *Feminist Theology* 9 (1995), pp. 12–50.
16 Taubes, *Occidental Eschatology*, p. 106, lists Bloch's book on Muentzer and commends it.
17 Mannheim's work is alluded to, but only in passing, Taubes, *Occidental Eschatology*, pp. 106–7.
18 T. Adorno, *Minima Moralia: Reflections from Damaged Life* (London: Verso), p. 247.
19 J. Taubes, *The Political Theology of Paul* (Stanford, CA: Stanford University Press, 2004), p. 75.
20 Ibid., p. 70.
21 W. Benjamin, 'Theologico-Political Fragment', *Reflections: Essays, Aphorisms, Autobiographical Writings* (New York: Harcourt, 1978), pp. 312–13.
22 Taubes, *The Political*, p. 74.
23 Noted in passing, Taubes, *The Political*, p. 71.
24 Benjamin, 'Theologico-Political Fragment', p. 312.
25 E. Jacobson, 'Understanding Walter Benjamin's theologico-political fragment', *Jewish Studies Quarterly* 8 (2001), pp. 227–8.
26 W. Benjamin, *Illuminations Edited and with an Introduction by Hannah Arendt* (London: Fontana, 1992), p. 249.
27 William Blake, *There Is No Natural Religion* B, Conclusion, in David V. Erdman (ed.), *The Complete Poetry and Prose of William Blake* (Berkeley, CA: University of California Press, 1988), p. 3, henceforth abbreviated as 'E', followed by the page number.
28 William Blake, 'Holy Thursday', in *Songs of Experience*, E19.

29 R.D. Williams, 'The human form divine: radicalism and orthodoxy in William Blake', in Z. Bennett and D.B. Gowler (eds), *Radical Christian Voices and Practice* (Oxford: Oxford University Press, 2012), pp. 151–64. William Blake, *The Marriage of Heaven and Hell* 16, E40.
30 Taubes, *Occidental Eschatology* (Stanford, CA: Stanford University Press, 2009), pp. 10–11.
31 Cf. L. Welborn, *Paul's Summons to Messianic Life: Political Theology and the Coming Awakening* (New York: Columbia University Press, 2015).
32 Taubes, *From Cult*, pp. 8–9 and in Saperstein (ed.), *Essential Papers*, pp. 556–7.
33 Something similar to that which Alan Kreider identifies: A. Kreider, *The Patient Ferment of the Early Church: The Improbable Rise of Christianity in the Roman Empire* (Ada, OK: Baker, 2016).

Epilogue

1 Gerrard Winstanley, *A New-Yeers Gift*, in T.N. Corns, A. Hughes and D. Loewenstein (eds), *The Complete Works of Gerrard Winstanley*, 2 vols (Oxford: Oxford University Press, 2009), ii.149, henceforth abbreviated as 'CHL', followed by the volume and page number.
2 Ibid., CHL ii.107.
3 A. Kreider, *The Patient Ferment of the Early Church: The Improbable Rise of Christianity in the Roman Empire* (Ada, OK: Baker, 2016).
4 G. Gutiérrez, *We Drink from Our Own Wells: The Spiritual Journey of a People* (London: SCM, 1984), pp. 37–8.
5 C. Bauman, *The Spiritual Legacy of Hans Denck: Interpretation and Translation of Key Texts* (Leiden: Brill, 1991), p. 113.
6 R. Paulson, *Book and Painting: Shakespeare, Milton, and the Bible: Literary Texts and the Emergence of English Painting* (Knoxville: University of Tennessee Press, 1982), p. 116.
7 Cf. Z. Bennett and C. Rowland, *In a Glass Darkly: The Bible, Reflection and Everyday Life* (London: SCM, 2016).
8 J. Moltmann, *The Coming of God: Christian Eschatology* (London: SCM, 1996) and H. Räisänen, *The Rise of Christian Beliefs: The Thought World of Early Christians* (Philadelphia: Fortress Press, 2009), p. 85.
9 William Blake, Preface to *Milton*, in David V. Erdman (ed.), *The Complete Poetry and Prose of William Blake* (Berkeley, CA: University of California Press, 1988), p. 95.

10 R. Radford Ruether, 'Ecofeminism and healing ourselves, healing the earth', *Feminist Theology* 9 (1995), p. 53.
11 Gerrard Winstanley, *Saints Paradice*, CHL i.357; *New Law of Righteousnes*, CHL i.550; cf. T. Altizer, *The Radical Christian Vision of William Blake* (Ann Arbor: Michigan State University Press, 1967) and T. Altizer, 'The Revolutionary Vision of William Blake', *Journal of Religious Ethics* 37 (2009), pp. 33–8; L. Freedman, 'Tom Altizer and William Blake: The Apocalypse of Belief', *Literature and Theology* 25 (2011), pp. 20–31.
12 My italics; A. Schweitzer, *The Quest of the Historical Jesus* (London: A & C Black, 1931a), p. 401.

Bibliography

Adorno, T., *Minima Moralia: Reflections from Damaged Life* (London: Verso, 1974).

Allison, D., 'Acts 9:1–9, 22:6–11, 26:12–18: Paul and Ezekiel', *Journal of Biblical Literature* 135 (2016), pp. 807–26.

Althaus-Reid, M., *Indecent Theology: Theological Perversions in Sex, Gender and Politics* (London: Routledge, 2000).

Altizer, T., *The Radical Christian Vision of William Blake* (Ann Arbor: Michigan State University Press, 1967).

———, *The New Apocalypse: The Radical Christian Vision of William Blake* (East Lansing: Michigan State University Press, 1967).

———, 'The Revolutionary Vision of William Blake', *Journal of Religious Ethics* 37 (2009), pp. 33–8.

'Antinomianism', *Encyclopedia of the Bible and Its Reception, 2 Anim-Atheism* (Berlin: de Gruyter, 2009).

Apetrei, S., *Women, Feminism and Religion in Early Enlightenment England* (Cambridge: Cambridge University Press, 2010).

Ashton, J., *Understanding the Fourth Gospel* (new edn, Oxford: Oxford University Press, 2007).

———, *The Gospel of John and Christian Origins* (Minneapolis, MN: Fortress, 2014).

———, *Revealed Wisdom: Studies in Apocalyptic in Honour of Christopher Rowland* (Leiden: Brill, 2014).

Aslan, R., *Zealot: The Life and Times of Jesus of Nazareth* (London: Westbourne, 2013).

Aune, D.E., *Prophecy in Early Christianity and the Ancient Mediterranean World* (Grand Rapids, MI: Eerdmans, 1983).

Avineri, S., *The Social and Political Thought of Karl Marx* (Cambridge: Cambridge University Press, 1968).

Aylmer, G.E., 'Collective mentalities in mid seventeenth-century England: III. Varieties of radicalism', *Transactions of the Royal Historical Society*

5th ser., 38 (1988), pp. 1–25.

Barth, K., *The Epistle to the Romans* (Oxford: Clarendon Press, 1933).

Barros Souza, M. de, *A Bíblia e a Luta pela Terra* (Petropolis: Commissão Pastoral da Terra, 1983).

Barton, S., 'Sanctification and oneness in 1 Corinthians with implications for the case of "mixed marriages" (1 Corinthians 7.12–16)', *New Testament Studies* (2017), pp. 38–55.

Bauckham, R., 'The delay of the Parousia', *Tyndale Bulletin* 31 (1980), pp. 3–36.

———, *The Theology of the Book of Revelation (New Testament Theology)* (Cambridge: Cambridge University Press, 1993; repr. Cambridge: Cambridge University Press, 2003).

Bauman, C., *The Spiritual Legacy of Hans Denck: Interpretation and Translation of Key Texts* (Leiden: Brill, 1991).

Baylor, G., *The Radical Reformation* (Cambridge: Cambridge University Press, 1991).

Beker, J.C., *Paul the Apostle. The Triumph of God in Life and Thought* (Edinburgh: T&T Clark, 1980; 5th edn, Philadelphia: Fortress Press, 1992).

Benjamin, A. (ed.), *Walter Benjamin and History* (London: Continuum, 2006).

Benjamin, W., *Illuminations Edited and with an Introduction by Hannah Arendt* (London: Fontana, 1992).

Bennett Moore, Z., 'On copy clerks, transformers and spiders: teachers and learners in adult theological education', *British Journal of Theological Education* 9 (1997/8), pp. 36–44.

Bennett, Z., '"Action is the life of all": the praxis-based epistemology of liberation theology', in C. Rowland (ed.), *The Cambridge Companion to Liberation Theology*, 2nd edn (Cambridge: Cambridge University Press, 2007), pp. 39–54.

———, *Your MA in Theology* (London: SCM, 2014).

Bennett, Z. and C. Rowland, '"Action is the Life of All": New Testament theology and practical theology', in C. Rowland and C. Tuckett (eds), *The Nature of New Testament Theology* (Oxford: Blackwell, 2006), pp. 39–54.

Bennett, Z. and C. Rowland, *In a Glass Darkly: The Bible, Reflection and Everyday Life* (London: SCM, 2016).

Bennett, Z. and D. Gowler (eds), *Radical Christian Voices and Practice: Essays in Honour of Christopher Rowland* (Oxford: Oxford University Press, 2012).

Bentley, G.E., *The Stranger from Paradise: A Biography of William Blake* (New Haven, CN: Yale University Press, 2001).

Bindman, D., *William Blake's Illustrations of the Book of Job: The Engravings with Related Material* (London: William Blake Trust, 1978).

———, *William Blake: The Complete Illuminated Books* (London: Thames & Hudson, 2000).

The Illuminated Books of William Blake

Vol. 1: *Jerusalem: The Emanation of the Giant Albion*, ed. Morton D. Paley (Princeton, NJ: Princeton University Press, 1991).

Vol. 2: *Songs of Innocence and of Experience*, ed. Andrew Lincoln (Princeton, NJ: Princeton University Press, 1991).

Vol 3: *The Early Illuminated Books*, ed. Morris Eaves, Robert N. Essick and Joseph Viscomi (Princeton, NJ: Princeton University Press, 1993).

Vol. 4: *The Continental Prophecies*, ed. D.W. Dörrbecker (Princeton, NJ: Princeton University Press, 1995).

Vol. 5: *Milton, A Poem*, ed. Robert N. Essick and Joseph Viscomi (Princeton, NJ: Princeton University Press, 1993).

Vol. 6: *The Urizen Books*, ed. David Worrall (Princeton, NJ: Princeton University Press, 1995).

Online versions of Blake's illuminated books, including all those mentioned in this book, as well as some of Blake's images of biblical stories, are available at: http://www.blakearchive.org/blake/indexworks.htm

Illustrations of the Book of Job are available at http://www.blakearchive.org/exist/blake/archive/work.xq?workid=bb421&java=yes

Illustrations of the Book of Job (The Butts set) are available at http://www.blakearchive.org/exist/blake/archive/work.xq?workid=but550&java=yes

Blanton, W., C. Crockett, J. Robbins et al., *An Insurrectionist Manifesto: Four New Gospels for a Radical Politics* (New York: Columbia University Press, 2016).

Bloch, E. *The Principle of Hope* (Cambridge, MA: MIT Press, 1995).

———, *Atheism in Christianity: The Religion of the Exodus and the Kingdom*, with an introduction by Peter Thompson (London: Verso, 2009).

Bloom, H., *The Anxiety of Influence*, 2nd edn (New York and Oxford: Oxford University Press, 1997).

Bocock, R. and K. Thompson, *Religion and Ideology: A Reader* (Manchester: Manchester University Press, 1985).

Boff, C., *Theology and Praxis* (Maryknoll, NY: Orbis 1987).

Boff, L., *Jesus Christ Liberator: A Critical Christology of Our Time* (London: SPCK, 1979).

———, *Church, Charism and Power* (London: SCM, 1985).

———, *Ecclesiogenesis: The Base Communities Reinvent the Church* (London: Collins, 1986).

Boldyrev, I., *Ernst Bloch and His Contemporaries: Locating Utopian Messianism* (London: Bloomsbury, 2014).

Boyd, J. and P. Esler, *Visuality and Biblical Text: Interpreting Velázquez' 'Christ with Martha and Mary' as a Test Case* (Florence: Olschki, 2004).

Bradstock, A., *Faith in the Revolution: The Political Theologies of Müntzer and Winstanley* (London: SPCK, 1997).

———, *Winstanley and the Diggers, 1649–1999* (London: Routledge, 2000).

———, *Radical Religion in Cromwell's England: A Concise History from the English Civil War to the End of the Commonwealth* (London: I.B.Tauris, 2011).

Bradstock, A. and C. Rowland, *Radical Christian Writings: A Reader* (Oxford: Blackwell, 2002).

Brownlow, K., *Winstanley: Warts and All* (London: UKA, 2009).

Brueggemann, W., *The Prophetic Imagination* (Minneapolis: Fortress Press, 1978).

Burr, D., *Olivi's Peaceable Kingdom: A Reading of the Apocalypse Commentary* (Philadelphia: University of Pennsylvania Press, 1993).

Burdick, J., *Looking for God in Brazil: The Progressive Catholic Church in Urban Brazil's Religious Arena* (Berkeley, CA and London: University of California Press, 1993).

———, *Legacies of Liberation: The Progressive Catholic Church in Brazil at the Start of a New Millennium* (Aldershot: Ashgate, 2004).

Burr, D., *The Spiritual Franciscans: From Protest to Persecution in the Century after Saint Francis* (University Park, PA: Pennsylvania State University Press, 2001).

Butlin, M., *The Paintings and Drawings of William Blake* (London: Yale University Press, 1981).

Caird, G., *The Language and Imagery of the Bible* (London: Duckworth, 1980).

Capp, B.S., *The Fifth Monarchy Men* (London: Faber, 1972).

Carruthers, M.J., *The Book of Memory*, Cambridge Studies in Medieval Literature, 10 (Cambridge: Cambridge University Press, 1990; repr. Cambridge: Cambridge University Press, 2004).

———, *The Craft of Thought: Meditation, Rhetoric and the Making of Images*

400–1200, Cambridge Studies in Medieval Literature 34 (Cambridge: Cambridge University Press, 1998; repr. Cambridge: Cambridge University Press, 2003).

Chester, A.N., *Messiah and Exaltation: Jewish Messianic and Visionary Traditions and New Testament Christology* (Tübingen: Mohr Siebeck, 2007).

———, *Future Hope and Present Reality* (Tübingen: Mohr Siebeck, 2012).

Clement of Alexandria, *Stromata* translation, *The Library of Christian Classics: Volume II, Alexandrian Christianity*, ed. J. Baillie, J. McNeill and H. Van Dusen (London: SCM Press, 2006).

Cohn, N., *The Pursuit of the Millennium* (London: Paladin, 1957).

Coleridge, S.T., *Collected Letters*, ed. E.L. Griggs (Oxford: Oxford University Press, 1956).

———, *Aids to Reflection*, ed. John Beer (London: Routledge; Princeton, NJ: Princeton University Press, 1993).

Collins, J.J., *Apocalypse: The Morphology of a Genre* (The Apocalypse Group of the SBL Genres Project) *Semeia* 14 (1979).

———, *The Apocalyptic Imagination: An Introduction to Jewish Apocalyptic Literature*, 2nd edn (Grand Rapids, MI: Eerdmans, 1998).

Collins, J.J., B. McGinn and S. Stein (eds), *The Encyclopedia of Apocalypticism*, 3 vols (New York: Continuum, 2000).

Como, D., *Blown by the Spirit: Puritanism and the Emergence of an Antinomian Underground in Pre-Civil-War England* (Stanford, CA: Stanford University Press, 2004).

Coppe, Abiezer, *A Fiery Flying Roll: A Word from the Lord to All the Great Ones of the Earth* (London, 1649; Exeter: University of Exeter Press: Rota, 1973).

Corns, T.N., A. Hughes and D. Loewenstein (eds), *The Complete Works of Gerrard Winstanley*, 2 vols (Oxford: Oxford University Press, 2009) (= CHL).

Croatto, S., *Biblical Hermeneutics: Toward a Theory of Reading as the Production of Meaning* (Maryknoll, NY: Orbis, 1987).

Crossan, J.D., *The Historical Jesus: The Life of a Mediterranean Jewish Peasant* (San Francisco, CA: Harper, 1992).

———, *The Birth of Christianity: Discovering What Happened in the Years Immediately after the Death of Jesus* (Edinburgh: T&T Clark, 1999).

Daley, B., *The Hope of the Early Church: A Handbook of Patristic Eschatology* (Cambridge: Cambridge University Press, 1991).

Damrosch, Jr., L., *Symbol and Truth in Blake's Myth* (Princeton, NJ: Princeton University Press, 1980).

———, *Eternity's Sunrise: The Imaginative World of William Blake* (New Haven: Yale, 2015).

Dancer, A., *William Stringfellow in Anglo-American Perspective* (Aldershot: Ashgate, 2005).

Davidson, D., 'What metaphors mean', reproduced in *The Essential Davidson* (Oxford: Oxford University Press, 2006) and in *Critical Inquiry* 5.1, Special Issue on Metaphor (1978), pp. 31–47.

Davies, W.D., *Torah in the Messianic Age and/or Age to Come* (Philadelphia: SBL, 1952).

———, 'From Schweitzer to Scholem: reflections on Sabbatai Sevi', in *Jewish and Pauline Studies* (London: SPCK, 1984); repr. in M. Saperstein (ed.), *Essential Papers on Messianic Movements and Personalities in Jewish History* (New York: New York University Press, 1992), pp. 335–76.

DeConick, A. (ed.), *Paradise Now. Essays on Early Jewish and Christian Mysticism* (Leiden and Boston: Symposium Series/Society of Biblical Literature, 2006).

Department of Education, *The Prevent duty: Departmental advice for schools and childcare providers* (London, June 2015).

Deppermann, K., *Melchior Hoffmann* (Edinburgh: T&T Clark, 1987).

Ditmore, M., 'A prophetess in her own country: an exegesis of Anne Hutchinson's "Immediate Revelation"', *The William and Mary Quarterly* 57 (2000), pp. 349–92.

Dunn, J.D.G., *Jesus and the Spirit* (London: SCM, 1975).

Ellacuría, I. and J. Sobrino, *Mysterium Liberationis: Fundamental Concepts of Liberation Theology* (Maryknoll, NY: Orbis, 1993).

Ellis, M., *Toward a Jewish Theology of Liberation* (new edn, London: SCM Press, 2002).

Emmerson, R.K. and B. McGinn (eds), *The Apocalypse in the Middle Ages* (Ithaca, NY: Cornell University Press, 1992).

Engels, F., 'The Book of Revelation', in *Marx and Engels on Religion* (Moscow: Progress, 1957), pp. 183–9.

———, 'The Peasant War in Germany', in *Marx and Engels on Religion* (Moscow: Progress, 1957).

———, 'On the history of primitive Christianity', in L. Feuer (ed.), *K. Marx and F. Engels: Basic Writings on Politics and Philosophy* (London: Fontana/Collins, 1959), pp. 209–35; also in *Marx and Engels on Religion* (Moscow: Progress, 1957), pp. 281–308.

Erdman, D., *Blake: Prophet against Empire* (Princeton, NJ: Princeton University Press, 1977).

——, *The Complete Poetry and Prose of William Blake*, ed. David V. Erdman (Berkeley, CA: University of California Press, 1988) (= E).

Ferber, M., 'Coleridge's "anacalyptic" Blake: an exegesis', *Modern Philology* 76 (1978), pp. 189–93.

——, *The Social Vision of William Blake* (Princeton, NJ: Princeton University Press, 1985).

Flannery-Dailey, F., *Dreamers, Scribes, and Priests: Jewish Dreams in the Hellenistic and Roman Eras* (Leiden: Brill, 2004).

Freedman, L., 'Tom Altizer and William Blake: the Apocalypse of Belief', *Literature and Theology* 25 (2011), pp. 20–31.

Freire, P., *Pedagogy of the Oppressed* (London: Penguin, 1972).

Fredriksen, P., 'Tyconius and Augustine on the Apocalypse', in R. Emmerson and B. McGinn (eds), *The Apocalypse in the Middle Ages* (Ithaca, NY: Cornell University Press, 1992), pp. 20–37.

Gadamer, H.-G., *Truth and Method* (London: Sheed and Ward, 1989).

Garrett, C., *Respectable Folly: Millenarians in the French Revolution in France and England* (Baltimore: Johns Hopkins University Press, 1973).

Garnsey, P., 'Peter Olivi on the community of the first Christians in Jerusalem', in Z. Bennett and D. Gowler (eds), *Radical Christian Voices and Practice: Essays in Honour of Christopher Rowland* (Oxford: Oxford University Press, 2012), pp. 35–50.

Geoghegan, V., *Ernst Bloch* (London and New York: Routledge, 1996).

Goertz, H.J., *Thomas Müntzer: Apocalyptic Mystic and Revolutionary* (Edinburgh: T&T Clark, 1993).

Gorringe, T., 'Gustavo Gutiérrez's *A Theology of Liberation*', *Theology* 120 (2017), pp. 246–52.

Gould, W. and M. Reeves, *Joachim of Fiore and the Myth of the Eternal Evangel in the Nineteenth and Twentieth Centuries* (Oxford: Oxford University Press, 2001).

Graham, E., *Transforming Practice: Pastoral Theology in an Age of Uncertainty* (London: Mowbray, 1996).

Gray, R., *Prophetic Figures in Late Second Temple Jewish Palestine* (Oxford: Oxford University Press, 1993).

Gurney, J., *Brave Community: The Digger Movement in the English Revolution* (Manchester: Manchester University Press, 2007).

——, *Gerrard Winstanley: The Digger's Life and Legacy* (London: Pluto, 2013).

Gutiérrez, G., *The Power of the Poor in History* (London: SCM, 1983).

——, *We Drink from Our Own Wells: The Spiritual Journey of a People* (London: SCM, 1984).

——, *A Theology of Liberation*, rev. edn (London: SCM, 1988).

———, *The Truth Shall Make You Free: Confrontations* (Maryknoll, NY: Orbis, 1990).

———, *Las Casas: In Search of the Poor of Jesus Christ* (Maryknoll, NY: Orbis, 1993).

Hagstrum, J., 'Blake and the sister – arts tradition', in D. Erdman and J. Grant, *Blake's Visionary Forms Dramatic* (Princeton, NJ: Princeton University Press, 1970), pp. 82–91.

Hall, D., *The Antinomian Controversy, 1636–1638: A Documentary History* (Middletown, CN: Wesleyan University Press, 1968).

Halperin, D., *The Faces of the Chariot: Early Jewish Responses to Ezekiel's Vision*, Texte und Studien zum antiken Judentum, 16 (Tübingen: Mohr Siebeck, 1988).

Hampson, D., *Theology and Feminism* (Oxford: Blackwell, 1990).

Hampson, D. and R. Radford Ruether, 'Is there a place for feminists in the Christian Church?', *New Blackfriars* 68 (1987), pp. 7–24.

Hanson, P., *The Dawn of Apocalyptic: The Historical and Sociological Roots of Jewish Apocalyptic Eschatology*, rev. edn (Philadelphia: Fortress Press, 1979).

Harink, D. (ed.), *Paul, Philosophy, and the Theopolitical Vision: Critical Engagements with Agamben, Badiou, Žižek, and Others* (Eugene, OR: Cascade, 2010).

Hart, P., *The Literary Essays of Thomas Merton* (New York: New Directions, 1981).

Hawes, C., *Mania and Literary Style: The Rhetoric of Enthusiasm from the Ranters to Christopher Smart* (Cambridge: Cambridge University Press, 1996).

Hayes, T. Wilson, *Winstanley the Digger: A Literary Analysis of Radical Ideas in the English Revolution* (Cambridge, MA: Harvard University Press, 1979).

———, 'The Peaceful Apocalypse: Familism and Literacy in Sixteenth-Century England', *Sixteenth Century Journal* 17 (1986), pp. 131–43.

Hegel, G.W.F., *Introduction to Lectures on the Philosophy of Religion of 1824*, ed. P. Hodgson, trans. R.F. Brown et al., Vol. 1: *Introduction and the Concept* (Berkeley, CA: University of California Press, 1984).

Hengel, M., *Judaism and Hellenism: Studies in Their Encounter in Palestine During the Early Hellenistic Period* (London: SCM, 1974).

Hennelly, A.T. (ed.), *Liberation Theology. A Documentary History* (Maryknoll, NY: Orbis, 1990).

Hill, C., *The World Turned Upside Down* (London: Penguin, 1972).

———, *Winstanley: The Law of Freedom and Other Writings* (Cambridge: Cambridge University Press, 1973).

———, *The Religion of Gerrard Winstanley. Past & Present* Supplement 5 (1978).

———, *The English Bible and the Seventeenth-Century Revolution* (Harmondsworth: Penguin, 1993).

———, *The Experience of Defeat: Milton and Some Contemporaries* (London: Bookmarks, 1994).

Hinds, H., *God's Englishwomen: Seventeenth-Century Radical Sectarian Writing and Feminist Criticism* (Manchester: Manchester University Press, 1996).

———, *Anna Trapnel: The Cry of a Stone* (Tempe: Arizona University Press, 2000).

Hoare, Q. and G. Smith (eds), *Selections from the Prison Notebooks of Antonio Gramsci* (London: Lawrence and Wishart, 1971).

Hobby, E., *Virtue of Necessity: English Women's Writing 1649–88* (Ann Arbor: University of Michigan Press, 1988).

Holstun, J., *Ehud's Dagger: Class Struggle in the English Revolution* (London: Verso, 2002).

Hopkins, J.K., *A Woman to Deliver Her People: Joanna Southcott and English Millenarianism in an Era of Revolution* (Austin: University of Texas Press, 1982).

Hudson, W., *The Marxist Philosophy of Ernst Bloch* (London: Macmillan, 1982).

Idel, M., *Messianic Mystics* (New Haven: Yale University Press, 1998).

Jacobson, E., 'Understanding Walter Benjamin's Theologico-Political Fragment', *Jewish Studies Quarterly* 8 (2001), pp. 205–47.

Jeremias, J., *The Eucharistic Words of Jesus* (London: SCM, 1966).

Jones, R., *Spiritual Reformers in the 16th and 17th Centuries* (Boston: Beacon, 1914).

Juster, S., *Doomsayers: Anglo-American Prophecy in the Age of Revolution* (Philadelphia: University of Pennsylvania Press, 2003).

Käsemann, E., *On Being a Disciple of the Crucified Nazarene* (Grand Rapids, MI: Eerdmans, 2010).

Kaiser, C.B., *Seeing the Lord's Glory: Kyriocentric Visions and the Dilemma of Early Christology* (Minneapolis, MN: Fortress Press, 2014.

Kishlansky, M., *A Monarchy Transformed: Britain 1603–1714* (London: Penguin, 1996).

Knight, J. and K. Sullivan, *The Open Mind: Essays in Honour of Christopher Rowland* (London: Bloomsbury, 2015).

Knox, J., *Chapters in a Life of Paul* (London: SCM, 1989).

Kovacs, J. and C. Rowland, *Revelation: The Apocalypse of Jesus Christ* (Oxford: Blackwell, 2004).

Kreider, A., *The Patient Ferment of the Early Church: The Improbable Rise of Christianity in the Roman Empire* (Grand Rapids, MN: Baker, 2016).

Kuhn, H.W., *Enderwartung und gegenwärtiges Heil* (Göttingen: 1966).

Lerner, R., *The Heresy of the Free Spirit in the Later Middle Ages* (Berkeley, CA: University of California Press, 1972).

Lewis, W., *Peter John Olivi. Prophet of the Year 2000: Ecclesiology and Eschatology in the 'Lectura super Apocalipsim', Introduction to a Critical Edition of the Text* (unpublished dissertation, Tübingen, 1976).

Lieb, M., *The Visionary Mode: Biblical Prophecy, Hermeneutics, and Cultural Change* (Ithaca, NY: Cornell University Press, 1991).

Lincoln, A., *Paradise Now and Not Yet* (Cambridge: Cambridge University Press, 1981).

Lockley, P., *Visionary Religion and Radicalism in Early Industrial England: From Southcott to Socialism* (Oxford: Oxford University Press, 2013).

Luz, U., 'Paul as Mystic', in G. Stanton, B. Longenecker and S. Barton (eds), *The Holy Spirit and Christian Origins* (Grand Rapids, MI: Eerdmans, 2004), pp. 131–43.

MacCulloch, D., *Silence: A Christian History* (London: Allen Lane, 2013).

Mack, B., *A Myth of Innocence: Mark and Christian Origins* (Philadelphia: Fortress Press, 1988).

Mack, P., *Visionary Women: Ecstatic Prophecy in Seventeenth Century England* Berkeley, CA: University of California Press, 1992).

Madden, D., *The Paddington Prophet: Richard Brothers's Journey to Jerusalem* (Manchester: Manchester University Press, 2010).

Magister, S., 'Clodovis and Leonardo Boff, separated brethren', www.chiesa (July 2008), available at http://chiesa.espresso.repubblica.it/articolo/205773?eng=y.

Makdisi, S., *William Blake and the Impossible History of the 1790s* (Chicago: University of Chicago Press, 2003).

Mannheim, K., *Ideology and Utopia: An Introduction to the Sociology of Knowledge* (London: Routledge and Kegan Paul, 1936; repr. 1960).

Marcus, J., *The Way of the Lord: Christological Exegesis of the Old Testament in the Gospel of Mark* (Louisville, KY: Westminster John Knox Press, 1992).

Marsh, C.W., *The Family of Love in English Society, 1550–1630* (Cambridge: Cambridge University Press, 2005).

Martines, L., *Fire in the City: Savonarola and the Struggle for the Soul of Renaissance Florence* (Oxford: Oxford University Press, 2006).

Martyn, J.L., *Galatians: A New Translation with Introduction and Commentary* (New York: Doubleday, 1997).

Marx and Engels on Religion (Moscow: Progress, 1957).

Matheson, P. *The Collected Works of Thomas Müntzer* (Edinburgh: T&T Clark, 1988).

———, *The Imaginative World of the Reformation* (Edinburgh: T&T Clark, 2000).

McDonagh, F., 'The struggle continues – in the family', *The Tablet* (3 January 2009), pp. 4–5.

McGinn, B. *Apocalyptic Spirituality* (London: SPCK, 1980).

———, *The Calabrian Abbot: Joachim of Fiore in the History of Western Thought* (New York: Macmillan, 1985).

———, *Visions of the End. Apocalyptic Traditions in the Middle Ages* (New York: Columbia University Press, 1998).

———, 'Apocalypticism in Western history and culture', in *Encyclopedia of Apocalypticism*, Vol. 2 (New York: Continuum, 2000).

———, 'The Concordist imagination: a theme in the history of eschatology', in J. Ashton (eds), *Revealed Wisdom: Studies in Apocalyptic in Honour of Christopher Rowland* (Leiden: Brill, 2014), pp. 217–31.

———, 'Image as insight in Joachim of Fiore's Figurae', in G. de Nie and T. Noble (eds), *Envisioning Experience in Late Antiquity and the Middle Ages: Dynamic Patterns in Texts and Images* (London: Routledge, 2016), pp. 93–118.

McLellan, D., *Marxism and Religion: A Description and Assessment of the Marxist Critique of Christianity* (Basingstoke: Macmillan, 1987).

McNeil, H., *Emily Dickinson* (London: Virago, 1986).

Mee, J., *Dangerous Enthusiasm: William Blake and the Culture of Radicalism in the 1790s* (Oxford: Clarendon Press, 1992).

Merton, T., 'Blake and the New Theology', *Sewanee Review* 76 (1968), pp. 673–82.

Mesters, C., 'The use of the Bible in Christian Communities of the Common People', in Norman Gottwald (ed.), *The Bible and Liberation* (Maryknoll, NY: Orbis, 2nd rev. edn 1993), pp. 3–16.

———, *Defenseless Flower* (London: Catholic Institute for International Relations, 1989).

Middleton, J.R., *A New Heaven and a New Earth: Reclaiming Biblical Eschatology* (Grand Rapids, MN: Baker, 2014).

Miranda, J.P., *Marx and the Bible* (London: SCM, 1977).

Moltmann, J., *The Church in the Power of the Spirit: A Contribution to Messianic Ecclesiology* (London: SCM, 1977).

———, *The Coming of God: Christian Eschatology* (London: SCM, 1996).

———, *Theology of Hope* (London: SCM, 2002).

Morgan, R., '*Sachkritik* in reception history', *JSNT* 33.2 (2010), pp. 175–90.

Morton, A.L., *The Everlasting Gospel: A Study in the Sources of William Blake* (London: Lawrence & Wishart, 1958).

Moule, C.F.D., 'Obligation in the ethic of Paul', in *Christian History and Interpretation: Studies Presented to John Knox*, ed. W.R. Farmer, C.F.D. Moule and R.R. Niebuhr (Cambridge: Cambridge University Press, 1967).

Munck, J., *Paul and the Salvation of Mankind* (London: SCM, 1959).

Myers, C., *Binding the Strong Man: A Political Reading of Mark's Story of Jesus* (20th anniversary edn, Maryknoll, NY: Orbis, 2008).

Niblett, M., *Prophecy and the Politics of Salvation in Late Georgian England: The Theology and Apocalyptic Vision of Joanna Southcott* (London: I.B.Tauris, 2015).

Nicholls, D., *Deity and Domination: Images of God and the State in the Nineteenth and Twentieth Centuries* (London: Routledge, 1994).

Oermann, N.O., *Albert Schweitzer: A Biography* (Oxford: Oxford University Press, 2017).

Ozment, S.E., *Mysticism and Dissent: Religious Ideology and Social Protest in the Sixteenth Century* (New Haven: Yale University Press, 1973).

Paley, M., *The Traveller in the Evening: The Last Works of William Blake* (Oxford: Oxford University Press, 2003).

Parábolas de Hoje (São Paulo: Edições Paulinas, 1982).

Paulson, R., *Book and Painting: Shakespeare, Milton, and the Bible. Literary Texts and the Emergence of English Painting* (Knoxville: University of Tennessee Press, 1982).

Perrin, N., *The Kingdom of God in the Teaching of Jesus* (London: SCM, 1963).

Petrella, I., *The Future of Liberation Theology: An Argument and a Manifesto* (Farnham: Ashgate, 2004).

Pinto, V. de Sola, *Peter Sterry: Platonist and Puritan* (Cambridge: Cambridge University Press, 1934).

Portier-Young, A., *Apocalypse Against Empire: Theologies of Resistance in Early Judaism* (Grand Rapids, MI: Eerdmans, 2011).

Radford Ruether, R., *Sexism and God-Talk* (Boston: Beacon, 1983).

———, 'Feminist interpretation: a method of correlation', in Letty M. Russell (ed.), *Feminist Interpretation of Scripture* (Philadelphia: Westminster Press, 1985), pp. 111–24.

———, 'Ecofeminism and healing ourselves, healing the earth', *Feminist Theology* 9 (1995), pp. 51–62.

Rahemtulla, S., Qur'an of the Oppressed: *Liberation Theology and Gender Justice in Islam* (Oxford: Oxford University Press, 2017).

Räisänen, H., *The Rise of Christian Beliefs: The Thought World of Early Christians* (Philadelphia: Fortress Press, 2009).

Ratzinger, J., *Church Ecumenism and Politics* (San Francisco, CA: Ignatius Press, 2008).

Reeves M., *The Influence of Prophecy in the Later Middle Ages* (Oxford: Clarendon Press, 1969).

Reeves, M. and B. Hirsch-Reich, *The Figurae of Joachim of Fiore* (Oxford: Clarendon, 1972).

Rensberger, D., *Overcoming the World: Politics and Community in the Gospel of John* (London: SPCK, 1989).

Rose, J., *The Woman Who Claimed to Be Christ: The Millennial Belief of Mary Ann Girling and Her Disciples 1860–1886* (DPhil dissertation, University of Oxford, 2007).

Rosso, G.A., *The Religion of Empire: Political Theology in Blake's Prophetic Symbolism* (Columbus: Ohio State University Press, 2016).

Rowland, C., 'The visions of God in apocalyptic literature', *Journal for the Study of Judaism* 10 (1979), pp. 138–54.

———, *The Open Heaven: A Study of Apocalyptic in Judaism and Early Christianity* (London: SPCK, 1982).

———, *Radical Christianity: A Reading of Recovery* (Cambridge: Polity, 1988).

———, *Revelation: The New Interpreter's Bible, Vol. 12* (Nashville: Abingdon, 1998).

———, 'Friends of Albion? The dangers of cathedrals', in S. Platten and C. Lewis (eds), *Flagships of the Spirit* (London: Darton, Longman and Todd, 1998), pp. 18–34.

———, *Christian Origins: The Setting and Character of the Most Important Messianic Sect of Judaism*, rev. edn (London: SPCK, 2002).

——— 'Imagining the Apocalypse', *New Testament Studies* 51 (2005), pp. 303–27.

———, 'The Temple in the New Testament', in J. Day (ed.), *Temple and Worship in Biblical Israel* (London: Continuum, 2005), pp. 469–83.

——— (ed.), *The Cambridge Companion to Liberation Theology*, 2nd edn (Cambridge: Cambridge University Press, 2007).

———, '*To see the great deceit which in the world doth lie*', *Christopher Hill's* 'The World Turned Upside Down', *Caught Reading Again: Scholars and Their Books* (London: SCM, 2009), pp. 54–67.

———, *Blake and the Bible* (London and New Haven, CN: Yale University Press, 2010).

———, 'Gerrard Winstanley: Man for all Seasons', *Prose Studies: History, Theory, Criticism* 36 (2014), pp. 77–89.

———, 'Thomas Müntzer', *Expository Times* 126 (2015), pp. 417–24.

———, 'Liberationist reading: popular interpretation of the Bible in Brazil', in K. Dell and P. Joyce (eds), *Biblical Interpretation and Method: Essays in Honour of John Barton* (Oxford: Oxford University Press, 2013), pp. 133–48.

Rowland, C. and M. Corner, *Liberating Exegesis: The Challenge of Liberation Theology to Biblical Studies* (London: SPCK, 1990).

Rowland, C., P. Gibbons and V. Dobroruka, '"A door opened in Heaven": an essay on the character of visionary experience,' in A. DeConick (ed.), *Paradise Now. Essays on Early Jewish and Christian Mysticism* (Leiden and Boston: Symposium Series/Society of Biblical Literature, 2006).

Rowland, C. and J. Roberts, *The Bible for Sinners: Interpretation in the Present Time* (London: SPCK, 2008).

Rupp, G., *Patterns of Reformation* (London: Epworth, 1969).

Ryan, R. *The Romantic Reformation: Religious Politics in English Literature, 1789–1824* (Cambridge: Cambridge University Press, 1997).

Sanders, E.P., *Paul and Palestinian Judaism* (London: SCM, 1977).

———, *Jesus and Judaism* (London: SCM, 1985a).

———, *Paul, the Law, and the Jewish People* (London: SCM, 1985b).

Saperstein, M. (ed.), *Essential Papers on Messianic Movements and Personalities in Jewish History* (New York and London: New York University Press, 1992).

Scholem, G., *The Messianic Idea in Judaism: And Other Essays on Jewish Spirituality* (London: Allen and Unwin, 1971).

———, *Sabbatai Sevi: The Mystical Messiah, 1626–1676*, Littman Library of Jewish Civilization (London: Routledge & Kegan Paul, 1973).

Schürer, E. *The Jewish People in the Age of Jesus Christ*, rev. edn by G. Vermes and F. Millar, 2 vols (Edinburgh: T&T Clark, 1972).

Schweitzer, A., *The Quest of the Historical Jesus* (London: A & C Black, 1931a).

———, *The Mysticism of Paul the Apostle* (London: A & C Black, 1931b).

Scott, J., *Domination and the Arts of Resistance: Hidden Transcripts* (New Haven, CN: Yale University Press, 1990).

Segal, A., *Paul the Convert: The Apostolate and Apostasy of Saul the Pharisee* (New Haven, CN: Yale University Press, 1990).

Segundo, J.L., *The Liberation of Theology* (Maryknoll, NY: Orbis, 1976).

———, *Jesus of Nazareth Yesterday and Today: Vol. 2, The Historical Jesus of the Synoptic Gospels* (London: Sheed and Ward, 1985).

Shaw, J., *Octavia, Daughter of God: The Story of a Female Messiah and Her Followers* (London: Jonathan Cape, 2011).

Shaw, J. and P. Lockley, *The History of a Modern Millennial Movement: The Southcottians* (London: I.B.Tauris, 2017).
Sklar, S., *Blake's Jerusalem as Visionary Theatre: Entering the Divine Body* (Oxford: Oxford University Press, 2011).
Smith, N., *A Collection of Ranter Writings* (London: Junction Books, 1982).
———, *Perfection Proclaimed: Language and Literature in English Radical Religion, 1640–1660* (Oxford: Clarendon Press, 1989).
Snyder, C.A., *Biblical Concordance of the Swiss Brethren, 1540*, trans. G. Fast and G. Peters, with an Introduction by J. Springer (Kitchener: Pandora, 2001).
———, *Following in the Footsteps of Christ: The Anabaptist Tradition* (London: Darton, Longman and Todd, 2004).
Sobrino, J., *Christology at the Crossroads: A Latin American Approach* (London: SCM, 1978).
———, *The True Church and the Church of the Poor* (London: SCM, 1984).
Stayer, J., *Anabaptists and the Sword* (Lawrence, KN: Coronado, 1972).
———, *The German Peasants' War and Anabaptist Community of Goods* (Montreal: McGill-Queen's University Press, 1991).
Stone, M., 'A reconsideration of apocalyptic visions', *Harvard Theological Review* 96 (2003), pp. 167–80.
———, *Ancient Judaism: New Visions and Views* (Grand Rapids, MI: Eerdmans, 2011).
Stringfellow, W., *An Ethic for Christians and Other Aliens in a Strange Land* (Waco, TX: Word Books, 1973).
———, *Conscience and Obedience: the Politics of Romans 13 and Revelation 13 in Light of the Second Coming* (Waco, TX: Word Books, 1977).
Sugirtharajah, R.S., *Voices from the Margins: Interpreting the Bible in the Third World* (London: SPCK, 1991).
———, *Still at the Margins: Biblical Scholarship Fifteen Years after the Voices from the Margins* (London: T. &T. Clark, 2007).
Taubes, J., 'The price of Messianism', in M. Saperstein (ed.), *Essential Papers on Messianic Movements and Personalities in Jewish History* (New York: New York University Press, 1992), pp. 551–8; (also in Taubes 2010, pp. 3–9).
———, *The Political Theology of Paul* (Stanford, CA: Stanford University Press, 2004).
———, *Occidental Eschatology* (Stanford, CA: Stanford University Press, 2009).

———, *From Cult to Culture: Fragments towards a Critique of Historical Reason* (Stanford, CA: Stanford University Press, 2010).

Thiselton, A.C., *The First Epistle to the Corinthians*, New International Greek Text Commentary (Grand Rapids, MI: Eerdmans, 2000).

Thompson, P. and S. Žižek (eds), *The Privatization of Hope: Ernst Bloch and the Future of Utopia* (Durham, NC: Duke University Press, 2013).

Thurman, H., *Jesus and the Disinherited* (New York: Abingdon-Cokesbury, 1949).

Tilley, M.A., *The Bible in Christian North Africa: The Donatist World* (Minneapolis: Fortress Press, 1997).

Tondelli, L., M. Reeves and B. Hirsch-Reich, *Il libro delle figure dell'Abate Gioachino da Fiore*, 2 vols (Turin: SEI, 1953).

Trevett, C., *Montanism: Gender, Authority and the New Prophecy* (Cambridge: Cambridge University Press, 1996; repr. Cambridge: Cambridge University Press, 2003).

Tuckett, C., *Christology and the New Testament* (Edinburgh: T&T Clark, 2001).

Underwood, T.L., *Primitivism, Radicalism, and the Lamb's War: The Baptist–Quaker Conflict in Seventeenth-Century England* (Oxford: Clarendon Press, 1997).

Turner, D., *Marxism and Christianity* (Oxford: Blackwell, 1983).

VanderKam, J. and W. Adler (eds), *The Jewish Apocalyptic Heritage in Early Christianity* (Assen: van Gorcum, 1996).

Vermes, G., *Jesus the Jew* (London: Collins, 1973).

Wallace, D., *Shapers of English Calvinism, 1660–1714: Variety, Persistence, and Transformation* (New York and Oxford: Oxford University Press, 2011).

Walsh, M. and B. Davies (eds), *Proclaiming Justice and Peace* (London: CIIR and CAFOD, 1984).

Walzer, M., *The Revolution of the Saints: A Study in the Origin of Radical Politics* (London: Weidenfeld and Nicholson, 1965).

———, *Exodus and Revolution* (New York: Basic, 1985).

———, *In God's Shadow: Politics in the Hebrew Bible* (New Haven, CN: Yale University Press, 2012).

Wannenmacher, J.E., *Hermeneutik der Heilsgeschichte. De septem sigillis und die sieben Siegel im Werk Joachims von Fiore*, Studies in the History of Christian Traditions, 118 (Leiden and Boston: Brill, 2005).

Weiss, J., *Jesus' Proclamation of the Kingdom of God* (London: SCM, 1971).

Welby, J., *Dethroning Mammon: Making Money Serve Grace: The Archbishop of Canterbury's Lent Book 2017* (London: Bloomsbury Continuum, 2016).

Welborn, L., *Paul's Summons to Messianic Life: Political Theology and the Coming Awakening* (New York: Columbia University Press, 2015).

Werner, M., *Die Entstehung des christlichen Dogmas* (Bern: Haupt 1941).

———, *The Formation of Christian Dogma: An Historical Study of Its Problem* (London: Black, 1957).

West, G., *The Academy of the Poor: Towards a Dialogical Reading of the Bible* (Sheffield: Sheffield Academic Press, 1999).

Weinstein, D., *Savonarola and Florence: Prophecy and Patriotism in the Renaissance* (Princeton, NJ: Princeton University Press, 1970).

Williams, C. and C. Rowland, *John's Gospel and Intimations of Apocalyptic* (London: Bloomsbury, 2013).

Williams, G.H., *The Radical Reformation* (Philadelphia: Westminster Press, 1962).

Williams, R.D., 'The human form divine: radicalism and orthodoxy in William Blake', in Z. Bennett and D.B. Gowler (eds), *Radical Christian Voices and Practice* (Oxford: Oxford University Press, 2012), pp. 151–64.

Wengst, K., *Pax Romana and the Peace of Jesus Christ* (London: SCM, 1987).

Winship, M., *The Times and Trials of Anne Hutchinson: Puritans Divided* (Lawrence, KN: University of Kansas Press, 2005).

Winstanley, G., see under T.N. Corns, A. Hughes and D. Loewenstein (eds), *The Complete Works of Gerrard Winstanley*.

Winterson, J., *Oranges Are Not the Only Fruit* (London: Pandora, 1985).

Wire, A., *The Corinthian Women Prophets: A Reconstruction Through Paul's Rhetoric* (Philadelphia: Fortress Press, 1990; 2nd edn, Minneapolis: Fortress Press, 1995).

Yoder, J.H., *The Politics of Jesus: Vicit Agnus Noster* (Grand Rapids, MI: Eerdmans, 1972).

Žižek, S., *The Puppet and the Dwarf: The Perverse Core of Christianity* (Cambridge, MA and London: MIT Press, 2003).

General Index

(including topics covered and names mentioned in the main body of the text)

Index of Hebrew Bible, Old Testament References and Other Ancient Jewish Sources

(following the order of books in the
New Revised Standard Version of the Bible)

Index of New Testament References and Other Ancient Christian Sources